CONVICTION

CONVICTION

THE UNTOLD STORY OF PUTTING
JODI ARIAS BEHIND BARS

JUAN MARTINEZ

WM

William Morrow
An Imprint of HarperCollins*Publishers*

Photos on pages 1–11 of the photo insert courtesy of the Mesa Police Department.
Photos on pages 12, 13, and 14 (*bottom*) courtesy of the Siskiyou County Sherriff's office.
Photo on pages 15 (*top left*) courtesy of Diane Melendez.
Photos on page 15 (*top right*) courtesy of the Mendes Family.
Photos on page 15 (*bottom*) courtesy of Angela Flores.

HarperCollins books may be purchased for educational, business, or sales promotional use. For information please e-mail the Special Markets Department at SPsales@harpercollins.com.

FIRST EDITION

Library of Congress Cataloging-in-Publication Data has been applied for.

ISBN 978-0-06-244428-8

16 17 18 19 20 OV/RRD 10 9 8 7 6 5 4 3 2

CONVICTION

On the morning of Jodi Ann Arias' sentencing, I woke up early. It's not every day that seven years' worth of work comes to an end, and this was like the ending of a bad relationship. The only things left to say were the words that Arias did not want to hear.

It had all begun on June 4, 2008, the day Arias' victim and former boyfriend, Travis Alexander, had been brutally murdered. And now, after years of motions and discovery, appearances and court dates, a conviction of first-degree murder, and two hung juries tasked with deciding whether Arias should receive the death penalty, we were back at the courthouse on April 13, 2015, ready to hear the sentence as determined by the judge. In the aftermath of the hung juries, the death penalty was no longer an option, but the judge could send her to prison for either natural life or life with the possibility of release after twenty-five years.

Courtroom 5C of the Maricopa County Superior Court was packed to capacity, as it had been for much of the trial. There had never been a crowd like this in our courtrooms—the interest in the case was unprecedented. Maybe it was the attractive defendant and the handsome victim, or the fact that they were both Mormon, or the buzz about the kinky sexual relationship between them. Whatever the reason, there were always more people than there were seats, and eventually it had gotten to the point where people started lining up early in the morning just to get in.

I took the same chair at the counsel table that I had taken every day during the trial. Looking around the room, I realized that I'd spent years of my life here—the judge's bench in front of me, jury box to my left, and defense table to my right. I glanced across the courtroom at Arias. It was hard to reconcile her to the woman she was at the start of all this. She was still a brunette, only now her hair was laced with strings of gray. She looked older in other ways, too, from the glasses she wore to the wrist brace on her left arm. But more than physical appearances, I couldn't help but think about her untruthful side, and the different airs she'd worn.

Arias had always struck me as the "bad waitress" type. I imagined her at the Purple Plum, a restaurant in Yreka, California, where she had once worked. She would probably be looking down at her customers, smiling at them with a fake happy look, like she always did, giving them bad service. It was easy to see her spending her days taking photos, pouring weak coffee, and dreaming of a different life. Instead she was standing in front of a judge ready to be sentenced for the premeditated murder of Travis Alexander.

Even now, I could picture her saying, "Judge, it wasn't my fault," just as she might say to her customers, "It's not my fault the coffee is cold." I had never heard her take responsibility for anything, and I didn't expect to hear her take responsibility today.

The proceedings got under way at 8:40 P.M., with the bailiff calling the courtroom to order and the judge announcing the case.

"It is now time to enter judgment and sentence," the judge said. "It is the judgment of the court that the defendant Jodi Ann Arias is guilty of the crime of first-degree murder."

Maricopa County Superior Court Judge Sherry Stephens had been with us through it all, witnessing up close the heated exchanges that marked so much of the case. She turned to me and asked if I had any comments.

I had something to say, but protocol was to let Travis Alexander's family members speak first. They were in the front row, on the left side of the courtroom, as they had been for the duration of the trial. The three rows behind them were filled with those members of the media who were able to get a seat. The overflow media used another room equipped with closed-circuit television.

Travis' aunt Heather spoke first. His sisters Hilary, Tanisha, and Samantha were next. Their statements were difficult and emotional, and I felt the weight of their loss as I rose to make my statement.

"Hope is never a bad thing," I started. "Hope is always a good thing. . . . The family of Travis Alexander, as you heard, hoped that a death sentence would be imposed by this case, but that is not to be. That will not happen . . . [but] they still have hope. They have hope now that you will see your way to a natural life sentence. . . . As they have told you, when they think of the stabbing, they can feel their brother's pain. They can feel the blade going into him and it burns them. When they feel him moving away, trying to get away from [Arias] as she continually stabbed him, they can hear his cries, his screaming. It rings in their ears and it's something they cannot stop."

After my statement, Arias' mother rose to talk on her behalf, and as expected she defended her daughter.

Finally it was Arias' chance to speak. From the start of the trial, people had wanted to see how I would handle the cunning, manipulative defendant who had the ability to be sympathetic and demure at a moment's notice. I knew I had been able to cut through her posturing and expose her for who she really was—a cold-hearted murderer who refused to own up to the especially cruel crime she'd committed. I had been hard on her, but I had to be. I had prosecuted 181 jury trials, seventy-two of which involved a charge of murder, but I had never seen a defendant quite as calculating as the woman standing before the judge now. If I'd allowed her to dictate the pace of the questioning during cross-examination, she might have had her way and gotten away with murder.

Her statement was much shorter than I had anticipated. Of course, as I had predicted, she still refused to take responsibility for anything. Instead she was the victim. *She* had had to defend herself during the over-the-top murder of Travis. *She* had had to protect his reputation both while they were dating and in the days and months after his death. *She* was not the one who wanted the case to go to trial, but Travis' sisters had rejected plea-bargaining. *She* was the one who needed sympathy, even pointing me out by name as one of her tormenters.

"I do remember the moment when the knife went into Travis' throat," she said. "And he was conscious. He was still trying to attack me. It was I who was trying to get away, not Travis, and I finally did. I never wanted it to be that way, Judge. The gunshot did not come last. It came first, and that was when Travis lunged at me, just as I testified to. And, just as the State's own detective testified to years ago before he and Juan got together and decided to change their story for trial."

As she said those words, Arias physically pointed at me and used my first name. She appeared to be losing her composure. In my long career, I'd been personally attacked in the courtroom before, and this was no different. But perhaps saying those things made her feel better.

As it turned out, her pointed gesture was just the start. As her statement continued, it seemed she remembered more about the attack than she had ever let on. For years she had said that she was in a fog about the details of the crime—only remembering certain fragments of images, her running around the bedroom, finding the gun, shooting Travis, and the knife dropping. Now, in an apparent moment of anger, she recalled another detail, an important one. Arias, seven years later, recalled that Travis was conscious when she slit his throat. This was typical of the selective memory she exhibited every one of those eighteen days she had spent on the stand.

Beyond the lifting of the "fog," there was something else to her words in this final statement, something more telling. As she stood in front of the judge trying to win the chance to be released after serving twenty-five years, she made it my fault that she had been found guilty, claiming that I had changed the facts about the gunshot to make my case easier to prosecute. Of course, medical science, not I, had proved that the gunshot came after Travis had already been mortally wounded by the multiple stabbings.

But the fact that she was using some of her final words to the judge to attack me, rather than take responsibility, spoke volumes about Arias and her character. This was the vengeful woman who had killed Travis, the woman with whom I had sparred for days on the witness stand, the woman I'd convicted of first-degree murder.

␣␣␣␣━━━━━━━━

CHAPTER 1

In central Arizona during the summer, no matter what time of day it is, it can always get hotter, and as I stepped out of my car on the morning of June 10, 2008, with the temperature already in the mid-90s, I had the distinct feeling it was going to be a particularly hot one.

I'd never been to this part of Mesa, Arizona, before, but taking in my surroundings, I noticed that the streets had the quiet feel of the suburbs. The neighborhood was the picture of urban tranquility, and if the empty driveways were any indication, most residents were already at work that Tuesday morning. There wasn't even a dry gust of wind stirring the trees or the sound of children playing, but I wasn't surprised by this apparent calm; I'd learned a long time ago that most murder scenes are eerily silent in the aftermath of the violence.

At 8:35 that morning, I'd received a phone call from Sergeant Dana McBride, a supervisor with the Mesa Police Department, notifying me of a homicide and asking me to respond to the scene so that I could conduct a walk-through before the victim's body was removed. The investigation was nascent and there was only very basic information he could share: a thirty-year-old man named Travis Alexander had been murdered inside his own home.

I was in my twelfth year with the Homicide Bureau of the Maricopa County Attorney's Office in Phoenix, Arizona, having transferred into the unit in October 1996. Prosecutors assigned to the Homicide Bureau are required to take on-call shifts, and in the event that a murder occurs during their shift, that prosecutor must go to the scene in order to become familiar with the intricacies of the case and meet with the detectives and officers working to make an arrest. Technically, my twenty-four-hour on-call shift had ended at 8:00 P.M., and the call had come in after this. But although the schedule indicated that I was done at 8:00, I didn't agree with such a strict approach; besides, given that the body had been discovered the previous evening while I was still on call, it only seemed fair that I respond rather than shirk the responsibility onto the next on-call attorney on the list.

The facts that I had learned from the sergeant on the phone were that the victim shared a home with two roommates who had not seen him in a couple of days. On the evening of June 9, 2008, a friend, Marie "Mimi" Hall, worried about Travis' recent lack of communication, had stopped by his house. When no one answered the door, she called two friends to come meet her so they could go inside together, because she was afraid to enter on her own. One of Travis' roommates who happened to be home and had not heard Mimi at the front door then unlocked the master bedroom door, and the group found Travis' nude, contorted, decomposing body in the shower of the en-suite bathroom. Mimi immediately called 911 and alerted police to the situation at 10:27 P.M. Sergeant McBride added that he did not know how the victim had been killed.

After hanging up, I left the office and began the approximately thirty-mile drive to Mesa, a city in the east valley. Travis Alexander's home was located in a bedroom community miles from the center of the city. As I'd driven through his neighborhood, it seemed the kind of place where people move to raise their kids, and while there are many places of worship for many denominations, I knew the area to be particularly Mormon. Grocery stores stay open late. Movie theaters and restaurants abound. Crime—even petty offenses—was infrequent, and usually the only violence that touched their lives was what the residents saw on television.

Travis' home was an upscale tract house similar in style to the others in the subdivision, tan with brown trim and a Spanish-style roof. When I arrived, I walked up to the officer standing at the front door and let him know that I was ready for my walk-through whenever the lead investigator, a detective named Esteban Flores, was ready for me. I hadn't worked with Detective Flores before, but I knew that he was reputed to be methodical and thorough in his investigations. A half hour later, I was allowed inside the home, and after I covered my shoes with protective booties, Detective Flores, a stocky former marine in his late thirties with close-cut black hair, met me just inside the front door.

As my eyes adjusted from the sunlight outside, I began to focus on each detail in the home as it was presented to me. The main reason for having prosecutors in the Homicide Bureau on call was that doing a walk-through of the location where the murder occurred gave us firsthand knowledge of the scene and victim. While we never assisted the police in their investigation, I always tried to use the walk-through to my advantage to get a head start on understanding the homicide I would be handling.

Glancing around the home's first floor, I was struck by how orderly everything was, giving no indication that there had been trouble here. It was immaculate, and nothing seemed to be out of place. I'd been to many murder scenes and in the majority of them the furniture and household items inside the homes are strewn about or knocked down. Here, the only out-of-place item was a steam vacuum cleaner, which had been left standing in the middle of the living room floor.

As always, in a scene like this, I had my hands deep in my pants pockets to make sure I didn't touch or disturb anything, a habit I had developed years earlier. Standing beside me, Detective Flores gave me the little information about Travis the police had been able to confirm at this early stage of the investigation. Travis sold memberships through direct sales and network marketing as an independent contractor for Pre-Paid Legal Services, a business that provided access to legal services for its members who paid a fee to join. His friends said he was Mormon and faithfully attended services at the local church.

Detective Flores motioned me to follow him up the stairs. At the foot of the staircase was a doggy gate that had been pushed aside by the same friends who had discovered the body. The victim's dog, Napoleon, a black pug, had already been removed from the house and was with one of Travis' friends. We speculated about whether the dog had been there for some time without food or water, but noticed that at least there was a pet door insert in the sliding door that opened into the kitchen from the backyard allowing him to go in and out of the house.

At the top of the stair landing on the right, there was a makeshift home theater, with beanbag chairs, a big-screen TV and DVD player, a projector, and movie posters on the walls, including ones of Humphrey Bogart, Al Pacino, the Rat Pack, and Marilyn Monroe. Nothing there was disturbed, although there was a camera case lying next to one of the beanbag chairs. The camera itself was missing.

To the left were double doors that opened into the master bedroom. The first thing I noticed when I walked in was that the room felt cool. The air conditioner had been set to the mid-seventies, making the room seem chilly compared to the heat outside. The king-size bed in the center of the room had been stripped bare; there were no sheets or comforter, and a white mattress cover was balled up in the middle of the bed. Light streamed in through two windows on either side of the bed. On the nightstand was a book, *1,000 Places to See Before You Die*, by Patricia Schultz. Two pillows missing their pillowcases were on the floor near a pair of flip-flops. Carpet remnants had been cut and glued to the upper sole of the flip-flops in an apparent effort to make them more comfortable to wear.

Taking my first steps into the room, I immediately noticed a large amount of blood on the carpet bordering the hallway leading to the bathroom. The blood was brown and crusted in an ovoid stain, with a concentration of bloody footprints around it oddly reminiscent of hoof prints left at a riverbank after a wildebeest migration. These footprints started and ended around the stain, indicating that the person had been careful to avoid tracking the blood anywhere else in the bedroom.

I didn't walk down the hallway that led into the bathroom, but I could see that the tile floor was dotted with blood patches and the walls intermittently smudged with blood. There were crime lab technicians inside the hallway attempting to find any latent fingerprints—a latent print is a chance impression left at the scene of a crime that may not be immediately visible to the naked eye—or biological material for DNA testing.

I also noticed a number of detectives busy searching the bed area, while others processed the large walk-in closet with a door leading from the bedroom on one end and the bathroom on the other. Detective Flores directed that we walk through the closet on our way into the bathroom where the body had been found. Although we were wearing "booties" over our shoes, we ran the risk of transferring the blood on the hallway floor to other areas of the crime scene should we go down the hallway.

As we passed through the closet, I noticed it was orderly and organized. Baseball caps were lined up in a row. Several pairs of Levis, each clipped to a hanger by the hem hung lengthwise. Casual shoes sat on a shelf above the dress shoes, each pair aligned with its mate. To the right were Travis' suits, and next to them were his shirts, which seemed to be arranged by color. In the middle of the closet was a bench for dressing and putting on shoes. A framed picture of Abraham Lincoln hung on the small space of wall between the two shelf units, as if watching over Travis' clothing. Some luggage was stored next to the door leading into the bathroom.

The orderliness of the closet stood in stark contrast to the chaos of the bathroom, and as I looked around I first saw a sink streaked with brownish-red blood. The blood covered the faucets and was splattered on the mirror. Blood was also strewn around the floor and on the baseboards, marking a grim trail either toward or away from the shower stall, where Travis Alexander's naked body lay on the floor crammed into a fetal position—legs bent to his chest, head pressed onto his right shoulder, feet pushing against the wall. After days in this cramped repose, his extremities were turning black. It was obvious that his throat had been slashed, but there were also stab wounds visible on the upper chest. The body had apparently been rinsed off, but there was still an active discharge emanating from the gash in his throat.

There was a clear sixteen-ounce plastic tumbler resting between his right arm and the wall of the shower. Detective Flores and I discussed two possible alternatives for the tumbler. One was that it had been used to wash the body. That explanation did not make sense, because the body was already in the shower. It was more likely used in an attempt to wash away the blood in front of the sink and down the hallway, which had only served to distribute the blood to different places on the tile floor. A cardboard box on the floor of the bathroom linen closet next to the sink had soaked up some of the blood and water, leaving a light pinkish-red pattern on its' sides.

The cut to the throat had almost certainly been delivered with a knife, and although I hadn't seen anything resembling a gunshot wound, there was a .25 caliber casing lying on top of a small concentration of blood on the floor in front of the sink, where I first noticed a variety of blood patterns, indicating that Travis had stood there before making his way down the hallway. Police had searched throughout the house, but no weapon—not a gun or a knife—had been found.

Standing there, taking in the spectacle, I couldn't help but think Travis must have suffered greatly. I'd seen a lot of crime scenes since I'd joined the homicide unit, and this one spoke to an over-kill. This murder seemed methodical and I didn't think it was a crime of passion. It also seemed less angry and more purposeful. Only later would I find out just how goal-oriented the murderer had truly been because as it turned out, Travis had been killed three times over—stabbed in the chest next to the heart, slashed across the throat, and shot in the temple.

My eyes moved slowly around the bathroom one more time. I knew that it would be memorialized in photos and diagrams and that the whole room would be cataloged and measured by the investigators now working in the master bedroom suite. I would revisit this disturbing scene many times in the future through the photographs taken and the reports yet to be written, but I wanted to preserve as much as I could in my mind, so that wherever the investigation led I wouldn't forget the bloody scene now in front of me.

Flores' voice stirred me from my thoughts.

"Several of Travis' friends and acquaintances keep talking about an ex-girlfriend named Jodi," he said. "They all think she may have done it. They say she is a real stalker type."

Flores said this "Jodi" had already called the police department asking to speak to a detective involved in the investigation and he was going to return her call as soon as he could. At this time, it didn't seem strange that an ex-girlfriend had called the station—more than anything it was just interesting.

As we left the upstairs bathroom, Detective Flores stated, "We found a camera in the washing machine on the first floor. Let's go downstairs so you can look at it."

The door of the top-loading washing machine was open, allowing me to bend over and peer inside. To the left of the agitator was a black camera nestled amid the wet clothing, indicating it had been put through the wash cycle and from the discolored look of the brown towel also inside, it appeared that bleach had been used.

"I don't know if we are going to get anything out of it," Flores told me, gesturing toward the camera, "but we are going to process it to see what we can find."

I also looked inside the dryer and saw what appeared to be the missing bedding from the room upstairs. It included the king-size comforter and sheets matching the bed in the master suite.

"All this took time, you know," Flores said, and I nodded in agreement. The clean up had not been restricted to the killing scene upstairs—it was throughout the house, including the downstairs laundry room.

Cleaning up after a murder scene is extremely rare; this was only the second time I had come across one manipulated to such an extent.

CHAPTER 2

━━━━━━━━━

Questions about the crime scene and motive swirled around in my head as I merged onto Interstate 17, heading toward my office in downtown Phoenix. I was anxious to get back and jot down some notes while the scene was fresh in my mind. I was still on the freeway, but knew I was getting close when I looked to the north and saw the copper dome of the Maricopa County Administration Building coming into view. The copper had started to turn green, which gave the building a classic look. I liked seeing it, knowing that I was almost back to my office in the nerve center of the city.

The Phoenix area is a sprawling metropolis of many smaller cities collectively known as the Valley of the Sun. Land is cheap, and although people build farther and farther from downtown, the feeling of wide-open space is not compromised. Over three million people occupy the metropolitan area's more than five hundred square miles, so there seems to be room for everybody.

I'd first arrived in the valley from my home state of California to attend law school at Arizona State University in August 1981. I remember driving past the school's campus in Tempe early one morning and thinking it was already quite hot. It probably seemed hotter than it really was because my car didn't have air-conditioning. As I drove around, I was listening to the radio and heard the disc jockey raise his voice and announce that it was "cool in Phoenix." I thought it was some sort of joke until I realized that the station's call letters were

KOOL. Despite the temperature that day, the pleasant year-round weather became the reason I stayed in the Phoenix area. On those very hot days, I just keep reminding myself that it is a dry heat. Besides, it really is always "cool" here in the valley.

My ten-story, cement-and-glass office building in downtown Phoenix spans the entire block between Third and Fourth Avenues on West Jefferson Street. When we moved into the offices in the mid-1990s, the Maricopa County Attorney's Office occupied four of the ten floors, and a few years later, the Homicide Bureau expanded onto another floor, the fourth floor. I chose the southeast corner office, which has a view of the Maricopa County Fourth Avenue Jail, and have been there ever since.

I like the layout of the courthouse facilities. Our building is connected to the Maricopa County Superior Court Complex, and I can walk across "the bridge," a glass-enclosed walkway, to the courthouse without ever going outside. This is especially convenient on those days when the temperature rises above 110 degrees. Ours is one of the largest prosecutorial offices in the country, with more than three hundred attorneys serving a population of about four million people. The number of employees varies, but there are usually around nine hundred full-time workers, including attorneys, investigators, paralegals, victim advocates, and support staff. The number of attorneys in the Homicide Bureau, now called the Capital Litigation Bureau, fluctuates, with an average of fifteen attorneys, including me. Everything that happens in the legal sense happens here, so I am in the middle of the action at all times, which suits me well.

It was shortly before noon by the time I finally parked my car in the garage. After a quick sandwich at the Change of Venue café on the second floor of my office building, I began filling out the incident report about my walk-through of the murder scene. It was only one page, asking for the basics—date, time, and place.

In this case, investigators didn't know the date Travis Alexander was killed. His body had been found on the ninth of June, but given the state of decomposition and that Travis hadn't been heard from in a week, police couldn't tell how long he had been there just based on what they recovered at the crime scene. Where the form asked for "suspects," I left it blank. But in the hours that followed, as the investigation deepened and Flores gathered more information from Travis' friends and roommates at the scene, the identity of the suspect gradually began to shift from "unknown" to "Jodi Arias."

Travis' friends described Arias as "clingy" and a "fatal attraction" type. Apparently the two of them argued a lot, so much so that one of Travis' roommates had been able to detail some of their disagreements. The main source of conflict related to Jodi Arias moving to Mesa *after* she and Travis had broken up. She had been living in Palm Desert, California, and in July 2007, a couple of weeks after their breakup, she moved to Mesa. One of Travis' best friends, Taylor Searle, told detectives about a conversation Travis said he'd had with Arias just the previous week, during which Travis let Arias know that he did not want to ever see or talk to her again. Searle said that according to Travis, this had made Arias very upset.

Of particular interest was the information provided by Mimi Hall. She had been one of the people who found Travis' body. She told police that she had met Travis at a singles function at the Church of Jesus Christ of Latter-Day Saints (LDS) in Mesa. They had been spending time together as friends since about February or March, and they even went out on a couple of dates.

Mimi was scheduled to travel to Cancún, Mexico, with Travis on June 10 and hadn't heard from him in about a week. She had made it clear that they were only going as friends, and even told him that he was free to invite someone else if that made him more comfortable. Apparently, it was too late to change the plans, so they agreed to go as friends. As the trip approached, Mimi became increasingly concerned when Travis failed to return her telephone calls, respond to her text messages, or answer her e-mail correspondence. The night before their scheduled trip, she finally decided to go over to his house to make sure nothing was wrong.

It was some time after 9:00 P.M. when Mimi arrived there. Before approaching the house, she called her mother and asked that she stay on the line with her as a precautionary measure. She was concerned because she knew an old girlfriend named Jodi had been stalking Travis, and he'd told her that she had actually followed them on one of their dates. With her mother on the phone, Mimi knocked on the door and rang the doorbell over and over again without receiving an answer. Although a light was on upstairs, no one came to the door. The only response was from Travis' dog, Napoleon, who kept barking and jumping at the door in an agitated state.

Mimi was now concerned that something might have happened to Travis and called mutual friends, Michelle Lowery and Dallin Forrest, to come over and help her try to enter the house. A short time later, the group gained entry into the garage using the pad access code, which allowed them to walk into the house through the unlocked pantry door.

They were greeted by Napoleon, who was running around downstairs. When they didn't find Travis on the first floor, they went upstairs to check his bedroom, but the door was locked and nobody answered when they knocked. Travis owned the house, but to meet expenses he rented rooms to roommates, Zachary Billings and Enrique Cortez, both of whom he'd met through the LDS church. Billings was with his girlfriend in an upstairs bedroom and offered to go downstairs to get the key.

After unlocking the door, Billings and Forrest entered the room to see if Travis was inside. They'd gone only a few steps when they saw the large spot of blood on the bedroom carpet. They followed the blood down the blood-streaked hallway and into the bathroom, where they found Travis' decomposing body stuffed on the floor of the shower. After seeing the body, the two men hurried out and told the others that Travis was dead and Mimi called police.

Mimi was a dedicated Mormon girl, which was part of the reason Travis said he found her so attractive. As a devout Mormon himself, he wanted to get married and raise a family, and he believed Mimi was someone with whom he could spend the rest of his life. The problem was that after going out a couple of times, Mimi found that she was not attracted to him in that way. For his part, Travis thought she was the one and believed it was a relationship he could still explore.

Mimi told police that Travis was always a gentleman during their dates, never did anything inappropriate, and didn't even try to kiss her. Although the relationship was platonic, she had agreed to travel with him to Cancún because she'd been there before and had enjoyed it.

Mimi said she didn't know much about Jodi Arias, but did know that Travis had been the one who baptized Arias into the LDS church and that she had moved to Mesa from California after their breakup to be near him. She described Arias as a stalker ex-girlfriend and was worried about her because she believed her to be "obsessive." Travis had told her that Arias would sneak into his house through the doggy door insert in the sliding glass door leading into the kitchen. Mimi had heard that Arias had hacked into one of his online accounts, either Facebook or e-mail, and had stolen his personal journals. She said Travis had confronted her about it. Mimi thought that Arias was dangerous enough that she feared for her safety.

Police also questioned Travis' roommate Zachary Billings. Billings said that he had started renting a room from Travis beginning in late January 2008 and was charged a monthly rent of $450. When asked about Jodi Arias, Billings said that she would hang out at the house all the time when Billings first moved in back in January. He knew she had moved to Arizona from California shortly after she and Travis broke up, and that she had rented a room in a friend's house just a few miles away to be close to Travis.

Billings said Arias' move had been a source of conflict between Arias and Travis. She would call at inappropriate times and show up at the house unannounced, which led to arguments between her and Travis. Billings recalled that Travis was dating someone else back in January. He couldn't remember the woman's name, but said they broke up in mid-February and that he believed Arias had been the cause. The new girlfriend didn't like that Arias was always "hanging around" and told Travis that until he "dealt with Jodi" things between them wouldn't work out.

Billings recalled that when he came home on either Wednesday, June 4, or Thursday, June 5, the furniture on the tile floor downstairs had been moved. He said Travis had just bought an upright floor cleaner and he noticed it standing downstairs when he first walked inside. He also said that the banister leading upstairs was "slick," as if it had been cleaned.

I had wondered about the upright floor cleaner when I first saw it during the walk-through of the scene. We'd passed it on the way from the upstairs bedroom down to the laundry room. And after I saw the cleanup efforts in the bathroom, I remembered thinking that the killer might have used it to clean something up in the downstairs living room area.

Billings said that eventually someone moved the furniture, with the exception of the floor cleaner, back to its proper place in the living room. He believed the other roommate, Enrique Cortez, might have done it.

Police also talked with the other roommate, Cortez. Cortez said he couldn't remember for sure, but he believed that the last time he saw Travis was when he got home from work on Wednesday evening. He recalled that Travis was downstairs and talking on the phone, perhaps on a conference call. There was nothing unusual about that night, but the next night when he got home from work he was surprised to find that the front door was locked. Travis never worried about break-ins and always kept the front door unlocked. Cortez didn't have a key and was forced to enter the house through the garage using the keypad. He recalled that as he walked through the living room he noticed that the furniture had been moved and pushed off the tile floor. He also remembered seeing the floor cleaner in the middle of the room and assumed that Travis was getting ready to clean the tile.

That evening, as he and his girlfriend were leaving the house to go to Temple, they noticed Travis' "CTR" ring sitting on the kitchen counter. Cortez found it strange because Travis typically didn't go anywhere without it. "CTR" stands for "Choose the Right," and is worn by Mormons to remind them to resist temptation. Also out of the ordinary was that the doggy fence was up on the landing, stopping Travis' dog from going upstairs. This was unusual because Travis only restricted Napoleon's access to the living room area of the house.

Detective Flores also told me about another ex-girlfriend of Travis', Lisa Andrews, who had dated Travis on and off for a number of months in 2007 and 2008. She was the one who'd mentioned Arias as the reason for her breakup with Travis. She recalled that she and Travis had fallen asleep one night while watching television in the upstairs loft area. They'd been awakened by the sound of Napoleon barking and noticed a light going off downstairs. When Travis went down to investigate, he found Arias standing in the kitchen area. She admitted to him that not only had she let herself into the house, but she had been upstairs watching them sleep.

Andrews told detectives she received a threatening e-mail from a "John Doe" the morning after she spent the night at Travis' house:

You are a shameful whore. Your Heavenly Father must be deeply ashamed of the whoredoms you've committed with that insidious man. If you let him stay in your bed one more time or even sleep under the same roof as him, you will be giving the appearance of evil. You are driving away the Holy Ghost, and you are wasting your time. You are also compromising your salvation and breaking your baptismal covenants. Of all the commandments to break, committing the act of whoredom is one of the most displeasing in the eyes of the Lord. You cannot be ashamed enough of yourself. You are filthy, and you need to repent and become clean in the eyes of God. Think about your future husband and how you disrespect not only yourself, but him, as well as the Lord and Savior Jesus Christ. Is that what you want for yourself? Your future, your salvation, and your posterity is resting on your choices and actions. You are a daughter of God, and you have been a shameful example. Be thou clean, sin no more. Heavenly Father loves you and wants you to make the right choices. I know you are strong enough to choose the right. Your Father in Heaven is pulling for you. Don't ignore the promptings you receive, because they are vital to your spiritual well-being.

Although Andrews believed it was Arias who sent it, she had no definitive proof.

Andrews also told police about an incident that had happened in February of 2008. She and Travis were at his house that evening when someone knocked on the front door. When they answered the door, there was no one there. They stepped outside to look around and still didn't see anybody, so they went back inside. The next day, they discovered that the tires on Travis' BMW had been slashed. They initially thought it was just a random act, until they heard the same knock on the front door the next night and found that Travis' tires had been slashed for a second time.

Travis called police that afternoon to report the second tire slashing. But after waiting for four hours for officers to respond, he left because he couldn't wait any longer.

I'd only been back at the office for a bit when Flores called me with another update. Apparently in the hours after Travis' body was discovered, Arias had made a number of phone calls to others in addition to the initial call she had made to police asking to speak to a detective. Arias started calling Travis' friends and according to them, Arias let them know she was just calling to find out what was happening. Police had encouraged one of the friends, Zachary Billings, who was standing outside of the house when his phone rang, not to answer her call. Apparently when her calls to other mutual acquaintances went unanswered, Arias called police for a second time.

"This time," Detective Flores said, "she was insistent, almost demanding to speak with the investigating officer." This message spoke of impatience, as she indicated that she was still waiting for detectives to return her call. Arias' earlier call asking to speak with an investigator had not struck either of us as particularly unusual. She was an ex-girlfriend who appeared to still care for Travis. As far as police knew, she had moved to Yreka, California, a couple of months earlier and hadn't returned for a visit, and they figured she probably didn't have any useful information. On the other hand, she might be able to provide a viable lead, so it was important to return her call.

"As soon as I call her, I'll get back to you with an update, but I'll hold off until I'm back at the station so that I can get the conversation on tape," Flores told me.

It was after 4:00 P.M. when I heard from him again. He told me he had returned Arias' call earlier that afternoon at 2:35 P.M., and found she was very cool and composed during their conversation. As he recapped the call, I found myself increasingly curious to hear it for myself, so I asked the detective to bring a copy of the forty-one-minute, fourteen-second audio recording of their conversation to my office, because I wanted to hear Arias' voice.

My first impression in listening to the call was that Arias genuinely seemed to want to help Detective Flores and sounded especially engaging as the conversation progressed.

"Well, I just wanted to offer any assistance that I might have," she began in a soft, even tone. "I was a really good friend of Travis'. I don't know a lot of anything . . ."

"What have you heard so far?" Flores asked her.

"I heard that he was—that he passed away, and that, um, it was, I, I don't know. I heard all kinds of rumors. I heard there was a lot of blood. I heard that, um, his roommate found him or his friend found him or, people were, I just, I'm sorry, it's all, I'm, I'm just upset . . ."

"Okay."

"I heard that, uh, he, he, nobody's been able to get ahold of him for almost a week, which, and that was about the last time I spoke to him, too."

"Okay," the detective said again, allowing Arias to fumble over her words. I knew he was purposely holding back information so he could see what it was she knew, as well as determine a possible motive for her call.

"Uh, which is actually why I thought I—my friend said I should call you anyway and let you know the last time I talked to him."

"Yeah, absolutely," Flores said, continuing the conversation. "Any help we can get from anybody who had any kind of contact with him, uh, any phone contact . . ."

"I used to talk to him quite regularly," Arias volunteered. "Um, I used to live there. I live in Northern California now. Um, but after I moved, I moved a few months ago, and after I moved we kept in touch very regularly, and, um, kinda fell back a little bit, but it got down to a couple times a week. But I hadn't heard from him. I—I—I talked to him on Tuesday night."

"Okay," Flores acknowledged, continuing to offer no details.

"Um, I looked at my phone records on, on the, on the Internet to check and, uh, so I definitely talked to him Tuesday night," Arias said, referring to the night of June 3.

That she had taken the time to check her phone records before speaking to police caught my interest. It seemed unusual that she would have this information at the ready in support of an alibi especially since police had not even attempted to question her yet.

Flores' tone remained steady. "Okay, so, and that was Tuesday night? Do you remember about what time?"

"Uh, I think it was, I wanna say, like, a quarter after nine. But I think—it was some time between eight and ten. But I know it wasn't as late as ten. Probably between eight thirty and nine thirty more so, to narrow it down."

Her failure to give a time also struck me as odd since the phone records she had supposedly reviewed include the time a call is made.

"Okay, and, uh, what did you guys talk about?"

"Um, it was brief," Arias recounted. "He—I was—um—I was driving out to Utah, and, you know, he was like, 'Are you gonna come out and see me?' And I'm like, 'No.' And, you know—he's—he's supposed to make a trip up here, um, at the end of the month because he—we—um—this thing we are doing, it's called, um—there's a book called *1,000 Places to See Before You Die*."

I remembered seeing that book on Travis' nightstand when I visited the crime scene, so I was curious to hear what Arias had to say about it.

". . . It's been featured on the Travel Channel and all that," she continued, her voice animated. "And we sorta got into that last year where we were starting to see all these different places on the list. And we thought, you know, one thousand places is a lot of places, but why not? That would be a fun goal. So we each kind of have that goal."

Arias' claim that she and Travis were intending to travel together later in the month also struck me as strange, because I knew Travis' friends had painted her as a kind of a stalker ex-girlfriend, so it didn't make sense that they would be making plans to go away together.

"Was that trip already scheduled, or is it just something you guys talked about?" Flores asked.

Arias stumbled over her answer. "Um, it was—it was—wasn't officially, like, dated. That's—I had been trying to reach him, so I could solidify my own schedule, because I was planning on making a trip down there . . . um, yeah. But, uh, it was supposed to happen in May and then, um, supposed to happen last week, and that didn't work out, so he was gonna leave for Cancún today and, um, and then he said as soon as he gets back from Cancún, he was gonna make the trip."

I could hear in the detective's voice that he was taking notes as he moved the conversation back to the subject of Travis' death. "Did he have any issues with anybody here in town? Any enemies, anybody that wanted to do him harm?"

"You know," Arias replied, "he got his tires slashed—it was last year. Um, he was, he—he said he was worried about that. Um, and I was worried about that. He never locked his doors. And I told him—I would tell him, 'Lock your doors.' And he'd be like, 'You're not my mom.' You know."

By now, Flores had already been told about the tire-slashing incident and knew that all of Travis' friends were pointing to Arias as the culprit, although he didn't let on what he knew. Instead, he asked her about her relationship with Travis. "How would you describe your relationship with him?"

From Arias' tone, which was upbeat and positive, it appeared she liked talking about this topic. "We dated for like five months," she recounted. "And we broke up and we continued, actually, to see each other for quite a bit . . . right up until I moved.

". . . We officially broke up June 29 of last year. . . . Even though we broke up, and we were no longer boyfriend and girl-friend, we decided to remain friends. But—you know, I—I kinda feel embarrassed talking about this, but it was more like—it was more than friends, but it wasn't boyfriend and girlfriend. It was more like kinda buddies. Do you know what I mean?"

"Okay . . . so you guys were not like, uh, romantically, uh, together at any time of . . ."

"We—we were intimate, um, but I wouldn't say romantic as far as the relationship goes," Arias responded in a matter-of-fact tone. "We were in no way headed toward marriage, uh, or talking about anything like that. We hung out probably . . . sometimes."

"Now, you say intimate," Flores repeated, in an attempt to verify what he had just been told. "Does—does that include, like, a sexual relationship with him?"

"Yeah, it does." Arias' confirmation added an interesting wrinkle to the story, one that would continue to unfold as the investigation into Travis' death continued. "If you could keep it confidential for now," Arias asked, implying a concern with protecting Travis' reputation. "Because I know that it's—you know—he's Mormon and it's . . . seriously looked down upon in—in our church and—I mean, I just—I'm telling you this to be helpful in any way I can," she explained.

When asked about the last time she saw Travis, Arias maintained that it was in early April. She couldn't remember for sure, but claimed it was sometime between April 7 and 10, when she left Mesa to return home to Yreka, California.

"Did you stop by the house, uh, when you rented the U-Haul, to say good-bye to him?" Flores asked.

"Oh yeah, in fact, um, I was, I was almost completely moved out of my house for about a week afterward, and I just stayed at his house the whole time. I mean, I practically lived there even when I was there. I spent—I spent the night there several times a week while I lived there. Um, I came over and cleaned his house a lot. He—he sorta—he paid me a little bit every month to keep his house clean and nice . . . sorta like a housekeeper."

"But, you haven't physically been here since you left?"

"Since I moved, no, I haven't," Arias said before launching into a lengthy explanation about her intention of staying at Travis' house while he was away in Cancún. She claimed that Travis' house was always open to her, as long as she gave him a heads-up.

"I was gonna go this week, actually, while he [Travis] was in Cancún and stay at his house. But I just—it's not in the budget."

"Okay, was that something that you guys had scheduled, that you were gonna come down and stay at his house when he was gone?"

"Yeah—or no—actually. Not—that's what I e-mailed him about last week 'cause it was kinda last minute," Arias claimed. " 'Cause I was gonna go—I'm looking at a calendar here. I was gonna go not this week but the next week and then he was gonna come up here that following week, which was the Fourth of July. And, um, I know it sounds kinda weird. We're all like travelers . . . And I figured, you know, it would be a good idea if I—I would have a place to stay. His house is open all the time to friends. I mean—anybody in his business or anybody that comes to visit, he gives up his bed. He'll sleep on the couch. He let them have the whole room. Um, so it just didn't seem he—he said that the door is always open, so I would have felt totally okay just showing up and staying at his house and eating his frozen dinners, et cetera, et cetera. And he would have been fine with that, too. And I just, you know, he said, 'Just always give me a heads up.' So, I—I asked him, you know, 'Let me know if that's cool. If not, I'll make other arrangements.' And I never heard back."

Something about Arias' tone and the way she stumbled over her words raised my suspicions. Her answers included too many details, all designed to paint an idyllic picture of their post-breakup relationship, which was clearly at odds with what others were saying.

"And, when was that e-mail sent out?" Flores asked.

"Uh, just a few days ago. I'm in front of my computer, so I can check right now for you," Arias told him. ". . . Um, let's see, I sent one on June 7, 'Haven't heard back from you.'"

That he was likely already dead when this e-mail was sent was not lost on me.

"He got a little bit upset when I said I wasn't driving out to see him," she pronounced, suddenly moving the conversation in a darker direction. "But he—he gets upset real easily. Um—I don't know. He just—he likes to hang it over me a little bit and we kinda guilt each other sometimes."

"So you guys still had a fairly decent relationship as friends?"

"We did . . ."

"'Cause the people that we talked to, uh, said that you guys, uh, that your relationship was kinda rocky and—uh—it got a little—it got a little crazy at times . . ."

Arias did not miss a beat in responding. "Um, what happened was when I—I broke up with Travis around last year—because—it was all really dumb. It was a bunch of drama. I, uh, had the suspicion that he was cheating on me and so I—I looked in his phone and found out, and I found all these text messages and, like, it just all blew up and it was, like, we realized we couldn't trust each other, so, I mean, we broke up at that point. But we were still—we were still attracted to each other and we still loved each other. So, it wasn't the best thing, but we still hung out all the time together."

Detective Flores kept the conversation moving with questions about the furnishings and bedding in Travis' bedroom, which Arias answered in great detail. I found her somewhat chatty for someone talking to a police officer about the death of an ex-boyfriend. When asked how she learned of Travis' death, she put forth the name of a mutual friend, Daniel Free-man. "I met him last year with his sister when we all took a trip out to the Grand Canyon and to Sedona," she offered.

"So he called you last night and told you what happened?"

"Yeah, yeah, he did. He didn't have a lot of information."

"Any idea what everybody's talking about? What everybody's saying? What their suspicions are?" Flores asked.

For the first time, Arias sounded flustered. She stepped over her words until she was finally able to formulate a coherent response. She explained that most of her information had come from the bishop from her church ward in Mesa, and that it mostly related to what police had done thus far in their investigation. "Um, he basically said that they took everybody and separated them. And I don't know who 'everybody' is."

After saying she'd called around to get additional information, she added, "And I heard from my friend, um, that there was a lot of blood," her voice filling with emotion. "And I don't know if that's just a rumor that's going around or if it's true . . ."

"Okay, well, I can tell you that we are investigating it as a homicide," Flores informed her.

She appeared eager to educate the detective on Travis' physical strength, explaining that in an attempt to get into shape for his impending trip to Cancún, he had begun a diet and exercise regimen that had him taking nutritional supplements and engaging in intense workouts with heavy dumbbells. "And he's so strong, I mean, there are a couple of times we've tried to wrestle just for fun and he showed me some moves and there's just no—like—I don't see how anyone—unless maybe there were two people—I don't see how anyone could overpower him . . ."

She seemed to be telling Flores to not even waste his time considering her as a suspect because her physical strength was no match for Travis'. But she didn't stop there and in what appeared to be an attempt to influence the investigation went even further by advising him to look for two people.

"Why would somebody want to hurt him?" Flores asked. "Did he owe somebody money? Did he have any worries or concerns about anybody?"

Arias claimed that Travis did owe people money, including one outstanding loan from a friend for about six thousand dollars, but she insisted the lenders were all "good friends," who would never harm him if he failed to make good on his loans.

Flores was about thirty minutes into the call when he advised Arias that "certain people" his detectives had interviewed had not portrayed her in the best light. "I don't want to make you feel bad . . . but they didn't have the best of things to say about you."

Arias' one-word reply belied no emotion. "Okay," she responded.

He went on to describe some of things that Travis' friends had told investigators, including some of the more hurtful comments. "There was also some talk about you," he added, "you know, spying on his e-mail and Facebook accounts, those kinds of things."

Arias sounded unfazed by the unflattering depiction, and even offered an explanation that appeared to counter what Flores had been told, although I would soon learn that her ability to tailor a response to negate a truth was one of her obvious strengths. "Oh, he gave me his, um, he gave me his Facebook password and his MySpace password, and I gave him my—which one? I gave him my Facebook password and my Gmail account password. And the reason we did that is because—it was kind of dumb—we did that months ago, and we thought, um, what's, what can we do to try to reestablish trust between us?

". . . And, um, you know, well, why don't we start with that? And so that's what we did. And, you know, it just didn't work. He got really upset finally and he's like, 'You know, this isn't working.' Um, and I said, 'All right. This is too much of a headache. Let's just change our passwords.' So we did. We changed our passwords after that."

"How long ago did you guys change them?" Flores wanted to know.

"I changed mine, gosh, not too long ago. Probably three weeks ago, maybe? And I don't know about his. Because I haven't—once he made it clear that he wasn't comfortable with that anymore, I didn't even try to get back into his accounts anymore."

Flores advised her that police intended to obtain a search warrant for Travis' e-mails, as well as his Gmail and Facebook accounts. "And we can tell where those things were accessed from by IP addresses. . . . I just want to make it clear that if you did access it from somewhere else at a certain time, you know, if you accessed it from California, we're gonna know."

"Yeah, I'll tell you right now that I did," Arias admitted.

As Flores continued to move the conversation along, he shifted to Arias' move to Arizona, and as I sat there, listening to the tape, the response he got to his next question gave me pause. When asked if she had moved to Mesa because of Travis, Arias told him, "I moved there because of him, and I moved away because of him." She added that financial pressures and a desire to be closer to her family were two other factors she considered when deciding whether to leave Mesa, but she made it clear that putting some distance between her and Travis was at the top of the list.

Flores said, "Yeah, because when we first arrived on the scene, and I started talking to people and—and some of his closest friends began mentioning your name as, 'You know, hey, you need to call her, because she probably knows what happened to him or she possibly had something to do with it.'"

"Oh, gosh," Arias replied coyly. "No, I had nothing . . ."

Flores barely acknowledged her denial. "That's how bad it was at the scene," he continued. "And, you know, I needed to talk to you to find out why they would say something like that. Uh, why would they start pointing fingers in your direction right away?"

As I would soon learn, Arias had a justification for every-thing. "I don't know. Maybe I'm—maybe because I am the ex-girlfriend. We've had lots of fights," she reasoned. "We started fighting because I did the wrong thing and got into his phone because I had a suspicion," she said, once again repeating the details of their subsequent fights and ultimate breakup.

Flores imparted his appreciation of her apparent candor. "Well, you know, I'm glad I did get ahold of you," he told her in a gracious tone. "It kind of clears up a lot of questions that I had. And, a lot of the concerns . . ."

As he attempted to sign off the call, Arias suddenly raised a red flag. "I should probably tell you that when he got upset, he would send me really mean e-mails," she offered without prompting. "Um, he would send me mean text messages and things. Um, you'll probably find some stuff on his Facebook. I know for sure you'll find it on his Facebook and definitely in his Gmail. And you're welcome to access all of my accounts, too, if you want."

Flores explained that police would probably subpoena Travis' Facebook and Gmail accounts to see with whom he had been communicating and what was being said. He then opened the door for Arias to impart her theories. "You know, in a case like this, we need to know who had some type of beef with him. . . . Why they would do something like this. . . . And I was just hoping maybe you could kinda point me in the right direction. . . ."

Arias immediately put forth a name, a former tenant of Travis' who she claimed had moved out on bad terms in the spring of 2007. "What happened was, he got kicked out be-cause he was considered like borderline sexual predator. Not like a rapist, but coming on to girls, and it's, you know, really looked down upon in the church . . . and so he was disfellow-shipped and Travis said, 'And you need to get out.' You know, 'Get your stuff out of my house.' It was said over the phone because he and I were in, um, Missouri. . . ."

Arias said the ex-tenant was a "really big guy," but added, "he doesn't seem violent. He seemed pretty gentle, like, a little bit thuggish. . . ."

"What about any of his neighbors? Any problems with anybody?" Flores posed.

Arias had one neighbor in mind, someone Travis had told her about, although she claimed she didn't know the guy personally. According to Arias, Travis had said, "He hates me," and when Arias asked him why, Travis' response was "I think he's jealous, because he's a forty-something-year-old that has to go to work every morning and I'm a successful, twenty-something-year-old that stays all day in my pajamas at home."

"This is more than jealousy. This is something else," Flores said of Travis' death. He asked Arias if she had any questions for him, and she listed several. "Do you know when all this happened?" she wanted to know. "You said that maybe multiple people because he was a guy, maybe you can talk about this, but was there, um, there, like, any kind of weapons used? . . . Was there a gun?"

The weapons used in the attack had not been made public yet, so it immediately struck me that she knew to ask about a gun.

"I can't say what type of weapon was used," Flores told her, "but, yeah, I'm guessing there was a weapon used by the type of injuries that were left behind. Um, do you know if he had any weapons in the house?"

"Uh, his two fists," Arias replied flatly, denying that he had any weapons.

"That's it? No handguns or rifles?"

"No, he wasn't one to keep any of that. . . ." Arias described Travis' interest in wrestling and the UFC, and recalled that he liked "beating the crap" out of his punching bag, seemingly implying that he was given to physical violence.

At the time, it was easy to see this characterization of Travis as being physically imposing as just an additional detail in the growing portrait of him. But in the months and years ahead, I often found myself returning to this initial call and thinking about how even back then she was attempting to portray herself as a victim by claiming that Travis had a bad temper as shown by the mean electronic correspondence he had sent her. It didn't matter that she hadn't been implicated; she was already laying the groundwork for her ultimate defense in her first conversation with police. As I would soon learn, Arias seemed to always be thinking several steps beyond her current story.

————————————

CHAPTER 3

Over the next three days, Detective Flores called me frequently, as he and the other investigators continued to process the crime scene and uncover new, disturbing details in the process. His updates weren't meant to seek my guidance, but to keep me informed, so that I would be prepared to make a decision on the charges to be filed once the person or persons who killed Travis came to light. While there was still no definitive suspect, Jodi Arias was on a very short list of one.

Flores told me the killing had been much more violent than the initial scene had suggested. There had been many more stab wounds than what we'd been able to see as we bent over to look at Travis while he lay crumpled inside the shower. Investigators from the Maricopa County Office of the Medical Examiner had unfolded the body to find multiple wounds to the upper back and several more to the torso. They also discovered that the gash to Travis' neck was much deeper than we had originally believed, and they noticed for the first time that he had been shot in the right temple, providing an answer to the empty shell casing found lying in front of the sink resting in Travis' blood.

The doctor conducting the autopsy, Dr. Kevin Horn, would later report that Travis Alexander received three mortal wounds, each of which alone would have caused his death: a stab wound near the heart, the slice to the throat, and the gunshot to the right temple.

In his opinion, Travis was stabbed first in the chest, with the

knife cutting into the protective sac around the heart and per-
forating the superior vena cava, a major vein that comes down
from the head and the upper body draining into the heart. This
stab wound did not cause Travis to lapse into unconsciousness
immediately, and he would have been able to move about for
a few minutes before he eventually died. Travis received many
defensive injuries to his left hand and one to the right, proving
he survived and was conscious long enough to either grab the
knife blade or raise his hands to protect himself.

According to the medical examiner, Travis' throat was then
slashed, cutting the jugular vein and carotid artery as the knife
was pulled from one side of his neck to the other. The cut also
severed his windpipe, preventing him from screaming or calling for help. It was approximately three to four inches deep,
reaching all the way back to his spine. This wound would have
been rapidly fatal, and Travis would have lapsed into unconsciousness within a few seconds of its infliction. Although
Travis was still alive when his throat was slashed, he would
not have been able to make any voluntary movements such as
putting up his hands after the wound was inflicted.

The medical examiner also found that the last fatal injury
was the gunshot wound to the right temple, which perforated
the brain and came to rest in Travis' left cheek. The doctor
could not determine how far away the gun was when the shot
was fired. But he could say that the shot would have caused
Travis to lose consciousness almost immediately, and he would
not have been able to engage in purposeful activity to defend
himself.

These details from the medical examiner proved helpful in
understanding how the actual crime unfolded, a picture that
would become even more clear through the blood spatter analysis of Lisa Perry of the Mesa Police Department. Perry's opinion was that the source of the blood, Travis Alexander, had
stood over the sink with blood falling onto the vanity. And
while he stood there, force was applied to his body, causing

the blood spatter patterns on the mirror. She also determined that Travis had already bled on the floor when the shot rang out, because the casing landed on top of blood that had been previously deposited near the sink.

Based on the autopsy and the blood spatter analysis, it was clear the attack started with Travis being stabbed in the chest while he was still in the shower, and continued with the assailant stabbing him in the back repeatedly as he stood over the sink, causing the blood misting on the mirror. The attack moved to the end of the hallway at the door breach to the bedroom, where Travis' throat was slit, as shown by the large ovoid stain on the carpet. His body was then moved back to the sink area, as corroborated by the contusions to the right leg, which were consistent with the body being dragged. The casing near the sink indicated that Travis had been shot in the face in that area, before his body was put back in the shower.

About a week into the investigation, Flores called my office with some curious news. Arias had traveled more than one thousand miles—fifteen hours on the road—from Northern California to Mesa on June 17 to provide biological swabs for use in DNA testing and to provide fingerprint samples. Given Arias' claim that she hadn't seen Travis since April, it was unusual that she would volunteer to drive that distance to give her fingerprints and her DNA to the police.

"This woman is calling us, coming out to see us, so clearly she doesn't think she is a suspect," Flores told me. "But we don't know anybody else who would want to kill Travis Alexander except for her." She claimed to have an alibi, that she wasn't even in Mesa at the time of the killing, but the investigation had no other leads and had uncovered no other enemies among Travis' business contacts or friends.

Her behavior struck us as peculiar, but all we could do was speculate. Maybe she believed that police would be less inclined to investigate her because she was so willing to assist us. At this point, there was still no case against her and no way to identify her as the killer.

Each time Flores and I spoke, our discussions about Arias were akin to a catchy song that you can't seem to get out of your head, where you sing the same lyrics and hum the identical tune. So it was with our conversations every time he called. We always said that it was Arias who killed Travis; but we agreed we just couldn't prove it at least for now.

All that began to change on June 19, when I got a phone call from Flores. I heard the eagerness in his voice, and I knew he had something important to tell me. The crime lab had managed to retrieve photographs contained in the memory card of the Sanyo camera that had been found in the washing machine at Travis' house.

"You're not gonna believe this," Detective Flores said with unusual excitement. "There are pictures of Arias naked at Travis Alexander's house on June 4, so she was there."

"How did you guys get them?" I asked. It seemed too good to be true.

"They were deleted, but we got them," he said.

He explained that although they had been deleted, a detective had been able to recover the photos from the unallocated space of the memory card. Police believed that someone had wanted these photos permanently gone, because they had taken the five separate steps to erase them.

Detective Flores started to describe the photographs to me over the telephone, but given that they placed our only suspect at the crime scene, I was anxious to see them for myself. So Flores offered to drive the thirty miles from the Mesa Police Department to my office. When he arrived, he already had the copies neatly arranged and separated into three groups in a blue three-ring binder, which he placed on my desk and opened to the first page. All but a small number of the photographs could be proven to have been taken on June 4, 2008.

The initial photograph in the first group, which was snapped at 1:42:53 P.M., placed Jodi Arias in Travis' bedroom on the afternoon of June 4, although she had denied being there no more recently than April. In this photo, Arias was lying naked on Travis Alexander's bed, her arms outstretched and her right leg bent at the knee, exposing the area between her legs. In the lower right-hand corner of that picture, barely visible, appears to be a knee, so police knew Travis must have been the photographer. Arias' hair was in pigtails, one resting just above her left breast. She was not looking directly at the camera, posing seductively with her head turned slightly to the right. Flores and I had a hard time believing that the person we suspected of killing Travis had apparently had sex with him that same day.

Flores then showed me the other five photographs that had been taken during the same afternoon session. One, snapped at 1:44:00 P.M., was a close-up shot of Arias' anal and vaginal areas.

Another, taken by Arias fifty seconds later, showed Travis naked and on his back, exhibiting his erect penis. In the foreground of that photograph was a bottle of KY personal lubricant. This photo confirmed that the other participant in the sexual activity that day was indeed Travis. There was now no disputing that Arias had been there on June 4, on the day of the murder, contrary to her protestations to Detective Flores during their June 10 phone call.

A fourth photo, taken at 1:47:14, was also of Travis. He was on his back and looking at the camera, with his right arm extended, as if motioning Arias to come over to him. The personal lubricant had been moved so that it was now closer to the head of the bed.

The next photo, which did not have a time stamp, showed Arias, propped up on her elbows, turning her body to the camera as if to show off her breasts and vaginal area, her left pigtail cascading over her shoulder onto the bed, the right one lying between her breasts.

The last of these six pictures showed Arias' legs spread to display her pubic area. It appeared she had either waxed or shaved in the recent past. Clearly, the couple was captivated by the moments now captured by the camera.

I can't say that I was shocked by the photos as I looked at them. Sexual picture-taking has become a commonplace activity these days, especially with the advent of smartphones, all of which are equipped with cameras. And it didn't surprise me that there was a sexual component to this killing. It seems the majority of the homicides that pass across my desk have some sexual element to them. If it isn't about sex, it is usually about money.

What was unexpected here was seeing Travis and Arias engaged in sexual activity, because they both practiced the Mormon faith, a religion that prohibits any type of sex before marriage. In all of these photos, Arias appeared extremely uninhibited in her poses and seemed very relaxed in front of the camera, indicating that perhaps she had engaged in this type of sexual foreplay in the past, perhaps even with Travis.

But to me, the lasting impression of these pictures had little to do with the explicit nudity they portrayed. What struck me as significant was that Travis was lying in his bed, a place of obvious emotional comfort, only a few short hours before he was bathed in his own blood.

As I was about to see, there was a tranquil lull that was documented in the second group of photographs. There were twenty in all, featuring a nude Travis Alexander in the shower. The first was snapped at 5:22:24 P.M. and the last one was taken eight minutes and six seconds later, at 5:30:30 P.M. All had been similarly deleted but not permanently erased.

The first sixteen captured him standing in the shower, water cascading down his head and body.

The last four were of him sitting on the shower floor. The first of these was snapped at 5:28:54 P.M. His solemn expression and the way the water was cascading down his cheeks gave the appearance that he was crying. The last one, taken at 5:30:30 P.M., is the last picture of Travis Alexander alive. Approximately forty-five seconds later, the killer, who we now believed was Arias, began her assault, as indicted in the final set of deleted photographs. This last set was comprised of three images that had been taken inadvertently. Two of the three had been snapped when the camera had been upside down, and had appeared dark when first viewed. The detective had enhanced them until he saw Travis' body in each of these photographs. These images were pivotal, because they showed someone dragging the body down the hallway as the attack was coming to an end—suddenly the events of the crime weren't conjecture because police could see what had happened at these two distinctive moments.

The first photo in this set of three was time-stamped at 5:31:14 P.M. It was blurry, but one could see the bathroom ceiling above the shower. It did not show either Travis or the person attacking him and Detective Flores and I agreed that it had been taken either immediately before or during the first part of the stabbing.

The second photo was snapped one minute and two seconds later, at 5:32:16 P.M. Travis was on his back in this one. He was at the threshold between the bathroom hallway and the master bedroom, with his head on the carpet and his feet on the tile. His throat had already been slashed and his head was partially elevated. There was blood flowing from the right side of his neck onto his upper back, spilling onto the tile floor and the edge of the carpet. This accounted for the large amount of blood I had seen on the carpet area during my walk-through of the crime scene. The person whose stocking foot is in the foreground looked to be grabbing or lifting Travis' right arm. There was a stripe running down the side of the person's pant leg. I asked Detective Flores if investigators had found any pants at the crime scene resembling those in the photograph, but they had not located any clothing like this.

Detective Flores then showed me the last of the three pictures of this set, which was taken one minute and sixteen seconds later, at 5:33:32 P.M. In this one, the killer is seen dragging Travis back along the hallway toward the bathroom, blood rolling down his back.

This last picture in the sequence was inadvertently snapped as Arias dragged Travis' body to the sink area, the place where she shot him in the head before continuing to drag him to the shower, where she stuffed his body into the standup stall. But, this also marked the beginning of her cleanup at the scene, which included the rinsing of the body and deleting the photographs. The cover-up also involved taking the plastic tumbler and throwing water down the hallway. It appeared Arias cleaned her feet at some point to avoid tracking any blood throughout the rest of the house and took the bedding and camera downstairs to put them in the washing machine.

As Flores turned the last page in the binder, we pieced together the day's chronology based on the time stamps. The police now had evidence that she had spent the early afternoon of June 4, enjoying a sexual dalliance with Travis, followed by a photographic session in the shower later in the afternoon after which she killed him.

It was Detective Flores' and my belief that Arias lured Travis into the shower to entice him into a vulnerable position, naked and defenseless. His shower ended with her stabbing him in the chest, slicing his throat, and shooting him.

Although Arias had denied being in Mesa within the last couple of months, the photographs proved otherwise. Not only could police place her at the crime scene on the day of the murder, they had a virtual flipbook of the crime itself, a series of images that showed how the events actually played out, in the form of time-stamped photographs. Though there was no photo of Arias' face, it was obvious that she was the one dragging him back toward the bathroom when the second inadvertent photograph showing her stocking foot and pant leg was snapped.

Based solely on the pictures, I was leaning toward charging Arias with first-degree murder, but I hesitated. While the photos supported our belief that Arias had been with Travis on the afternoon of his killing and provided the story of how his life ended, they still didn't prove that she hadn't walked out before Travis was killed.

"How can we be absolutely certain that Arias didn't leave the house in between the photos time-stamped earlier in the afternoon and when Travis was killed?" I asked.

"We don't know," Flores answered. "We'll have to wait for the fingerprint results to come back," referring to a latent palm print found in blood on the wall in the hallway leading to the bathroom. "I put a rush on the request."

That meant I'd still have to wait a little longer to make a determination whether to charge her.

As Flores packed up the binder, I found myself thinking over the disturbing implications of what the photos had shown. It now seemed clear that Arias' apparent cooperation with police was nothing more than a ruse to divert suspicion away from her. Detective Flores smiled wryly as he reminded me of their telephone conversation on June 10, where she had offered to "help" him with the investigation.

She had played the part of the grieving ex-girlfriend well.

CHAPTER 4

T he police might have had a collection of incriminating photos and an actual timeline of the crime itself, but they were only beginning to build the case against Jodi Arias. While the photographs from the camera were significant— certainly the most significant piece of evidence against her— police still had to proceed cautiously when speaking to Arias, whether it be in person or by telephone. They had to be strategic about what information to share with her.

Arias continued to maintain that the last time she visited Travis Alexander was in April 2008, two months before his murder. Backing up this assertion was a complex yet well-thought-out alibi in which she claimed that on the day of the killing she was traveling to visit a prospective beau in Utah.

In a phone conversation with Detective Flores on June 25, she laid out the details of her supposed alibi, saying that she left Yreka on June 2 and had expected to arrive in the Salt Lake City area on the morning of June 4 for a Pre-Paid Legal conference and to spend some time with a potential love interest. She then detailed a nightlong escapade of driving in the wrong direction on various highways after getting lost. According to her, the errant path taken explained why she arrived a day late, on June 5.

When contacted by police, the boyfriend-in-waiting, a man named Ryan Burns, confirmed that Arias had not shown up in Utah until the fifth day of June, a day later than she had told him to expect her. He could not account for her whereabouts in the days leading up to June 5.

Arias' alibi continued to unravel from there.

A fingerprint examiner with the Mesa Police Department confirmed on June 26 that the bloody latent palm print found on the west wall of the bathroom hallway belonged to Arias. The palm print put Arias in the hallway near the area where one of the inadvertent photographs captured the body being dragged. But it only proved that Arias was there at some point. It didn't tell us when.

The latent print results moved me one step closer to filing criminal charges, but I still wanted to wait for the results of any DNA testing from the scene. Helpful as they are, latent prints are limited in their use because they cannot be dated and examiners are unable to pinpoint the day a print may have been left. They make a strong case as supporting evidence, but taken alone, the palm print couldn't place Arias at the crime scene while the killing was taking place. Only the DNA results could do that by confirming whether or not Arias had left any blood behind.

A week later, on July 3, the DNA results from the bloody left palm print showed there was a mixture of blood from two individuals—Travis Alexander and Jodi Arias. There were also DNA results from a strand of hair that was found attached to the wall with blood. It, too, was from Jodi Arias. Like latent prints, the hair's presence was not enough to tell us when it was left at the house or how it ended up becoming stuck in his hallway. Arias had been to the house many times, so the hair could conceivably have been left there and only disturbed and attached to the wall later, during the attack.

The combination of the latent prints, the DNA, and, most importantly, the photos made me feel it was finally appropriate to charge her. The pictures chronicled the couple's activities during the entire afternoon, starting in the bedroom, followed by Travis taking a shower, and ending with the in-

advertent photographs of the body being dragged. This timeline from the camera made it clear that both the palm print
and hair were left during the attack as Arias stabbed and shot
Travis.

Although I had palm print and DNA results, the importance of the photographs retrieved from the camera was hard
to overstate. If Arias had simply taken the camera from the
crime scene and disposed of it on the drive to Utah instead of
leaving it behind after deleting the incriminating photographs,
I might never have charged her with the murder because the
remaining evidence may not have been enough to prove her
guilty at a trial.

It was hard to understand what caused Arias to put the
camera in the washing machine rather than take it with her.
The effort she put into cleaning the scene was difficult to reconcile with the apparent carelessness of leaving the camera
behind. Perhaps she mistakenly believed that once the photographs were deleted, they could never be recovered. Or maybe
she was confident that the deletion of the photos combined
with putting the camera through the wash cycle would erase
the images on the camera's memory card. Her reasons for leaving it behind were of little consequence. What was important
was that her mistake allowed police to place her at the scene,
even though she vehemently denied it.

During the June 25 phone call, Detective Flores had let
Arias know that police had found Travis' camera in the washing machine, but led her to believe that they had been unable
to recover any of the photographs on the memory card, telling
her the camera was "completely destroyed."

In response, Arias boasted of being a photographer and
claimed that Travis had sought out her advice before purchas-
ing this Sanyo camera. She then offered the detective solace
by advising him that he might consider sending the camera to
outside data recovery services that had been successful in re-
trieving data in situations like this where it seemed impossible.

Whatever her motivation in providing the detective this advice, it seemed she had been undermined by her own arrogance and the mistaken belief that because she had put the camera through the wash cycle, the water and bleach would destroy the images, leaving her safe from scrutiny.

Police discovered the remaining part of Arias' cover up plan in the penumbras of her electronic communications. Within days of the murder she made a cell phone call, sent a text message, and delivered an e-mail to Travis in an attempt to show that she had nothing to do with his death.

Arias left a voice mail on his cell phone around midnight on June 4, 2008, detailing the same story about getting lost on her way to Utah that she would tell Flores after her arrest in Yreka:

> *Hey, what's going on? It's almost midnight, anyway, right about the time you're starting to gear up. I know Leslie called you, so I already talked to her, so you could call her back if you want. But, it's not really necessary, um. My phone died, so I wasn't getting back to anybody, um, and what else? Oh, and I drove one hundred miles in the wrong direction—over a hundred miles, thank you very much. So, yeah, remember New Mexico? It was a lot like that, only you weren't here to prevent me from going into the three digits, so fun, fun. I'll tell you about that later. Also we were talking about when, we were talking about your upcoming travels my way. I was looking at the May calendar, duh, so I'm all confused. Um, Heather and I are going to see Othello July 1, and we would love for you to accompany us. Uh, I don't know when Teen Freedom's event is though. It's on "the list." We could do, we could do Shakespeare, Crater Lake and the Coast, if you can make it. If not, we'll just do the Coast and Crater Lake. Anyway, let me know and we'll talk to you soon. Bye.*

Less than two days after she left Travis the voice message on his cell phone, Arias sent him a text message on June 6, 2008, at 9:58 P.M., asking about a check in the amount of $200 dated May 25, 2008, she had mailed him as partial payment for the BMW that he had agreed to sell to her: *Hey, I need to know when you're going to deposit that check,* she wrote.

The following day, June 7, at 10:21:03, Arias sent an e-mail to Travis in which she related her concern at not hearing back from him in response to her phone call and text message:

SUBJECT:
FROM: "Jodi Arias" jodiarias@gmail.com
DATE: Sat, 7 Jun 2008 10:21:03
TO: "Travis Alexander" travis.alexander@gmail.com

Hey You . . .

I haven't heard back from you. I hope you're not still upset that I didn't come to see you. I just didn't have enough time off. It's okay, sweetie, you're going to be here in less than two weeks—we're going to see the sites, check things off, "The List" and all kinds of fun things. Oregon is BEAUTIFUL this time of year. Yaaay!. . . . be happy!

Anyway, I wanted to let you know that I'm thinking about pushing my visit up to next week, but it depends on my budget, so I'm not for sure yet. I know you'll be in Cancun, but I'll probably crash at your house in your cozy bed anyway . . . eat some of your oatmeal and frozen dinners, you know, the usual—jk. =) I know you said the door is always open, but I wanted to give you a head's up. If for any reason that won't work, let me know and I'll make other arrangements. Your home has always been my second home, although it's a bit more lonely without NAPS around. =/

You're probably in CA right now, but wherever you are get ahold of me at least before you head to Mexico.

                                        Thanks, hon—Jodi

With the discovery of these communications, the Mesa Police Department had now completed their investigation. The end result showed that Arias had been at Travis' house on June 4, 2008, and that they shared a sexual interlude hours before she killed him by stabbing him repeatedly, slashing his throat, and shooting him in the face. She had then attempted to cover up the crime by deleting the photos and staging her communications with him posthumously. With these pieces in hand, I decided to seek a charge of first-degree murder.

On July 9, 2008, I presented the case to a Maricopa County Grand Jury, and that same day the grand jury returned a true bill charging Jodi Ann Arias with the first-degree murder of Travis V. Alexander. The proceedings had been conducted in secret, as required by law, so Arias had no idea that she had been charged—she wouldn't learn of the charge until she was actually arrested. Ironically, the day the grand jury returned the true bill charging her with murder was her birthday. She was turning twenty-eight.

Within days of the indictment, police in Mesa called the Siskiyou County Sheriff's Office, one of the law enforcement agencies in Northern California that held jurisdiction over Yreka, where Arias now lived, and asked them to assist in her arrest. Detective Flores called me on July 14 to let me know that he, his sergeant, and another detective were flying to Yreka to arrest Arias and execute a search warrant on her home. He mentioned that they knew she was living in Yreka, but weren't sure of her exact address.

The Siskiyou County Sheriff's Office attempted to find Arias' car, a 2004 Infiniti Coupe with a California license plate reading 2ASCEND. It was registered to her parents' address on South Oregon Street in Yreka, but it was nowhere to be found. The deputies ran a computer search and learned that the car had been repossessed by Oregon Adjusters at the request of the lien holder on July 9, 2008, and was in a lot in Medford, Oregon, just across the state border.

With the car a dead end, investigators with the Siskiyou Sheriff's Office turned to searching the Yreka area. They found Arias was employed at a Mexican restaurant called Casa Ramos in Yreka, but they didn't find her there. They explored other leads where she could be, eventually locating her around 9 P.M. on July 14 at the Pine Street home of her maternal grandparents Caroline and Carlton "Sonny" Allen. A surveillance unit was sent to that address to monitor her movements, and as it started getting dark, Arias and her mother were seen talking in an animated fashion while they sat in her mother's car parked in front of the home. It appeared they were engaged in an emotional conversation, because Arias seemed to be crying. After about an hour, Arias got out of the car and went back inside as her mother drove off.

The surveillance team continued their watch rather than attempt a nighttime arrest of Arias. All arrests carry an inherent danger of injury to police, which may include being killed, a risk that increases once it is dark. The better course is to proceed with caution, preferably in the daylight hours when the suspect's movements can be best observed.

From their vantage point in the street, the surveillance team was able to see inside the house through the windows, where they observed Arias moving around in a northwest bedroom and it appeared to them she was packing for a trip. They ended the surveillance for the night after the lights in the house went off around midnight.

When the officers returned the next morning, July 15, they noticed that a white Chevy Cobalt rental car was now parked in front of the house. Several packing boxes were in the backseat, some with "Jodi" written on them in black marker. Fearing that Arias might leave town, police decided they needed to move quickly, and came up with a plan to arrest her. An officer from the Yreka Police Department, who was also assisting in the investigation, went up to the door under the guise that he was following up on an open burglary report that had been filed by Arias' maternal grandfather almost two months earlier on Wednesday, May 28, 2008.

In response to a call from Arias' grandfather phoning to report a burglary, Yreka police had responded to the residence around 3:30 P.M. that May afternoon. When officers arrived, they learned the elderly couple had been out for much of the day and had returned home some time around 3:00 P.M. to find that someone had broken into their house by forcing open a side door. That exterior door led to an enclosed patio or porch area, which, in turn, led to the kitchen. They mentioned that their granddaughter Jodi was still at home when they left at approximately 10:00 that morning.

Arias' grandmother Caroline told police she had already called Jodi to inform her of the "break-in," and Arias showed up at the house shortly thereafter, within fifteen minutes. Arias told police that she left home earlier that day at approximately 1:00 P.M. She also said that the doors and windows were locked before she stepped out.

The investigation by police cast doubt on the legitimacy of the burglary. Investigators found it unusual that only one item was taken from each of the house's four rooms. A CD player with cassette and radio was missing from the grandparents' bedroom. Also taken was a DVD player that had been sitting on top of the entertainment center in the living room. Arias indicated that $30 had been stolen from her room, a $20 bill and a $10 bill, both of which had been lying on top of the dresser.

Whoever broke in also took a .25 caliber handgun belonging to her grandfather that he kept secured inside a dresser in one of the other bedrooms. This was the same caliber weapon that had been used in Travis' killing. Police noted that other guns stored next to the .25 caliber pistol were left behind. It struck them as strange that other items of value were similarly untouched throughout the house. A large amount of change sitting in the dresser where the gun was kept remained undisturbed. It was mostly quarters, which could have been easily carried away.

Arias reported that her laptop was undisturbed in the clothesbasket underneath some clothing where she left it. She claimed she normally kept the laptop covered up in the basket, so that it would not be stolen if there ever were a burglary.

When Arias answered the door that Tuesday, July 15, she had already been notified by coworkers from Casa Ramos that police had called the restaurant and were looking to speak with her, so finding the Yreka officer on her front stoop that morning was probably not a surprise. She was compliant when the officer told her he wanted to get more information about the burglary and asked her to step outside, at which time she was arrested for the first-degree murder of Travis Alexander arising out of the indictment issued by the Maricopa County Grand Jury less than one week earlier.

After Arias was driven to the Siskiyou County Sheriff's Office, police executed a search warrant on her grandparents' house and the rental car. They began with the bedroom Arias had been using. There, they found a number of things that could prove useful, including journals, phones, a personal computer, an external hard drive, and an Airwalk brand shoe-box. When police looked inside the shoebox, they found miscellaneous papers and receipts from her trip in June.

Police then turned their attention to the rental car parked in front of the house. The three boxes in the backseat were mostly filled with clothes and personal items. Police did find two kitchen knives in one of the boxes. In a suitcase they saw a plethora of condoms. They later recovered a Hi-Point 9mm semiautomatic handgun that had been put in the spare tire compartment in the trunk of the car. The weapon was in a handgun case, along with an unloaded magazine. It seemed unusual that a gun and knives would be making another trip with Arias. She did not volunteer any information about where she was headed on her impending excursion.

Once Arias was taken to the sheriff's office, Detective Flores began his first in-custody interview with her. As he would tell me later that evening when he called, he started out by advising Arias of her Miranda rights and telling her that she did not have to answer questions that made her uncomfortable. Arias responded, "I would love to help you in any way that I can," which was almost exactly what she told Flores on June 10 when she ostensibly called the Mesa police department looking to find out what happened to Travis.

According to Flores' evening phone call from Yreka briefing me on the interview, he confronted Arias with pointed questions about the DNA results on the bloody latent palm print and the photographs retrieved from the memory card on Travis' camera. He told me Arias remained steadfast in her denial that she had been at Travis' house on the day of the murder, even after he showed her some of the photographs of her posing nude on Travis' bed on June 4.

Arias was booked into the Siskiyou County Jail later that day after her interview with Flores. The white pants and gray top that she was wearing when she was arrested were taken away and replaced by orange jail garb worn by all inmates. During the booking process, as her mug shot was taken, she managed to coquettishly tilt her head to the right and smile for the camera, almost as if she were posing for her high school yearbook. It didn't seem to impress her that she was being booked into jail because she was being accused of killing Travis.

Flores called me again the following day on July 16 and told me there was a second interview with Arias, this time with a female detective from the Siskiyou Sheriff's Office. The rationale behind introducing a female voice to the interrogation room was that Arias might be more forthcoming with a woman, but the change in the gender of the person conducting the interview produced the same results. Arias continued to say that she had not been in Mesa and had not hurt Travis.

Detective Flores told me that while speaking with the female detective, Arias asked to see him. He said that once he entered the interview room, her story from the day before changed and she finally admitted that she was at Travis' house on June 4. But, she did not admit killing him and instead told Flores a story of a man and woman who surprised the two of them as she took pictures of Travis in the shower. Arias claimed that she survived the attack because the assailants were only there to kill Travis. Flores mentioned that Arias even attempted to cast herself in the role of heroine by saying she had fought against the female attacker even though the woman was armed with a knife.

According to her revised tale, Travis was alive at the time she made her escape, and shortly before she fled, he had managed to ask her to go get help. When asked if she had called the police, Arias admitted that she had failed to contact anyone, claiming that her cell phone was dead, preventing her from using it.

In checking out her story, police visited the rental car company in Redding, California, a city approximately 100 miles south of Yreka, where Arias rented a car for her supposed trip to Utah on June 2. The rental car employee, Ralphael Colombo, remembered the transaction.

When police showed him a photographic line-up composed of six photographs of women, which included one of Arias smiling during the booking process as her photograph was taken, and five others with similar facial features to hers, he immediately recognized Arias and blurted out that her hair had been blonde when he rented the vehicle to her. Neither Flores nor I really understood the implications of Arias' change in hair color at the time, but it would later became clear that dying her hair was part of her plan to enter and leave Arizona undetected.

Colombo recalled that when he initially offered her a red car she declined and asked for one that was lighter in color, with Arias ultimately choosing a white Ford Focus. Not lost on any of the investigators was the fact that Arias drove for approximately an hour and a half to rent a car in Redding, although there were two other car rental agencies only minutes away in Yreka. But, Yreka is a small town with a population of approximately 7,500, so perhaps she figured there was less of a chance she would be recognized at the airport in Redding, where she could blend in as just another customer.

Colombo told police that in addition to renting Arias the car, he had also been the one to clean the vehicle after it was returned. He remembered that the floor mats had been missing, and that there were stains resembling "Kool-Aid" on both the backseat and the front passenger seat, leading him to assume that kids had been in the car. He also expressed surprise at the odometer reading, which showed that she had driven over two thousand miles, because she had told him she would only be using the car locally.

Arias remained at the Siskiyou County Jail until she was extradited to Phoenix, where she made her initial court appearance on September 6, 2008. Upon arrival at the Maricopa County Jail, she was brought before a commissioner who, based on my recommendation, set her bond at two million dollars. Five days later, Arias appeared for her arraignment and formally entered a plea of not guilty to the first-degree murder charge. The Office of Public Defense Services was appointed to represent her.

The first time I saw Jodi Ann Arias was at a status conference on October 22, to discuss the progress of the case with the court. She was sitting in the jury box, where she looked out of place. She seemed somewhat small and frail, almost virginal in her black-and-white-horizontally-striped jail garb. I took note that a jury might find her sympathetic because of her seemingly unpretentious façade. It was hard for me to see how all that violence could have come from this person. She didn't look like someone who could have committed this type of killing—but then, no one does.

Prior to Arias' case, I'd tried ten death penalty cases in Arizona. Deciding that the death penalty should be sought is not a decision that is taken lightly. If the Maricopa County Attorney elects to seek the death penalty, the State must file a notice within sixty days of the arraignment informing the court and defense counsel of its decision. In this case I filed such a notice on November 6, 2008, indicating that the State would be seeking the death penalty should Arias be convicted of first-degree murder. The basis for my request was that the killing was especially cruel. In Arizona, "especially cruel" describes the infliction of physical or mental anguish upon the victim before death. It also requires that a defendant know or should have known that suffering would occur.

The killing in this case was especially cruel because Travis Alexander suffered as he staggered in the bathroom and made his way down the hallway trying to escape Arias as she carried out her relentless attack. Travis suffered with each stab wound to his back, chest, hands, and head. He didn't die immediately. It was a slow and painful death.

Arias' excessive use of force reminded me of another case in which I'd sought the death penalty some years earlier. The victim in that case had been a man by the name of Joseph Andriano, who had been killed in October 2000. The similarities between Joe Andriano's murder and Travis Alexander's were uncanny, even though they were not related. Both murder scenes were bloody, both men were killed by more than one means, and both had been found with gaping wounds to their throats, the result of being sliced with a knife.

In the case of Joe Andriano, he had been killed by his wife, Wendi, a cute thirty-year-old blonde. The two had been married only a few years and had two children when Joe learned that a lump on his neck, once thought to be benign, was malignant and terminal. Wendi saw his misdiagnosis as an opportunity to make money and contacted a lawyer about initiating a medical malpractice suit. She even attempted to obtain a life insurance policy on Joe after she learned he had incurable cancer.

She began dating other men soon after they were told of his cancer and almost immediately fell in love with Rick a tenant in an apartment complex she managed. The complex was in the Ahwatukee section of Phoenix, and once their relationship started, she let him live in the apartment rent-free. Somehow Rick found out that Wendi's husband was dying, and he was unnerved enough to end their relationship.

The breakup did not sit well with Wendi. She would randomly show up unannounced at Rick's apartment, but he still wouldn't take her back. So she hatched a plot to kill her husband. She started the process by creating the fictitious name of Anne Newton, which she used to buy some sodium azide, a propellant for air bags. Sodium azide is not immediately fatal if ingested but can cause respiratory failure leading to death.

Wendi began implementing her plan to kill Joe by emptying some of her husband's medication capsules and refilling them with the poison, intending to give them to him to end his life. Apparently, she could not wait the six or so months it would take for his cancer to kill him.

On the last night of his life, Wendi took Joe to a barbecue at his parents' house in Casa Grande, a city in Pinal County halfway between Phoenix and Tucson. It was the fourth day of Joe's chemotherapy regimen and he was not feeling well. Once they returned home after midnight, Wendi gave him the capsules laced with the sodium azide. Wanting to make sure it was enough, she also added sodium azide to the stew that she was warming up for him. The dose wasn't immediately fatal, but Joe started throwing up and asked her to call 911.

Moments later, Wendi told Joe she had placed the call, but claimed that emergency responders were too busy to come out. In truth, she hadn't called at all. She later phoned a female friend Chris to come over, hoping she would then have a witness to her husband's death. When Chris arrived, Wendi was waiting for her outside the apartment and admitted that she had not called 911. After the two finally entered the apartment, Chris saw Joe lying on the floor, conscious but very ill and literally begging for help. He told Chris that he had been lying there for forty-five minutes without any aid. It was then that Wendi went to another room and finally placed the 911 call.

Within a few minutes, the sirens could be heard approaching the house. Chris walked outside to meet the fire department, but realized she had left her purse inside. When she tried to reenter the apartment, she found the front door had been locked and instead of letting her in, Wendi threw her purse out into the breezeway.

When the paramedics knocked on the door, Wendi failed to answer. After approximately five to ten minutes of knocking, one of the paramedics called the dispatcher, who reached Wendi by telephone. The dispatcher convinced Wendi to come out and speak with the paramedics. Rather than coming out the front door, Wendi went out the back, jumped the fence, walked around the apartment building and met the paramedics in the breezeway outside the locked front door. She informed them that Joe had a DNR, (do-not-resuscitate order), and their services weren't needed. With that information, the medical emergency response unit left the scene without ever seeing the patient, a protocol that would later be changed.

Several hours passed before Wendi again called 911, this time claiming her husband had attacked her after she complied with his dying wish to know if she had been unfaithful. She confessed to him, and he attacked her, forcing Wendi to kill him in self defense. When paramedics finally got inside, they found a bloody scene. Joe had been beaten with a barstool in excess of twenty times before ultimately being stabbed in the neck with a knife. At the autopsy, it was discovered he had also been poisoned.

I prosecuted Wendi Andriano in 2004. After an emotional trial that lasted three and a half months, she was convicted of first-degree murder. The jury imposed the death penalty, finding the killing to be "especially cruel." She was the first woman to be sentenced to death by a jury in the state of Arizona. She has been on women's death row ever since, sharing the distinction with only one other woman.

If sentenced to death, Jodi Arias would be the third woman on death row in the state of Arizona.

———————————

CHAPTER 5

The period of time between the arraignment and trial can be a lengthy one. Following Arias' arraignment, roughly four years would pass before the trial would actually get underway. And while that may seem to be "dead time," with little happening in the courtroom, much work is being completed behind the scenes. This preparation time allows both sides to review documents, interview potential witnesses, and formulate strategies they will employ at trial.

It has always been my practice to start the case review as soon as I receive a copy of the police report, which was delivered to me shortly after Arias' arrest. As a prosecutor, I am not a part of the police investigation and rely on periodic updates from the lead detective, in this case Detective Flores, to keep me apprised. While I am alerted to important developments, there are things the investigators do that I am not privy to as they happen. Reading the police reports allows me to see what they have done in their investigation on a day-to-day basis, including the items they have seized, witnesses they have interviewed, and any photographs and other materials they have collected.

I always try cases alone without the assistance of other lawyers, which are normally referred to as "second chairs." I favor this single prosecutor approach although it may mean more work. Because of this, it falls on my shoulders to read every document associated with the case from any source, such as those provided by defense counsel. I sit through every interview of any potential witness, whether or not I believe they are going

to be called to testify at trial. I also view every video created at
any point of the investigation, including statements made by a
defendant to the police.

Preparing the case for trial without the assistance of another prosecutor requires that I make decisions regarding
which witnesses to call at trial and the order of their appearance. I am solely responsible for the documents, photographs,
or other items to be introduced for the jury's consideration.
Of course, any cross-examination of witnesses called to testify by defense counsel will likewise be left to me. Opening
statements and closing arguments are strictly my province.
This approach requires me to be versed in every aspect of the
case.

In addition to reading the police reports Flores provided me,
I began by creating a more detailed portrait of the victim. I
learned that Travis was born on July 29, 1977. He was five
feet, nine inches tall, weighed 180 pounds, and had green eyes.
He was one of eight children, four boys and four girls. He grew
up near Riverside, California, in an area commonly referred
to as the Inland Empire. According to a book he was writing about his life called *Raising Me*, which was posted on the
internet, Travis' parents were methamphetamine addicts, and
at a young age, he went to live with his grandmother Norma
Sarvey, who introduced him to the Mormon faith. He em-
braced its teachings and attempted to live by church doctrine.
After high school, he went on a church mission to Denver,
Colorado, and ultimately settled in Mesa, Arizona, because of
its strong Mormon community.

I looked into Travis' employment at Pre-Paid Legal Services, which today is called LegalShield. Travis worked from
home, but he was also a motivational speaker for the company, and appeared periodically at meetings to help encourage
sales of new memberships. Although Travis portrayed himself
as financially successful, it seemed that he was struggling to
maintain the lifestyle he had built for himself. He had taken

in two roommates to help with his mortgage and sometimes borrowed money from an ex-girlfriend to pay his bills.

One of the first things I did was check whether Travis Alexander had ever been in trouble with the law, and I found that he hadn't. The only contact he had ever had with police was when he called the Mesa Police Department in February 2008 to report that the tires on his BMW had been slashed while his car was parked outside his house. Although there was only that one call, I learned from Detective Flores' police report that his tires had been slashed on consecutive nights. While all of Travis' friends pointed the finger at Arias, Travis himself vacillated between blaming her and saying he didn't know who had done it.

From all that I had read in the police reports it seemed that Jodi Arias had been obsessed with Travis. But, as her interviews with Flores made clear, the irrational nature of her behavior was not reflective of her ability to maintain her composure in the most dire of times. Because Flores had told me that Arias had been so in control during the two days of interrogation in Yreka I needed to look for myself at those interviews to see if she'd made any missteps, however slight.

Detective Flores provided me copies of the videotaped interviews he had conducted with Arias on July 15 and 16, after her arrest in Yreka. I had a transcript of the tapes prepared, which I checked for accuracy by reading while listening to the actual words being spoken, because it had been my experience that transcriptions always contain mistakes by the transcriber. Even though the transcript is not admissible at trial, I still wanted to make sure it was as accurate as possible, so that I could use it in my trial preparation. Closing the door to my office, I turned on the videotape of the July 15 interview on my computer.

The first image on the video showed Arias shortly after her arrest still dressed in white pants and a gray top, resting her head on a small table at the center of the room, her long brown hair falling forward onto the tabletop. She remained in that repose for several minutes, never flinching, to the point where it appeared she was asleep.

She then stood up, and shook out her arms, and seemingly angry that police had left her in handcuffs, plopped down on the floor with her back to the wall. "Can you take my handcuffs off, please?" were the first words she spoke when Siskiyou Sheriff's detective Rachel Blaney pushed open the door to check on her.

I found it telling that she was so focused on her own comfort, when faced with a much bigger issue—that she was in police custody and accused of first degree murder.

Arias appeared irritated when Blaney advised that she'd have to wait for Detective Flores to remove the handcuffs. She lodged her next complaint as soon as Blaney left the room. *It's so fucking cold in here,* she mumbled, her shoulders shuddering.

The arrival of Flores appeared to mollify Arias, who immediately rose to offer her handcuffed wrists so he could remove the cuffs.

Flores' offer of a bottle of water was met with several requests, "Any chance you could get my purse? . . . Any way they can turn the heat up in here? Or like do you have a sweater I can borrow or something?"

In his relaxed, casual manner, Flores, dressed in a blue button down shirt and tie, agreed to look into adjusting the temperature and the whereabouts of her purse, which had been taken during her arrest. "So you remember me?" he asked once she had finished her litany of requests.

"Of course I do," Arias acknowledged.

"I traveled all the way up here to come talk to you because— you know, I've been working on Travis' case ever since it happened. And I know exactly when it happened, when he was killed. I know a lot of details and just recently we found quite a bit of evidence and I'll discuss that with you. The main thing that I'm looking for though is answers on why certain things happened and why they went so far, and also to get your statements.

"Um, a lot of details on this case haven't been released to the public and not even to Travis' family. And those details are known only by us and the person who did it, okay, and that's one of the reasons I'm here is because I believe that you know some of those details.

"And, I think you can help us."

"I would love to help you in any way that I can," Arias responded, leaning in toward the detective, her pale, thin arms, crossed at the elbows and stretched on the table.

She appeared to be listening as Flores read her the *Miranda* rights and set out the purpose of the interview. "What I'm gonna do is just ask some questions, ask you what you've been doing . . . kind of clarify some things . . ."

As I watched this interview what struck me most was Arias' ability to be so controlled and devoid of emotion right from the start. Most people get extremely apprehensive just being stopped by police for a traffic infraction. Yet, Arias demonstrated no reaction as her *Miranda* rights were read and she was advised, amongst other things, that she had the right to remain silent. But as I was going to see, remaining silent was not something she would ever do.

"Is this recorded at all," she asked, looking behind her. "Or should we, I mean?"

Before the detective could respond, she reached behind her to retrieve two tape recorders from a small wooden table in the corner of the room, placing them on the table in front of Flores. "I don't know if these are voice recorders, I noticed them, if they have video cam, or they have audio . . . or batteries or what."

Arias was so aware of her surroundings that she noticed two small recorders lying on the table in the corner behind her. I took note of her acumen and concluded that she would probably never lose her composure, whether it be in an interview room or a courtroom.

Flores lifted the recorders and looked at them as if to be checking their status. "I don't think they are on," he assured her. To which Arias again complained of being cold and reminded the detective that she had asked that the heat be turned up.

Flores sidestepped the temperature issue, bringing the conversation back around to the homicide. "What have you been up to since Travis' death? What have you been doing?"

"Um, well I've been working," Arias replied. "I haven't been really working for Prepaid Legal. There's not a whole lot here in this marketplace . . ." she said, referring to her hometown of Yreka.

"It's small here and really that could be seen as an opportunity rather than a hindrance, because that just means the market is untapped in a large way, so I could have it if I wanted to, but I have—I'm kind of like a deer in the headlights when it comes to Prepaid Legal and I kind of, I just have a fear of approaching people.

"So, I've been working in a Mexican restaurant on the north end of town. Um, I've been, I've been in kind of a daze, at least for the first few weeks."

"Like everybody, you know," Flores concurred, obviously trying to keep her talking.

Without prompting, Arias turned the conversation to the online tributes and news coverage surrounding Travis' death. "I know that a lot of people have been posting on Facebook really nice things, and memories, and at one point I was like well maybe I should do that, so I posted this thing and I just said all of my memories and I realized looking back on it that it was kind of, it kind of sounded immature, it's more like my 'Dear Travis' kind of letter. And so I took it down because . . ."

Arias was referring to her June 14 comment posted on the Internet site called Guest Book. *"Travis, what can I say to you that I haven't already said? I am so grateful for the endless hours of conversation and amazing experiences we've shared. Thank you for having the courage to share the Gospel with me. You've had one of the greatest impacts on my life, and have forever altered it's* [sic] *course for the better. I love you, my friend, and always will. —Jodi Arias, Yreka, California."*

Responding to Arias' decision to remove the post, Flores suggested that he understood that she likely felt her tribute should probably have been less personal.

"Yeah, some of it was details that were a little more personal, not too personal, nothing inappropriate . . . I just felt funny, I think because I'm a photographer I tend to communicate more through pictures, so I posted a ton of pictures that I had of him, and I have a ton more that I just can't access right now, and videos and things that I know his family would want," Arias answered.

"I've been on Facebook and MySpace, looking at his profile, looking at his pictures, reading things, um, about his obituaries and um, any news updates and, you know, there's Legacy.com, right, you can write something about him."

"I've seen a lot of those postings," Flores admitted.

Arias indicated that since Travis' death, she had also been spending a good deal of time speaking to Ryan Burns, whom she described as her "potential possible maybe person that you might start dating." She explained that she and Ryan tried not to speak about what happened to Travis, "'cause it's kind of like, 'oh,' And plus, Travis is my ex-boyfriend at the same time he's my friend, so while I'm mourning my friend, how do you talk to your new potential, possible maybe person that you might start dating about your friend, even if he was your ex-boyfriend, so it's kind of a gray area. I try not to talk about him too much, but he comes up a lot."

Arias told Flores that it was through Burns that she first learned that she was emerging as a suspect in Travis' killing. "He said, 'you know, if you come out to Utah things are really

weird 'cause everyone is, everyone thinks that you could have
had a hand . . .' "

Flores took the opportunity to interject, "And I've talked
to a lot of people, and everybody's pointing the finger at you.
You know, everyone is saying, 'I don't understand what happened to Travis. I don't know who killed him, but you need
to look at Jodi.' And sometimes the simplest answers are the
correct ones, and that's one of the reasons I've started looking
at you a little bit closer. . . . So one of the reasons I am here is
to talk to you to figure out what was going on between you
two. I know the relationship that you guys had was of conve-
nience sometimes. Obviously, you weren't boyfriend/girlfriend
anymore.

"But you were still having a sexual relationship, which you
know . . ."

Flores' declaration appeared to stir something in Arias.
"Does his family know about that?" she asked, the first time
in the interview she expressed concern over something. She
claimed it was because she wanted to protect Travis and how
he was remembered.

Even after Flores assured her that Travis' family didn't know
anything, Arias continued to steer the interview in this direction. She seemed overly concerned with the photos police had
recovered from their afternoon sexual encounter on June 4th,
2008. Her preoccupation led me to think that perhaps there
were more than six photographs taken that afternoon during
their sexual romp.

"The reason I care about that is because he was adamant
about that, and a couple times we prayed about it. It didn't
work or we didn't stick to our, you know, guns on it and um,
one time a girlfriend of mine just said, 'Why don't you just go
to the Bishop and talk and ask Travis the same?' And I talked
to him about it and he got really angry. He said, 'I've already
had problems with this in the past. I'm embarrassed by it, I
don't want to go to the Bishop.' And so we just kind of stopped

for like a few weeks, and then that must have been in, I think it was August and then it just resumed."

As I watched the video over the course of several hours, I came across numerous things that would be helpful in my preparation of the case—ranging from small incongruous details in her story to Arias' ability to maintain her composure. More than anything, though, I was able to discern how she attempted to manipulate the situation to her advantage and buy herself time to respond to Flores' questions.

Detective Flores wanted Arias to know that as part of the police investigation, he'd read Travis' journals, and he told her that they indicated that Travis felt his relationship with Arias was unhealthy. "Maybe you didn't understand why he didn't believe it was healthy?"

"No, I didn't think it was healthy, either, spiritually at least and probably emotionally, but mostly spiritually. . . . And once you have something that's not healthy spiritually, it filters through all aspects of your life."

Arias continued, saying that while that was one of the reasons she moved back to Yreka, it was not the primary reason. Instead, she cited financial hardship, followed by a desire to be closer to her family, particularly her younger siblings, as her number one and two reasons. But also, as she put it, "too much of my nightlife was about" Travis.

She went on to describe Travis' supposed late-night requests to see her, saying that "he would text me and, 'Hey, I'm getting sleepy,' dot, dot, dot, and a bunch of Zs, and that was code to, like, come on over kind of thing . . ."

As I listened to her describe the relationship, it was easy to see the routine that their relationship had apparently taken. As Arias described it, "I lived five minutes away to maybe ten, depending, and it was just too convenient and too easy, and it was fun and we had fun when we were together, and so it wasn't healthy and I totally agree with that."

At different points during the interview, Arias talked about how she and Travis struggled with the sexual dynamic of their relationship. When she was trying to find work, Travis offered her a job cleaning his house to help her pay her bills, and she grew animated as she described a photo of a French maid's outfit that he purportedly e-mailed to her, instructing her to wear this kind of ensemble on her first day of work. For a tumultuous period of time, the two of them had carried on a secret sexual relationship, characterized by fits of jealousy and deceit. According to her, Travis' friends warned Arias that he was actively dating and looking elsewhere for a mate, and she recalled how one of his friends in particular had even confronted Travis about his behavior, asking, "Why do you kiss Jodi in the dark and then act like you guys aren't even together in the daytime?"

Throughout the two days of interviews, it seemed clear to me that Arias was playing the part of the victim, whether it was crying about her father's failing health, expressing her love for her family, or complaining of Travis' infidelity. But that was not a role that was written for her, at least not under these circumstances. It appeared she thought her sob story would go a long way in making things easier for her, but given the accusations being leveled, it showed remarkable self-centeredness. She seemed to exude a confidence that she could control the interview, and by extension Detective Flores, if she came across as sympathetic.

Flores remained undeterred, digging into each facet of Arias' relationship with Travis as he tried to have his questions answered. I found it interesting that she was evasive with Detective Flores as to why she moved to Mesa after the breakup. Rather than address her stalking behavior, she chose to ramble about different living arrangements she had worked out that would allow her to be in Mesa, but within a safe and appropriate distance of Travis and his church ward. She even claimed that it had been Travis who had talked her into moving back to Arizona, suggesting that when she entertained the idea of moving to Southern California, he had offered up a litany of reasons why Mesa would be the more desirable location. "And he's really, he's, he's really persuasive," she said, smiling.

"He persuaded you to stay there in Mesa?" Flores asked, a tone of disbelief in his voice.

"Uh, he's, he kind of was playing up all the advantages if I did come to Mesa . . . you know, 'It's a great place. We could still see each other and hang out on occasion. Um, this church is very strong, you know, you'll probably make a lot of friends.' And I already knew all this stuff prior because I had, we'd talked about that. So I went ahead and just made the move. It sounded at the time like a good idea."

No more than five minutes later, Arias contradicted herself when she told Flores that when one of her roommate situations in Mesa didn't work out and she moved again to a place that was closer to Travis', "he freaked out about it." This was the kind of discrepancy that revealed how she could meld a story to her benefit.

Other inconsistencies in Arias' story were revealed when Flores began to question the route that she claimed to have taken to Utah. He began his questions by talking about the car she rented for the trip. At first, Arias tried to stymie the investigation altogether by failing to name the rental car company that she used to reserve a car for the drive, as if withholding it would make it impossible for the police to track her movements. Despite not remembering the rental car company itself, she did recall every other detail about the car she rented, including that she had rented it at the Redding Airport, that it was a white Ford Focus, and that it didn't have cruise control.

"Instead of going to Utah, you went straight out to the Los Angeles area?" Flores asked.

Arias' voice was soft and steady as she recounted her movements for the detective. "I went to Santa Cruz first . . . I stayed the night in Monterey, and the next day I drove to Pasadena." She explained that she had arranged to meet the sister of an ex-boyfriend to do a photo shoot of her new baby. She said when she first arrived in town, she left a voice message on the woman's answering machine, but she didn't get a call back until she'd already left the Los Angeles area.

"And which route did you take from there?" Flores asked. He already knew the route she claimed to have taken from their previous conversations, but now he was prepared to dispute her story. The detective listened intently as Arias recited her itinerary.

"I was supposed to get on the 15 and go all the way up . . . and I somehow got off the 15," she explained.

"And where did you end up?"

"Um, for a while I was lost, and I'm not above sleeping in the car, so I slept for a while . . . I'm a heavy sleeper and I sleep a lot, so . . ."

"But you were on the 15 for a while and you ended up getting off the 15 somewhere?"

"Yeah, I looked at a map and I'm pretty sure I know where I went . . . Can I draw you a map?"

Detective Flores offered Arias the yellow legal pad he had been using to take notes, and she sketched the circuitous route that took her to Las Vegas and then south into Arizona. She said she first took Interstate 15 North toward Las Vegas on the way to Utah. She then began talking about another freeway, Interstate 40, which runs east and west through northern Arizona.

"Did you actually cross over into Arizona? Is that how far you went?"

"I crossed over twice, I think," Arias said with a giggle.

She next provided an elaborate account of traveling on various freeways, starting with Interstate 15, which runs north from the Pasadena area to Salt Lake City. She claimed that once she arrived in Las Vegas, she mistakenly began driving south on Highway 93 past the Hoover Dam and into Arizona. She said she became disoriented and further lost her way when she ended up on Interstate 40 driving east towards Flag-staff. She said she finally turned around on that interstate and made her way back to Highway 93, heading north back toward Las Vegas, where she finally was able to be reunited with In-terstate 15, allowing her to head north toward Salt Lake City.

"I have a problem with this trip," Flores declared. "I've gone over this trip over and over in my mind and on paper, and even if—there's still twenty-some-odd hours, even if you pulled over to sleep a couple of times . . ."

The detective's inquiry appeared to be a warning that Arias' alibi was not airtight, but she remained impassive and revealed no sign of anxiety. "Did I tell you I got stranded?" she asked, harkening back to her earlier claim.

"Yeah, you mentioned that . . . but if you slept for ten hours . . . it would still leave eighteen-some-odd hours for something else, okay."

Flores then shifted his line of questioning to a discussion of Arias' cell phone.

"I pulled your cell phone records," he said, referring to a cell phone tower report that police had obtained. "Your cell phone was turned off between here and here," he told her, indicating a stretch of land east of Pasadena, California, to a location south of the Nevada border. "The next place it was turned on was here," he said, pointing to a site on Highway 93. "What does that show me?"

Flores was alluding to the fact that a cell phone cannot be traced if it is powered off. While this piece of evidence alone did not prove anything about where Arias had driven, it would become important to the case because it helped shed light on her plan. Turning off the cell phone was a deliberate way for Arias to avoid being tracked. It seemed too much of a coinci-dence that her phone lost power as she approached the western part of the Arizona border only to have it powered on as she reached Nevada.

Still, Arias didn't budge.

"Oh, well, I began—oh, no, no, no . . ."

"Is there plenty of time for you to do that? Yes. And I, do I believe that you had come to visit Travis? Yes, I truly believe it. Did you have the opportunity? Yes, you were traveling alone; there are no other witnesses. Your phone just happened to turn off from here to here?"

"Well, I didn't turn it off physically, but it died."

"And then it magically, you found your charger here?"

"I got it, it was, it was under the, back under the seat of the passenger side, and it was when I was . . ."

"When you were lost, you couldn't have maybe pulled over and found it or . . ."

"Well, I did finally start looking when I was stranded. I wouldn't, I wouldn't have pulled over when I was lost," she answered, parsing out that she would only stop if she were stranded.

"I've been focusing on this and going over and over in my mind why this happened, why your phone turns off here, outside of Los Angeles," the detective posed, indicating a location on Arias' makeshift map.

"What city is that? 'Cause I got this far . . ." she responded, pointing to a similar area on the map.

". . . It's not cities, there's towers," Flores explained, referring to the cell towers that had pinged with Arias' locations. Flores was trying to show her that based on the data from the cell phone tower, she had eventually turned her phone on as she approached the Nevada border, but while she was still in Arizona. "There's towers dotted all over this place. . . . One tower hit here," he said, highlighting various spots on the map. "The other tower here on the 93. There is no way somebody can get on that 15 and magically get on that 93, 'cause the 15 goes right through Las Vegas, right there, and continues this way. It never goes through Arizona again. . . .

"This tower here, it's not just over the border in Arizona, it's quite a distance inside of Arizona that it hit, because there is a mountain range all along here, and if you are on this side of the mountain range, a pretty good distance, that signal is not gonna come, not gonna hit Utah or Nevada or California. It's only gonna hit in Arizona."

After going back and forth on her impossible route, Arias again went to the map, but when Detective Flores confronted her about the freeways, and the impossibility of her trip, she started to lose composure and for the first time, admitted that she took Interstate 10. In her haste to cover up, she mistakenly said she traveled west on Interstate 10, which, if true, would have taken her to the beach in Santa Monica.

"I honestly got lost. It's—it's bad timing," Arias said, hiding her face in her hands.

"Were you at Travis' house on Wednesday?"

"Absolutely not, I was nowhere near Mesa . . . I was nowhere near Phoenix . . ."

Detective Flores let out an audible sigh in apparent frustration. Her unwillingness to surrender even in the face of compelling proof showed just how much it would take to get her to concede a point. It was becoming clear that I would need tangible evidence contradicting her statements when the time came for me to cross examine her at trial. But I was about to see that even approach that would not shake Arias.

"What if I could show you proof you were there? Would that change your mind?"

"I wasn't there . . . I was not at Travis' house . . . was not."

"You were at Travis' house, you guys had a sexual encounter, which there are pictures, and I know you know there's pictures because I have them. And I will show them to you, okay? So, what I'm asking you is for you to be honest with me. I know you were there."

"Are you sure those pictures aren't from another time?"

"Positive. Absolutely positive."

Arias' body language did not change. She sat hunched over the table, her arms folded in front of her, and in a soft voice recited her mantra: "The last time I had any kind of sexual contact with Travis was in April."

Detective Flores reminded her of the camera police had found in the washing machine during the initial investigation at the crime scene, the one she had offered to help police retrieve items from the memory card. "Remember I told you about the camera?"

"Mm-hm."

"Remember I told you that card was destroyed?"

"Mm-hm."

"I didn't tell the truth, 'cause I wanted to make sure those photos were accurate. And we can pull deleted photos . . . we can pull every photo that was ever on there, pull the pixels together, get the time stamps on them, not all of them, but most of them have time stamps on them and we can verify those time stamps. . . .

"And I have pictures of you in Travis' bedroom with Travis, pictures of him, and it's obvious you guys are having sex, taking photos of each other, and they're dated and time-stamped on the day he died."

"Are you sure it's me?" Arias asked incredulously. "I mean that—'cause I was not there."

Flores forged ahead, advising Arias that the camera had actually taken pictures by accident during the time that Travis was killed.

For the first time, there was a reaction. "Really?" she asked, the muscles in her forehead tightening, perhaps indicating that the detective had struck a nerve.

Watching Arias skillfully manipulate the realities being presented to her, I couldn't help but think ahead to a possible trial. If she were to take the stand, she would be difficult for me to deal with, because her stories streamed forth so effortlessly. If I was going to show she was untruthful, I would have to come up with something factual like a receipt, something that she was not aware of or that she had forgotten about. Otherwise, there was a real chance a jury might be taken in by the seamless delivery of her answers.

I turned my attention back to the video just in time to hear Flores make mention of a gun. "A record check shows that you guys reported a gun stolen, a .25 auto, that just happens to be the same caliber as the weapon used to kill him," he told Arias referring to the burglary her grandfather had reported to Yreka police that past May.

"A .25 auto was used to kill Travis?" she whispered, acting as if she were surprised at the revelation.

"Yeah, along with multiple stab wounds," Flores responded.

But the information about the caliber of the gun used wasn't enough to change her story either, and as Flores prepared to show her the photos that proved their sexual encounter, she seemed to double down on her innocence.

"If I killed Travis, I would beg for the death penalty," she said.

Detective Flores continued to push, in what seemed a calculated effort to draw out a confession. But as hard as he pressed, he still couldn't stop the conversation from going around in circles, with him laying out what police had found and Arias deflecting her involvement.

"I was not at Travis' house on Wednesday the fourth," she repeated.

"You were, 'cause that is when the bloody palm print was left on his wall," Flores advised her. ". . . I've got pictures of you that I've blown up and you've got that little mole right there . . ." he said, pointing to a small mark on her left lower cheek. "It's you, it's obvious . . ."

"I wasn't there," Arias maintained.

". . . There's pictures of you laying on the bed in pigtails."

"Pigtails?" she asked incredulously, cocking her head to the side as if in disbelief.

". . . I can show you some of these pictures. Do you want to see the pictures? Will that change your mind?" Flores suggested they take a short break so he could retrieve them. Arias called out to him as he rose to leave the room.

"Detective," she wailed with a hurt look. "I am not a murderer."

—————————

CHAPTER 6

When Detective Flores returned to the interview room, he was carrying the same blue three-ring binder he had brought to my office at the start of the investigation.

"What kind of gun is that?" Arias asked him, referring to the weapon in his holster. It appeared she wanted to show some interest in him, and maybe even flirt with him a little.

"It's a Glock."

"I just got a gun."

"Did you?"

"Mm-hm."

"They've probably found it by now," Flores told her, referring to the police officers executing the search warrants on the homes of her grandparents and parents, as well as the rental vehicle in which she had packed three boxes and a suitcase. The 9mm gun would later be found stashed in the trunk of the rental car.

Arias remained impassive as the detective sat down in the chair across from her, held the binder in his lap so as to shield the pictures from her view, and began to leaf through its pages. "These are just a few photos, and I want to be careful showing— not showing you certain photos because some of them . . ."

"Please don't show me . . ." Arias pleaded with seeming anguish.

After reviewing several of the pages, Flores placed the book on the table opened to a photograph of the exterior of Travis' house that had been taken by police at the crime scene. "Remember that?"

Arias hid her face in her hands and began to sob. "If Travis were here today, he would tell you that it wasn't me."

"No, my job is to speak for Travis right now, and everything Travis is telling me is that Jodi did this to me," Flores explained in a stern but mild voice. Returning the binder to his lap, he again glanced through its pages, momentarily stopping to consider several photographs before deciding on one. Sliding the book toward Arias, he showed her a close-up shot of Travis' face, his hair wet and water cascading down his face. "Remember him?"

"Is he naked—in the shower?"

"Yes, he is . . ." Flores replied. "Soon after you and he had sex on his bed."

Looking directly at the detective, Arias tried to neutralize the impact of the photographs now before her. "Travis would never go for that," she stated matter-of-factly. "The last time we had sex in his bed was in April."

Flores was undeterred. "This didn't come out very good 'cause they're copies of actual photos," he explained, purposefully placing his legal pad over the lower portion of the next image—a shot of Arias naked and lying back on Travis' bed in a sexual pose. "That's you—and I wanted to cover you up because . . . that's all of you."

"Oh!" Arias uttered with an air of surprise. "That looks like me," she confirmed, perhaps her way of avoiding having to admit the obvious.

". . . You can look at the rest of it if you want," Flores suggested, prompting her to lift up a corner of the legal pad so she could view the full image.

"There's a few of those," the detective told her, "and there's a few more, which I'm trying not to show you, because I don't want to put you out there like that to people.

"Let's just say I've seen all of you, and I've seen all of Travis, but the one that sticks out in my mind is of Travis on the autopsy table. And I'm not gonna show you that one, or should I?

"But this one," he said, flipping the page to one of the snap-shots that had been taken by accident, "it's your foot, Jodi." He used his pen to highlight parts he wanted to call to Arias' attention.

"Those are your pants. That's Travis."

"This is his bathroom," she agreed, appearing to study the image before again starting to cry. "That is not my foot!"

Flores did not give an inch. "Those are your pants," he told her.

"I have . . . those pants at home, if these are the same ones. I don't have a zipper there, though, not on mine . . ."

Next came another round of photographs. "You see the date, 6/4/08 at 5:22 P.M., that's when it started . . . Right there, see that?"

Arias picked over the little details in the photos that Flores highlighted.

"Do you see the spots here?" he asked her now showing her the photograph of the latent print on the west wall. "They look a different color because we used a chemical to enhance this . . . that right there is blood. It's a mixture of yours and his, and that's your palm print of your left palm."

"I don't have any cuts on my left palm," Arias offered.

"Nobody said that your cut was on the palm. Do you have any recent cuts that are healing?"

"Well, my cat scratches me . . . little things, these are all her work. You can see," she said, pointing out little marks on her left arm before again challenging the results of the latent palm print identification. "How can that be my palm print?"

" 'Cause you were there," Flores replied, moving his chair to sit closer to Arias. "There is no doubt in my mind that you were there. There is no doubt in my mind that you did this, none. So, you can go until you're blue in the face and tell me you weren't there and you had nothing to do with this, but I won't believe you. I will not believe you, because Travis is tell-ing me that you did this to him."

The interview seemed to drag on. While Flores finally got her to agree that the photographic evidence was "very compelling," she diffused its value, suggesting the images could have been "modified" or "altered," and the date and time stamps could have been "tampered with."

"I didn't modify anything," Flores countered.

"I don't think you would," Arias responded, perhaps sensing she might alienate the detective if she continued in this vein.

After watching her repeated denials, I was momentarily caught off guard when suddenly Arias appeared to change course—from accusing the police of manipulating the time stamps on the photos to questioning whether it was Travis' camera that may have taken those photographs.

"Can I, can I ask you, I don't know if you know this, oh, I have a camera and it's in my storage unit that I don't use anymore, but that Travis used frequently," Arias began. "And we took pictures with it. Um, this is, I don't know . . ."

"Do you remember taking *these* pictures?" Flores asked, directing Arias' attention back to the collection of photographs in the blue binder on the table between them.

"There were many pictures . . . we took tons and tons of pictures, some I saved, most we deleted," she claimed. It was clear Detective Flores didn't know where she was going with her answers, but he continued to lead her along in the direction of what he thought would be an admission.

"We took a bunch the week before I left . . . We took a bunch over the last six or seven months. Last year, even when we were still dating, but we would delete them mostly. There were some he sent me that I didn't delete. Um, what I'm asking is, is it possible that, you know, that my memory card would have been in his camera? They're interchangeable."

And with that Jodi Arias had another possible explanation for how those photographs came to be in Travis' camera. When initially confronted by the existence of the images from the camera found in the washing machine, she tried several different possible denials, ranging from the images not being of her, to the police tampering with the time stamps on the images, and now something far more complicated and wholly implausible. She advanced the notion that someone had switched the memory card in the camera found in the washing machine with the camera she had previously used to take photos of herself and Travis.

Though she'd been at an apparent dead end, she was unwilling to cede the point. She seemed prepared to keep evading, creating ever more elaborate fictional scenarios—anything to avoid the truth. She had clearly realized the photos' significance and was looking for a way to discount them, thereby removing what appeared to be the only indisputable piece of evidence placing her at the crime scene. It seemed she thought she knew enough to explain away the DNA evidence collected at the scene, the blood, the hair, and perhaps even the palm print, but she was at a loss to find a rationalization for the time-stamped photographs.

Detective Flores realized what she was trying to do and pointed out that her theory of switched memory cards was completely implausible. "Your camera's here, his camera's there, he just bought that camera."

"Well, the other camera that I used before that is broken. Now it's in my storage unit."

"Are you saying those pictures are on that camera?" Flores asked in an attempt to clarify what she was alleging.

"What I'm saying is I had several memory cards for this camera that I don't have anymore, so I guess . . . it's so far-fetched," she conceded. "But, I guess it's possible that my card could—"

Flores interjected. "So you're saying somebody took your pictures or card and is framing you and put that into his camera?"

"I'm just saying that if my memory cards were left at his

house, he could have, he would have used those for his camera.
I don't know. I can explain the blood, though, and I can explain the hair. I don't know about the palm print."

There it was. She really did believe that she could smile at
the detective and have him believe that such a scenario was
possible. Even in light of the scientific results, she held true
to her story. Flores had spent two hours and forty-seven minutes with her and was no closer to an admission than when he
started. The interview drew to a close with Arias asking to use
the restroom.

As soon as the detective left the room, she let out an audible
sigh and threw her entire body back in the chair, her arms
outstretched to the wall.

"You should have at least done your makeup, Jodi, gosh,"
she whispered aloud.

She next sang part of Dido's "Here With Me." She then
spent a few seconds searching through the plastic garbage pail
on the floor behind her. I was surprised when she suddenly
stood up, placed her head on the floor and did a handstand,
her body perfectly aligned with the wall.

Returning to the table, she sat quietly for a few moments
before breaking into eerie laughter and then a few verses of
"O Holy Night." Her search of the small table in the corner
yielded a piece of paper and a pen that she used to scrawl as
she waited for someone to come for her.

After reviewing Jodi Arias' interview of July 15, I turned my
attention to the videotaped statements of her parents, William
(Bill) and Sandy Arias.

Detective Flores interviewed the couple the same day,
shortly after having spoken to Arias. I was curious to see if
they had provided any information that would either support
or undermine their daughter's unwavering claim that she had
nothing to do with Travis' death. Detective Flores had already

told me that they had no information, but I wanted to hear what they had to say.

The couple were celebrating their twenty-ninth wedding anniversary in September 2008. Jodi was the oldest of their four children. Bill also had a daughter from a previous marriage. Their interviews were conducted separately, so that they would not have a chance to tailor their stories. Investigators typically don't meet with the parents of suspects, because they seldom have much to offer related to the killing. However, in this case, Arias had returned home to Yreka, and both of her parents could speak to her daily activities and movements in the days before and after the killing.

Interestingly, Jodi's father, Bill Arias, had some concerning things to say about his daughter. He had just celebrated his fifty-ninth birthday, but appeared older, likely because of health issues involving his kidneys. Without prompting, he began to paint an unflattering picture of a young woman who didn't really get along with either of her parents.

"She's a strange person," he said at one point, "because some—you know, after she left the house, you know, she just kind of got strange, you know. She's really friendly sometimes. She'll call and be real sweet, and ten minutes later, she'll call in a rage, you know, just screaming at my wife. And she did that for, uh, gee, the last year and a half she was doing that."

What began to emerge was that the story of the relationship with Travis she had told to her family was in stark contrast to the way Travis' friends and people who knew the couple had described it.

Arias had indicated to her parents that she and Travis had considered getting married. Bill described a phone call he received from his daughter shortly after she had moved to Mesa. "She called me hysterically crying," he recalled. ". . . She snuck up at his house and she looked in the window and she saw him on the couch with another woman. And here they—she was planning on marrying this guy. So she just left.

"But then she stayed there, you know, for I don't know how many months . . . six months or something . . . and Jodi would not let anybody say anything or discredit him, either. 'Cause I did say a few things after she told me that he was with another girl, I said, 'You need to get the hell out of that town and leave that guy alone.' But then, every time I called her, she was over his house, every time I called her."

In listening to the conversation, Flores and Bill Arias seemed like they were old friends sharing stories about a distant relative. Arias' father recounted a three-hour conversation he and his wife had with Jodi soon after Travis' death. Bill was on the dialysis machine when Jodi had stopped by for a visit. He and Sandy were trying to find out why she believed she needed to leave town. "And she goes, ''Cause I might be blamed for something.' I go, 'What?' And she goes, 'I can't tell you.' She goes, 'I just won't tell you.' And she—she refused, never told us."

Bill went on to say that Jodi quit her job at Casa Ramos after learning police had called the restaurant asking to speak with her. "I said, 'Well, what are you running away for if you're not guilty?' " To which she replied, " 'Cause I don't want to be a part of it."

Flores took the opportunity to relate the challenges he had confronted when trying to speak to Jodi. "Well, I talked to her for over an hour and a half and—and I left with some more questions than I had answers for. You know, I, I, still don't know why. She just refused to tell me."

"She don't talk to us, either," Bill commiserated with Flores, telling him that Jodi treated her mother "like crap . . . I mean verbally abusive on the phone with her. You know, we could never ask her anything about her personal life ever since the day she left the house." As it turned out, neither Bill nor Sandy had ever even seen a picture of Travis until after he'd died. Jodi never showed them a thing.

The information Bill shared next was of particular interest.

He indicated that Arias had not been honest with her parents since she was fourteen. "You know, she doesn't trust us 'cause we're parents. And when she was in eighth grade, she got busted for growing marijuana with our Tupperware, putting it on top of the roof.

"We found it, and we called the sheriff's department, and they busted her, and then, I don't know . . . we searched her room. And after that, she was kind of like, uh, something turned in her head that we were nosy parents and we were gonna search everything she had. So she hid everything from us . . . and she has never been honest with us since then."

Bill also told Flores that Jodi asked him to pick her up at her grandparents' house at 7:30 P.M. on the morning of July 15 and give her a ride to the rental car place. "And I thought it was gonna be for good, you know, and I'm thinking, hmmm . . . And then when I was talking to her, she goes, 'Oh, don't worry, Dad, I'm only gonna be gone for three days.'"

According to Arias' father, her plan was to visit with friends in the Monterey area of California. He told Flores that Jodi had indicated she was planning to visit a couple of ex-boyfriends, Darryl Brewer and Matthew McCartney. But police were never able to establish her true destination based on what she had packed into the car.

Jodi's mother, Sandy, was also of the belief that her daughter was only intending to leave Yreka for a short jaunt, something her parents had come to expect from her.

"That's Jodi," she told Flores during a painful interview. Sandy Arias, a pleasant-looking brunette who had just turned fifty that past March, entered the interview room in tears. She was visibly distraught over her daughter's circumstances and broke out sobbing the moment she sat down at the table with Flores.

The biggest hurdle for Sandy was her inability to reconcile Jodi's seemingly ordinary behavior with the police's accusations that she had taken a life. She described her daughter's demeanor in the days after her trip to Utah in June as completely "normal."

Jodi's "normal" behavior was in sharp contrast to what Sandy experienced at other times, when she described her daughter as someone with "mental problems" who would "freak out all the time."

"I had quite a few of her friends call me and tell me that I needed to get her some help," she said, weeping. "She would call me in the morning all happy and call me an hour or two later in tears, crying and sobbing about something she didn't want to talk about, and it happened constantly."

Like her husband, Sandy seemed to harbor her own initial suspicions about Jodi's involvement in Travis' death, saying that was the first thing she asked her about when she came home. She went on to describe how on the day Jodi learned of Travis' death, she went not to her mother but to her younger sister for comfort. "She was totally in tears. She cried for two or three, four or five days. And, um, that's the first I asked her. I said, 'Did you go to Arizona?' And she said, 'No, I was nowhere near Arizona and I have gas receipts and everything to prove it.' So, of course, I believed her. You know, but I questioned her about it."

The significance of what Sandy was saying—that she, Jodi Arias' own mother, had her suspicions about Jodi's involvement in the murder—was not lost on Flores. "But you had enough suspicion to ask her?"

"Well, yeah."

Sandy Arias explained that her daughter guarded her privacy so vehemently that she wouldn't even let her and her husband stay with her when she lived in Palm Desert with a previous boyfriend, Darryl Brewer. "She was afraid I would snoop through her stuff. That's the kind of relationship we had.

"I told her one day, 'You need some help, Jodi.' I said, 'You've got this fantasy in your head that you had a rotten childhood and that we searched your room all the time and we did all this stuff, and we didn't. And you need some help,' I said, 'because that didn't happen . . .' "

Sandy told Flores about a late-night visit she had with Jodi the previous evening. She couldn't sleep and had called her daughter to ask if Jodi could borrow her grandfather's car to drive over to the house, so they could spend some time together. Instead, Sandy ended up driving to her parents' on Pine Street, where they sat outside in the car and talked. "In the last couple of weeks, since Travis' death, we've had the best relationship we've had in our whole life, and I said, 'Maybe this death has made her see that life is short and, you know, you can't be this way, and it's changing her.' So, the last few weeks . . . I didn't spend a lot of time with her, but I talked to her more than I have ever talked to her since she left the house at eighteen. . . ."

At certain moments during the interview, Arias' mother appeared willing to entertain the idea that her daughter might have killed Travis. "I don't know, maybe she did do it," she conceded, wiping tears from her eyes, before continuing, "I just cannot imagine her doing it."

I paused the video on those words and turned them over in my head. It is always difficult to watch parents of the accused struggle with their children's crimes. No matter how strained the relationship, few parents can really believe that their child is capable of taking a life. Sandy Arias was no different.

But conflicted as Sandy may have been about Jodi's possible involvement in Travis' death as well as her apparent mental instability, one thing that Sandy was not conflicted about was Jodi's intelligence.

"Jodi is a very intelligent person," she told Flores confidently. Her mother's words echoed what I'd already come to observe, that I was dealing with a highly intelligent woman who happened to be a killer. It was apparent from her conver-

sations with Flores that Arias brought a level of careful fore-
thought to each response, even though she had limited time to
formulate her answers.

"She's extremely intelligent, and the more I've talked to her
over the last month and a half, I know she's intelligent," Flores
said.

The detective's comment elicited a response from Arias'
mother that shone a light on an aspect of Arias' personality
that I would encounter again, an inflated sense of intelligence,
a belief that she was smarter than everyone else. "She gave us
a hard time because I never went to college and she kept telling
me, 'Mom, you need to read. You need to do this. You need
to better your life.'" Arias had made these criticisms although
she herself had not graduated from high school.

"I don't know. I just can't even imagine. My God, I can't. I
just can't even think about it," Sandy said, trying to absorb the
significance of the allegations against her daughter.

"Unfortunately, the evidence that we have is completely
convincing to me. . . . I mean, we have everything from fingerprints at the scene of the crime . . ." Flores told her.

"Well, I know her fingerprints are there . . ."

"Her DNA, things like her hair . . ."

"Well, you know she spent time with him, you know . . . so,
does that prove that she killed him? She cleaned his house."

It was symbolic that Arias' mother was ending her interview
in the same place as her daughter, by trying to excuse away
what police had found at the crime scene.

———————

CHAPTER 7

For the July 16 interview, it had been decided that Siskiyou County Sheriff's Detective Rachel Blaney would conduct it, while Detective Flores waited outside the room monitoring what was being said. Looking back and now knowing Jodi Arias, it is obvious that she would never have bonded with a female detective because she seemed to know that she would have a more difficult time manipulating a woman.

During her nearly two hour interrogation with Detective Blaney, Arias twice asked to see the crime scene photos that Flores had declined to show her the previous day, and once again, her requests were denied. For her part, Blaney made little headway and it got to the point in the interview where Blaney asked if Arias would prefer to continue with Detective Flores.

". . . If you want to speak to Detective Flores as opposed to me, you can do that. . . . I thought it would be easier for you to talk to a woman who could relate to some of these feelings," Blaney told her.

"I kind of do want to talk to him because he's always been in contact with Travis' family a lot," Arias replied, without actually knowing what Flores' contact with the family had been. When Flores arrived a few minutes later, dressed in a brown button-down shirt and a pair of slacks, Arias greeted him with a "hey" and a smile.

"Rachel said something about you wanting to see some photos, but I don't think I can show you any more photos,"

Flores told her, obviously uncomfortable with the idea of tip-
ping his hand any further by allowing her to see the remaining
photographs. He had called me after the first interview and
expressed concern that Arias undoubtedly wanted to see the
pictures to learn what police had observed at the scene. Her
next statement confirmed his suspicions.

"The reason I asked was because I just feel like it might help
me piece some things together . . . and this is more of a selfish
reason. I think it might give me some sense of closure. I know
it's kind of morbid. I don't even think I really deserve closure.
His family does. But I wasn't able to attend his funeral. And
it's just, I don't know, that's just why mostly."

"What is it you want to know about the photos?" Flores
asked her. "Do you want to see the room? You want to see the
bathroom, or do you want to see him, or is it the photos before
it happened that you want to see?"

She told him she wanted to see the pictures of everything,
but the ones she was really interested in were the ones in the
bathroom, the ones of Travis' body in the shower.

"I don't want to show you those, not in good conscience."

"Okay, is there any that you can?" By this point it was
clear that Arias' interest in the photographs was beyond an
obsession.

When she realized that Flores was not going to let her view
the crime scene photos, she turned the conversation back to
Travis' family. She wanted to know which relatives he had
spoken to, showing particular interest in Travis' grandmother
Norma Sarvey. She'd already told Flores about Travis' close
relationship with his grandmother, who had raised him since
he was a boy. It was as if she wanted Flores to see how close
her relationship with Travis had been, otherwise she wouldn't
know so much about his family and those closest to him. She
even went so far as to ask if Flores would be willing to deliver
a message from her to them.

"I'll let you decide what to say and I'll relay it exactly how you want me to," he assured her. His willingness to oblige her desire to reach out to the family seemed a calculated effort to gain her trust.

As frustrating as it must have been to indulge Arias' many deflections, I admired Detective Flores' single-mindedness as he pressed on.

"So, were you there that day? Please tell me. Did you just miss him? Did he call you? Did he miss you? The only explanation I can think of is that you went there for one purpose, and that's to hurt him . . . Were you guys alone? . . . Answer that for me. Should I be looking for somebody else? Was there anybody else with you besides you and Travis? Are you protecting somebody else?"

Flores' questions were met with a lengthy silence.

"Jodi?"

"I'm sorry, I'm just—I just don't know what to do. I'm just trying to figure things out."

It was obvious by her statement that she was trying to work out a new story and buying time so she could concoct it.

Arias maintained that it was all a blur, before again requesting to see the photos to help her bring it into focus. Flores didn't close off the possibility, telling her detectives had taken them to Redding when they went to pick up the rental car, and that perhaps she could view them once the investigators returned to Yreka.

"Oh, because there's something in the rental car," Arias suggested.

"Like what?"

"Maybe blood," she said matter-of-factly.

"In the trunk? In the backseat? That's what we are going to look for, so . . ."

"I was thinking maybe the handle, the steering wheel, and things that get touched."

It appeared Arias was almost confessing when she alluded to the possibility that there might be blood in the rental car.

But investigators were never able to recover any biological material to be used for DNA testing because the car had been cleaned by an employee after she returned it. She had also removed the floor mats before returning the car.

Even though Arias continued to deny being in Mesa on the day of the murder, Flores began to premise his questions as if she had been. He asked her whether she'd been worried that Travis' roommates would find her there, how long she was in the house after it happened, why she threw the camera in the washing machine.

"Do you remember those things?" he asked.

"Mmm, no," Arias replied.

They started to talk about the white Ford Focus that Arias had rented for the drive. The investigation into the car had determined that Arias had actually rejected the first car the rental company had given her, another Ford Focus, but a red one, and he wanted to find out more about it.

"I know they were going to rent you another car, but then something happened with the first car, either you didn't like it or I don't know if it had problems."

This was a detail that I considered important because it spoke to her planning. She claimed she hadn't wanted a red car because it would be more noticeable, akin to a red flag— that police were more likely to stop someone in a red car, but I suspected she chose a more neutral color to blend in.

After discussing the fact that Travis had apparently canceled plans to see her at the end of May, Flores returned to his questions.

"Did Travis know you were coming?" Flores watched for a reaction. "He knew?" he coaxed. "I saw you kind of shake your head a little bit."

"This is hard," Arias said, her voice cracking. For the first time, she looked away from the detective, her gaze fixed to a point on the wall. It appeared she was trying to buy time to come up with her next line.

"That's okay," he said as he tried to coax her along, peppering her with questions. "Did he know you were coming? Did you guys talk on the phone? What was the discussion about? Did you guys talk when you were en route to Phoenix?"

Arias' reply was barely audible. "Yeah," she mumbled, looking down at her feet. And with that she had placed herself at the crime scene, finally succumbing to the evidence left behind in Travis' camera. "Just briefly. I told him my phone was dying, which was true. I thought I left my charger in Monterey. I really honestly thought I left my charger there and I had been talking all day, just on the phone.

"I take a lot of pictures of myself," she smiled.

"I noticed," Flores replied with a laugh, referring to several selfies police had found on the cell phone they seized from her at the time of her arrest.

"I am kind of picky about it. I take like twenty, and I am like delete, delete, delete, and I keep two or three."

"So he knew you were coming. He was expecting you?"

Arias did not respond, instead remaining quiet, with her hands folded in her lap.

"Obviously you guys had a little encounter. Is that when those pictures were taken?" Flores asked, referring to the six photographs of their sexual rendezvous. "Did he even show you those pictures?"

This was the longest silence I had seen from Arias since the start of her two-day-long interview. Unlike other times, when she would close herself off in the fetal position or hide her face in her hands, this time she looked off toward the corner, apparently thinking about how much she was going to reveal and the style with which she was going to deliver the line. She'd already put herself at the house, and was on the brink of having to explain what happened inside.

"It's going to be all right, Jodi."

"I feel really powerless in here," she whimpered, appearing to finally realize that she was caught and for the first time couldn't figure out how to explain that she'd been merely present at the crime scene but had not committed the crime. Her repeated requests to see the photographs had been denied, so she had been unable to craft a story based on the evidence police had gathered. Her only way out was to change the subject.

The detective let enough time pass to demonstrate his concern before moving ahead with his inquiry. After talking to her about whether Travis' roommates were home when she arrived, Arias explained that she got in at three in the morning.

"Did you guys spend all day together then? . . . Did you go anywhere, did you stay in the house?"

"Slept," Arias said.

"Well, after a long trip I would sleep, too."

Arias recalled that when she got there, Travis was watching some stupid music video with people dancing with foil boxes on their heads. Suddenly, she grew animated, mimicking the characters' hand movements. She was speaking to Flores as if they were friends, sharing stories about a mutual acquaintance. "It was weird. It was robotic kind of music. It's just like stupid, pointless stuff. Being as driven and deep as he is, it is just funny that he watches stuff like that."

The detective laughed along, obviously hoping that this somewhat bonding experience would give her the impetus to share what really happened. He redirected her to the afternoon photographic session. "Is that when those were taken that day?"

In a barely audible whisper, Arias shared with Flores something that he didn't know. "We also made a video, and we deleted it."

"On that camera?"

"On his camera," Arias confirmed.

Her admission came as a surprise to me. She hadn't said much of anything up to that point and now she was volunteering information that was not even known to the detective.

I wondered what her motivation for this new disclosure was, and the only thing that seemed logical was that in her mind she and Flores were sharing a moment. It was clear to me now that her preoccupation with the photos was partially an effort to try to find out if their sex video had been recovered.

If Flores was surprised by this revelation, he didn't show it.

"Videos are hard to get when they are erased," he told her. "They take up so much room, whereas pictures are a little different." The video would not have offered any clues that the pictures hadn't already given him, so it was not surprising that he moved on to the bigger question of motive.

"What happened after that? What went wrong? I know that the last photos of him were taken at 5:20, 5:30. And you said he doesn't like you to take pictures of him."

"He was very private about the shower," Arias disclosed and added that so was she.

Laughing, Flores asked, "Is that why you were taking pictures of him in the shower? Trying to get back at him?"

Arias denied that was the reason.

"I am surprised he allowed you to take pictures of him in the shower. The first few looked like he wasn't that comfortable, but obviously whatever you were saying to him appeared to make him a little more comfortable. . . .

"What went wrong? Did he say something to you?"

Arias took several deep breaths and turned her face away as the detective pressed her for an answer.

"Were you angry about something? Were you frustrated? What was it?"

Her face was almost completely hidden behind strands of her long brown hair, but I could tell she was listening closely. It appeared she was weighing her options and had come to a place where she was finally ready to free herself of the tremendous burden she had been carrying around for the past month. It looked as though she was about to say something when suddenly the sound of Flores' pager going off interrupted the pin-dropping silence. Sixteen seconds ticked by as Flores checked his phone and looked at the message.

It appeared the short reprieve allowed her to collect herself enough to sit up in her chair, push her hair back away from her face, and take a breath as she waited for the detective's attention to return to her. "What are you going to do with the rental car?" she asked, immediately redirecting the focus of the questioning away from the precipitating incident to something completely unrelated. "Are they gonna bring it here?"

"There were several photos of him," Flores continued, trying to return the conversation to the moments before the killing. But Arias was now focused on the present and the search of the rental car currently under way.

I could feel Flores' frustration as he inhaled deeply and let out a sigh. Still, he did his best to bring Arias back to the scene in the bathroom. "There were several photos of him, and the last one is of him sitting in the shower. That's when I think it happened.

"What did you do? What happened, Jodi? We've come this far. . . . Did you plan on doing that the whole time?"

"No," she answered, clearly disengaged, as she began running her fingers through her hair and staring blankly as the staccato of Flores' questioning increased.

"Then why? Tell me. I don't believe you planned it," he told her. I was familiar with the interrogation technique Flores was now employing, where the officers are taught to minimize the suspect's involvement in hopes that they will admit something. "But then I don't understand why, why you took a gun with you?"

"I didn't," Arias insisted.

"Then where did you get it? Did you bring it with you? Did you get it there in Arizona?"

"I didn't have . . . actually, like have it my possession."

"Then who had it? If you didn't have it, and Travis didn't have it, then who had it? Jodi," Flores implored, "please."

"I can't," she said in her best B-actress angst.

"Why not? Are you protecting somebody else? Why would somebody else do this?"

"I don't know."

"Did someone catch you there, someone not expecting you to be there?"

Arias' reply was inaudible.

"Then who was it?"

"I don't know," she said, looking up at the ceiling and nervously pulling on her hand, likely trying to figure out which direction her story should pivot to next.

"Okay, what do you remember from the time you were taking pictures and the time you left, what happened? What happened after that last picture was taken?"

After they went back and forth, Flores finally began to push her. "If somebody else was there with you, we need to know that. Why would somebody do that just because you're there with Travis?"

"They didn't say," she replied. For the first time, there was an answer—not much, but something he could build off.

"Hmm . . ." he murmured.

"They didn't say," Arias repeated in a faint voice.

"*He* didn't say?"

"*They.*"

And with that, Arias had the beginnings of her second story, one in which she had been present for Travis' death, but it wasn't her committing the crime, it was "they."

"What was the first thing they did to him? You were there, you saw it."

Flores hoped that what Arias was about to tell him might actually be what happened, because it could be that two people had done this. If she were to give him names, it wouldn't be so implausible.

"I actually didn't see it. I heard it . . . first," Arias began.

"Was there an argument?"

"Not between Travis and them."

"Any argument between anybody?"

"Yeah." She paused, patting tears from her eyes. "Is there any way I can see those pictures?" It was a telling moment of lucidity during a moment that at least superficially appeared emotional, and it was a strategy of hers that I would encounter later on. Even in the midst of crafting this new story, she had not lost sight of her true aim—the crime scene photos and how they could enable her to fabricate a story that matched the events depicted in the photographs.

"No," he told her. "Not right now."

"Can I see them soon?" she begged. By this point, her request had morphed into a desperate plea.

"You need to start letting me know what happened," Flores instructed her. "You are saying that other people were there, you know how much that concerns me?"

"I don't know . . . They . . . they know where I live, or they know where my parents are. I don't know if they know where my grandparents are. They know my address. They know where my family is," Arias contended, sobbing and wiping at her tears. "Sorry."

"So you are trying to say you're doing this to protect your family? Why would somebody do this to you and to him?" Flores asked incredulously.

"I don't think they really intended to do anything to me."

"So you are saying somebody followed you all the way to Arizona from here?"

"I think I was an element of surprise for them."

"You were an element of surprise?" Flores parroted, an air of frustrated disbelief in his tone.

"I am guessing . . ."

"They didn't expect you to be there?"

"I mean they had to have seen my car."

"Is this someone who lives in Mesa locally?"

"I didn't recognize them."

"Well, you have to give me a motive," Flores told her. "Why would they do this? Were they going after Travis?"

Arias collapsed onto the table, resting her head in the crook of her elbow.

"You tell me this, but you give me no reason."

"They didn't discuss much," Arias said, popping back up to look at Flores. "They just argued."

"About what?"

"About whether or not to kill me."

"For what reason?"

"Because I'm a witness."

"A witness to what?"

"Him . . . to Travis," Arias said, cupping her face in her hands.

"Travis' murder?"

"Yeah, but I didn't really witness it. I didn't see much," she said, hiding her face in her hands as if frightened at the recollection.

"You need to make this believable, because this is *not* believable to me right now," Flores directed. "You need to give me something."

Arias seemed eager to indulge the detective. "Okay, just listen . . ."

"Jodi, I am listening, and it doesn't make any sense to me. People just don't go in somewhere and kill somebody for no reason and then let a witness go. That doesn't happen. They've already killed one person, why not just take care of the other? You know who they are, if you are telling me the truth."

"I don't know them."

"Then I don't believe you. I can't. You can't expect me to."

As if to buy more time, Arias then launched into a long-winded rendition of the events of June 3, her first day on the road, beginning with her departure from Yreka and going through her arrival at Travis' house in the middle of the night. After arriving there, she said they slept in until about 1:00 P.M.

the next day, June 4, and almost immediately upon waking, they engaged in sexual interplay, which as she told Flores earlier, included videotaping as well as photographs. At least this part of her story appeared to have been true, since the photographs from the camera confirmed them posing nude starting around 1:30 in the afternoon.

She claimed afterward that they went downstairs to his study, where they tried to view some CDs that she had brought with her containing pictures of various trips they had taken, but they were having problems because either the computer couldn't play them or the CDs were damaged. It was around this time that they engaged in sex for a second time. She said they went back upstairs, where Travis shaved before he took a shower. As he stood in the shower, she convinced him to allow her to use his newly purchased camera to photograph him. She believed that the photograph of him with the water running down his face was a very nice image.

That was where her story took a drastic detour, once again stretching the boundaries of credulity. As she knelt down outside of the shower reviewing the photos, she said she heard a pop and almost simultaneously felt a strike to the back of her head, which she believed caused her to lapse into unconsciousness for a short period of time. Upon regaining consciousness, she saw two attackers wearing ski masks, a man and a woman, one armed with a gun and one armed with a knife. She turned her attention to Travis and realized that he had been shot and was screaming and bleeding profusely. He told her to go to his neighbors and "go get help." She did not follow his instruction because, she said, the attackers prevented her from leaving.

According to her story, in the middle of this melee, the male attacker took the time to find her purse and rummage through it, looking to find her identification information. He found both her driver's license and car registration, which included her parents' address in Yreka. She was then told by the male attacker that she must be "that bitch from California," leading her to believe they somehow knew her.

She immediately became afraid for her family and decided to follow the attackers' instructions. After returning the registration and driver's license to her purse, the male attacker went through the pockets of her Levi's, which she claimed were in a backpack she had brought with her, and found eighty dollars, which he pocketed.

According to her, the attack took a more serious turn when the female assailant tried to convince her companion that Arias should also be killed. But he prevailed, saying "That's not why we are here."

At some point, Arias claimed that she began to fight with the woman, who apparently was now holding the knife. Although Arias was barefoot and unarmed, she appeared to have escaped the encounter unharmed, with the exception of a cut to one of the fingers on her left hand.

The attackers finally decided to let her leave with a stern warning, counseling against telling anyone what she had just lived through. They allowed her to take her purse and backpack and shoes, and leave out the front door, apparently confident that their threats would silence her and stop her from calling police to aid a dying Travis.

"You just left? You didn't run to the neighbors, you didn't try calling?" Flores asked with a tone of disbelief. "You knew they were in his house. You had time to run to the neighbor, why didn't you do that?"

"I was really scared," Arias whined. "I was freaked out of my mind."

"I don't believe you," he responded, in a raspy Godfather-type voice, extending his left hand to emphasis his point. "I came in here hoping you would tell me the truth, and this is not the truth, Jodi."

After some final back and forth, Flores left the room, and the lined legal pad he had left behind on the table became the focus of her attention. Tearing three sheets from the pad, she folded them and stuck them in the chest pocket of her orange top. But when she looked down at them, she appeared to realize that they would be visible to anyone who entered the room, so she tucked them into the waistband of her orange pants, making sure her top was covering them.

When Detective Blaney entered the room a few moments later, she asked if Arias had any paper. The police had been monitoring her from outside the room and saw what she'd done. Arias hesitated for a moment before lifting her top to reveal the hidden papers. Although Blaney ultimately allowed her to keep the items, her attempts to hide them showed she had no compunction about trying to get away with as much as she could, even if it was something as insignificant as three sheets of paper.

Approximately two weeks later, Arias mailed a letter from the jail to Travis' grandmother Norma Sarvey, who lived in Riverside, California. Interestingly enough, Arias listed the return address on the envelope as her parents' address on Oregon Street, although the jail's official address was stamped in black ink over her handwritten one.

"Of all of the letters I must write, this is one of the most difficult, second only to the one I must write to my parents," Arias began the eighteen-page handwritten letter, which was dated Monday, July 28, 2008—which would have been Travis' thirty-first birthday.

"I don't have all of the answers that you seek," the letter continued, "but as I sit here today and put pen to paper, even on Travis' birthday, I'm going to try to answer as many as I can. . . . Since things have culminated in this way, and since the detectives have already made it clear that my case is hopeless and theirs rock-solid, I have no reason to hold anything back at this point. . . ."

She proceeded to provide a "brief synopsis" of the history of her relationship with Travis.

"I met Travis at the Rainforest Café at the MGM in September 2006. We later marveled and mused at the irony of meeting in such a place, as we later discovered our mutual passion for a healthy planet and the environment in general. He confidently walked right up to me, stuck out his right and said, 'Hi, I'm Travis.' I cordially responded with the usual niceties and figured that would be it, since in that moment, he was just another of the many new names I was trying not to forget."

Arias claimed she didn't feel any sort of "magnetic attraction" to him, but also did not turn her back on his entreaties. Although she tried to meet and mingle with other people, he monopolized her attention by walking alongside her and keeping up a running conversation. In the short time they talked, they discovered they had a few things in common: traveling, the 49ers, the UFC, and "the drive to create an amazing life." She said she didn't expect to hear from Travis again, but "surprisingly," he called her the very next day. As she described it, the relationship was on a very fast track.

Within days, he invited her to spend the weekend at the home of his friends Sky and Chris Hughes in Murrieta, California, one of the reasons being so that she could attend church with them, and the following Wednesday, he gave her a copy of the Book of Mormon. By November 2006, Travis was baptizing her as a Mormon at the church in Palm Desert, California. "He said he'd never met anyone more prepared to receive the Gospel," she wrote. Arias went on to say she was very happy, because she claimed joining the LDS church was one of the best decisions she ever made. "I know that Travis will be richly rewarded for the role he played in bringing me into the fold."

Arias explained that they were mutually attracted, but they were not officially dating. By Christmas of 2006, Travis had grown to mean a lot to her. For his part, he was determined to

"Mormonize" her, so he gave her gifts to serve that purpose, including a CTR ring and scriptures with her name engraved on them, a painting of Jesus Christ, and a biography of church president Gordon B. Hinckley. "His generosity never wavered the entire time that I knew him, not once."

Arias wrote in that same letter that on February 2, 2007, they began to officially date. "Things went really well despite one small hangup: Deanna Reid." Deanna Reid was one of Travis' former girlfriends, whom he had dated during two separate periods, and the two had remained very close friends. According to the letter, she and Travis even talked of marriage. This included discussions about baby names and the number and sexes of children they wanted; she believed this was a "natural progression."

According to her letter, in May 2007, Arias could no longer handle the mortgage of her home in Palm Desert and she had to move out. "Travis insisted that I move closer to him, so that we could have a more normal relationship," although he expressed concern for Deanna's reaction, saying that if she found out it would be "World War III."

The two took a trip to Daniel's Summit, Utah, in June 2007, and after their return, according to Arias, she did something completely dishonest. "I acted on an impulse and a gut feeling. . . . You see, I had been in a few relationships before when my partner was not being completely faithful, and there is a distinct feeling that comes with it. Travis had been interacting with some girls in my presence that gave me cause for concern. I knew he was a flirtatious type, and I had witnessed it on countless occasions prior to that point.

"I am not a jealous person, but something about the way he conducted himself at that time caused me to question his level of commitment to our relationship and to me. The dishonest deed that I had mentioned was that I looked at the text messages in his phone. I thought to myself, he said he had nothing to hide, so why not? A flawed logic, I know. I fully expected to find a few mild flirtations with other girls, as this was his MO anyway. And he was not secretive about it. What I found, however, was far more, including several references made of the many, separate, intimate rendezvous he had with other girls including plans in the making for further associations of the same kind."

Arias said she attempted to verify that he had been dishonest by checking the dates; as she feared, the activities that she'd uncovered had been during the time they had been dating, supposedly exclusively.

But rather than confront Travis, she chose to go on vacation with him, and they traveled to Niagara Falls and the Sacred Grove, in New York State, as well as to Huntington Beach, California. It was only after they returned from their trip that she spoke to him about her concerns. Although he was very apologetic, she found there was no way she could forgive him, so she broke up with him on June 29, 2007, because she could not trust him. "This was a very difficult decision for me, because I loved him very much. It was especially difficult because he begged me to marry him that same day. Up to that point, a proposal was expected at any time, but once the trust is gone it is hopeless."

In July 2007, Arias wrote, she decided to move to Mesa, after Travis persuaded her to make the move, reiterating the story she'd told Flores. She used to wonder what it would have been like to accept his marriage proposal, but she didn't think things would have changed, because a month before she moved back to California in April of 2008, she and Travis had a conversation about previous relationships, and he confessed that most of the time that she'd been living in Mesa, he'd been dating Lisa Andrews. She had asked him about it, and he had lied by telling her he wasn't dating anyone. She said she'd never had a reason not to believe him, so she couldn't understand why he hid it from her, since she was not the "type to have a crying emotional meltdown over something like that."

She would have been happy for him. The shock that she experienced was related not to the fact that he had lied again, not that he cheated on yet another girlfriend, but that this time, *she* was the other woman, and it made her feel ashamed. Arias claimed her first thought was not of herself, but of "poor Lisa." She said she even thought about telling her, but decided that it would destroy her relationship with Travis and "cause a lot of unnecessary drama and pain."

According to Arias, when it was her turn to come clean his attitude changed and "all hell broke loose. . . . He lost his temper completely and flew into a rage, he began punching himself in the head so hard that he injured his neck and his back and could barely turn his head from side to side." She even claimed that he beat her on two separate occasions, but she never told anyone about it because he was not her "part-ner" any longer, and "besides, it would be a matter of days before she rolled out of town in a U-Haul truck."

"I know you all probably hate me even more than before you started reading this letter," Arias wrote on page 8 of the eighteen-page attempt to exonerate herself in the eyes of Travis' grandmother. "Well hang on, because the plot thickens, and by the time you're done reading this, you most likely won't consider me worthy of your own spit."

She went on to describe Travis' killing in the same fashion as she did to Detective Flores, with a few embellishments. In this version, the male assailant "held the gun to my head and tried to fire but nothing happened, just a click." She also de-tailed a scuffle with the female attacker who she claimed came at her with a knife and during the struggle, stomped on her bare feet. "I didn't notice the pain, maybe it was adrenaline, but my left foot was later throbbing and bruised so I know she got me at least once, probably more on that foot, and she had caused two of the toenails on my other foot to bleed, which I didn't discover until later as well."

She also claimed that she felt awful because she hadn't looked before backing out of the driveway as she fled the scene. "I probably should've never been driving in that kind of state."

Her seemingly heartfelt letter sent to Travis' grandmother, supposedly offering solace, appeared more like a taunt, as she described a scenario that was impossible to believe.

———————

CHAPTER 8

Almost two years after Travis' murder, the case should have been ready to go to trial according to the timeline set out in the Arizona Rules of Criminal Procedure. The police reports had been reviewed, witness interviews were under way, and Jodi Arias' version of events had been consistent ever since she told Flores that she had merely been present when two strangers broke in and killed Travis. But in spring 2010, the defense began to shift in ways that would permanently alter the makeup and tone of the case.

These changes had actually started to take root in August 2009, when Arias' initial court-appointed counsel was allowed to withdraw and a second set of attorneys, also appointed by the court, took over the defense. Laurence Nurmi was assigned as lead attorney, with Victoria Washington assisting him. I didn't know much about either attorney—our paths had never crossed before—but I understood that Nurmi was qualified to represent defendants charged with a capital crime.

On the face of it, the presence of these new attorneys wasn't particularly significant because my interactions with Arias' defense team were fairly limited. As is standard, the only time I would see them was during our periodic status conferences, which occurred every thirty to forty-five days. During these appearances, the prosecution and defense were asked to update the judge on their progress and alert the court to any problems that had arisen. In these conferences, neither side is required to disclose details of the approach or tactics they intend to use, enabling the prosecutor and defense counsel to pursue avenues that best advance their cause without having to tip their hand.

But with the arrival of these new attorneys came new requests. The prosecution is required to provide defense counsel copies of police reports, photographs, and other documentary items. Over the course of this prosecution, more than twenty-four hundred pages of documents alone were provided to defense counsel. The state is also required to list the names and addresses of those it expects to testify at trial.

Defense counsel has a similar duty to disclose the claims that will be advanced at trial, along with the names of persons who may be called to testify for their side. Their disclosure obligation includes providing the state with copies of any materials that they think are important and might be used at trial.

In April 2010, Arias' defense counsel requested that the prosecution provide text messages from Travis' cell phone and instant messages and e-mails from his computer. The production of this electronic correspondence initially proved problematic for different reasons. Technology had not advanced sufficiently to allow recovery of the text messages without making it unduly burdensome and extremely time consuming. As for the instant messages and e-mail, the service provider, in this case Google, had ignored the subpoena I sent requesting the correspondence. Eventually each of these issues was resolved once the electronic correspondence was made available to the prosecution, allowing for copies to be made and turned over to the defense.

The state provided defense counsel with thousands of texts, e-mails, and instant messages from Travis' various accounts. It was a massive trove of information with the messages and e-mails covering everything from the mundane to the inflammatory. What emerged was a portrait of a tumultuous relationship, one laced with sexual overtones and bad feelings on both sides.

The instant messages were particularly troublesome because they portrayed Travis as someone who may have verbally crossed the line of good taste as he and Arias argued
via electronic means. In one angry instant messenger chat between the two on May 26, 2008, Travis complained that Arias
was "nothing but a liar from the beginning." It was clear that
she had done something to upset him greatly, but that catalyst
wasn't discernible from the lengthy exchange. What was clear
was that Travis felt that she had lied to him:

> TRAVIS: you have not felt as much pain in all your life than
> what you have repeatedly caused me with your lies and
> your invasions and the phycho [sic] shit you have subjected
> me to
> TRAVIS: you have made me want to die
> TRAVIS: on countless occasions
> TRAVIS: you have hurt me so bad over and over again
> TRAVIS: and how do you repay me forgiving you by doing
> the same thing
> TRAVIS: couldnt you ever try to love me
> TRAVIS: you only showed that you hated me
> TRAVIS: never love
> TRAVIS: only hate
> TRAVIS: ur words were lies . . . cant you just tell the truth

Throughout the entire exchange that followed, Arias
avoided answering Travis' ongoing requests for the "truth."
Instead, she portrayed herself as the victim, writing:

> JODI: There have been times when you've screamed into
> the phone so loud at me that the speaker was distorted and
> then you hung up. The pain was so sharp and so deep that
> I just couldn't process it. I could only scream in response
> to the air. And I would scream at the top of my lungs until
> my throat was raw, "I HATE YOU! I HATE YOU! I HATE

YOU!" until I had no energy left to say it and it had wittled [*sic*] down to a little whimp [*sic*], ". . . i hate you . . ." And I just sobbed and cried until I couldn't breathe.

JODI: But you know what? I deserved all of that. Every angry phone call. Every unpleasant word.

JODI: doesn't compare to what I've put you through.

The conversation continued with Travis attempting to get Arias to admit that she had slashed his tires. He also accused her of stealing his journals. At one point, Travis' frustration with Arias' refusal to take responsibility was boiling over when he said: "write something you stupid idiot."

Arias picks this moment to respond, "I may be a liar, I may be a whore, I may be evil, I may be a coward, I may not be worth the air I breathe, I am most like the most horrible person you've ever had the misfortune of knowing, but one thing I am NOT, is violent. I did not and would never slash your tires."

This appears to infuriate Travis, who again demands that Arias "tell the truth." The heated exchange continues for several more pages until his anger finally boils over and he lashes out in derogatory fashion, calling her a "3 hole wonder."

The first time I read those words, I realized that they were extremely harsh, so I went back to the beginning of this section of the conversation to understand the context of the remark. The way this conversation had been reproduced required it be read from the bottom of the page to the top, rather than the customary top to bottom. This time, I read the conversation from top to bottom rather than the way I had been reading it before. I wanted to make sure that I hadn't been mistaken, that Travis had actually referred to Arias in this way. Either way I read it, it brought me to the same uncomfortable place.

While I understood from the conversation that Travis had made the comment in anger, it felt inappropriate under any circumstance because it was so derogatory. Even if they were talking in a sexual context, and even if Arias prompted the comment by saying she was a "whore," it still didn't lessen its impact. It was the kind of comment that could shape a jury's opinion and garner sympathy for Arias.

I took solace in the belief that this comment would probably not be admissible at trial because it was hearsay and would unfairly go into an area of Travis' character that had nothing to do with the killing. Up to this point, Arias was still maintaining that Travis had been killed by two intruders as he posed for pictures in the shower so his being verbally abusive to Arias was irrelevant to the reason he was murdered.

In the same conversation, Travis also indicated that he felt he was meaningless to her, writing that he "was little more than a dildo with ah eartbeat [sic] to you." It seemed that Travis had very conflicted feelings about his sexual relationship with Arias and believed that she had been using him for her sexual gratification.

Arias was no shrinking violet and pushed the sexual envelope by sending Travis explicit text messages encouraging the sexual interaction between the two. She sent the following on February 25, 2008: "The 'things' I had to do today consisted of waxing my pussy so it was nice and smooth—just in case, showering so I was fresh and clean for U. . . ." Arias sent other text messages along the same lines in January and February 2008: "Will do. The reason I was asking about later tonight is because I want to give u a nice bj and I'd like a generous facial in return. Waddya say?"; "O-my-Gosh!!! That is so freaking hot I want to lick it up and then sit on it! U are so tasty. My goodness. . . ."; "Oh yes. I want to fuck you like a dirty, horny little schoolgirl."

Although Arias may have been a willing participant in their sexual repartee, defense counsel's inordinate interest in Travis' texts, instant messages, and e-mails hinted that they might be contemplating a change in strategy and moving away from the story that Arias had been alleging for the nearly two years since her arrest.

Another change in her story would be risky because it would contradict both her allegations to Flores that two masked intruders killed Travis, and the tale she'd told during interviews with two national television news magazines in which she said the same thing, tying herself to that fantastical rendition of events.

One of the TV interviews had actually occurred in Yreka less than a month after she was taken into custody, when she had granted a jailhouse interview to *48 Hours*. She then did a follow-up interview with that same news show in September 2008 after her extradition to Phoenix. She also spoke to *Inside Edition* around the same time as the second interview with *48 Hours*.

Her interview with *Inside Edition* aired first. Arias, dressed in black-and-white-striped jail garb, her long brown hair neatly brushed and falling over her shoulders, smiled demurely as she emphatically proclaimed her guiltlessness. "I know that I am innocent, God knows that I'm innocent, Travis knows I'm innocent. . . . I absolutely did not kill Travis Alexander. I had nothing to do with his murder. I didn't harm him in any way."

She again went on to tell the story of two assailants who entered Travis' home and "attacked us both." "In a nutshell, two people took Travis' life, two monsters," she claimed, her voice never higher than a raised whisper.

As believable as her denials may have sounded, what was most compelling about this interview was her indignation. "No jury is going to convict me," she said with certainty. She then followed up this statement with an even more emphatic one, "Because I'm innocent. You can mark my words on that one . . ."

The interview with *48 Hours* aired some months later, and it was telling for totally different reasons. When asked about her childhood, Arias described an idyllic upbringing and maintained that she and her parents and siblings were very close. I couldn't help but think back to the interviews Detective Flores had conducted with Sandy and Bill Arias and how they had described a secretive, disrespectful daughter who had been shutting them out of her life since she was fourteen. As far as I was concerned, here was yet another indication that she would make things up if it suited her, even under inconsequential circumstances such as a media interview.

More importantly, though, she had made it difficult to present a story of an abusive childhood as a possible excuse for her behavior or to help understand the killing because she had told a national audience something contrary to what Bill and Sandy had expressed to police. Her statements had served to effectively preclude her parents from testifying at trial, because the idyllic family portrait she had just painted for the television audience was in stark contrast to the statements her parents had made to police about her inability to get along with her mother and being extremely secretive.

When it came to the murder of Travis Alexander, Arias stuck to her story, continuing to adamantly deny any plans to visit Travis in Arizona on that fateful day. She again recited her masked intruder story, making sure it was consistent with the one given to Detective Flores and to *Inside Edition*. In addition to the incredible nature of the story itself, her failure to alert police immediately or to tell them about the two intruders during her first interviews with Detective Flores continued to stand out as problematic. It sounded more like a slip of the tongue than a reason when she told the interviewer she hadn't called police because she "didn't want to implicate" herself.

The highlight of the *48 Hours* interview was the assertion that she intended to take the witness stand and testify at trial. That told me that she was confident in her public speaking abilities and that she believed she was persuasive enough to make the charges go away just by telling her story. She was masterful in front of the camera, playing the part of someone who couldn't have committed this murder. The way she could look straight at the camera lens and answer the interviewer's questions with apparent sincerity was impressive. She clearly wasn't going to be intimidated.

"I don't believe that I am going to be convicted," she confidently told *48 Hours*' Maureen Maher, just as she had advised the interviewer from *Inside Edition*. "I don't think that I'm going to spend one day in prison."

While she hadn't given another interview in the almost two-year span since these aired, her initial decision to tell her story to the media had elevated both the case and her account to mythical heights. It was one thing to concoct this kind of narrative when confronted with overwhelming evidence during a police interview, but quite another to volunteer those same claims to a national audience. The account of the masked intruders had become synonymous with the case.

Perhaps the feedback from Arias' TV interviews, which called into question the believability of her story, led her and her defense counsel to rethink their approach in defending the case. Even though no notice of a change in defense had yet been filed with the court, I could see that one was in the offing. The graphic and hurtful nature of the text messages, IM chats, and e-mails had the potential to taint Travis' reputation and character, which would only be important if Arias changed her existing story.

It didn't take much to foresee that defense counsel were considering self-defense as an option. Pleading self-defense would allow Arias to say that Travis was such a bad person he deserved what she doled out to him on June 4, 2008. It appeared from their requests for the electronic correspondence that defense counsel was motivated by their intent to use Travis' words to cast him into the role of villain, a role they would insist he play. And Arias was being recast as a victim, a role she'd sought as hers from the beginning of the case.

In June 2010, not long after the e-mail and text messages were made available to them, defense counsel made an unexpected disclosure to me. It was printouts of ten letters they had received via e-mail on Sunday, April 11, 2010, from someone with an e-mail address identifying himself as "Bob White." Accompanying the letters was a single sentence written by "White," ostensibly seeking to distance himself from the case, "I came across these but don't want to be involved."

As indicated in existing public filings, each of the letters attached to the e-mail was supposedly written by Travis where he mentions sexual acts and fantasies, and purportedly admits conduct that would be considered deviant or unlawful. By order of the court, the specific content of the letters was sealed on July 15, 2010.

Anyone can create an e-mail account under a fictitious name, and it seemed that was the case in this instance, because "Bob White" was never identified beyond the name provided on the electronic correspondence. Even more suspect was that the whereabouts of the original letters was never disclosed by defense counsel. The method in which they came to light and the fact that the letters were not originals immediately raised a red flag and signaled that an investigation into their authenticity was in order.

Three weeks after the disclosure of the Bob White letters, defense counsel advised me through a "notice of defenses" filed with the court that they would now pursue a justification defense related to domestic violence, commonly known as self-defense. Despite previously claiming she either hadn't been at the scene or that the killing was committed by intruders, Arias was changing her story again and now admitting that she had killed Travis and had done so for a justifiable reason.

In her latest version of events, Travis became angry and attacked her, making her fear for her life, because she dropped his camera while she took pictures of him in the shower. She admitted that no one else had been in the bathroom with them, contrary to what she had told Detective Flores back on July 16, 2008, when he interviewed her in Yreka. Arias was also claiming that on several occasions Travis sexually and physically abused her and had slapped her and choked her.

This was in sharp contrast to the Travis Alexander she had previously described to Detective Flores during their telephone conversations and her face-to-face interviews with him. Changing stories would normally be the death knell for a defendant because any testimony with inconsistent stories would surely be rejected by a jury, except that Jodi Ann Arias was different in her physical appearance, affect, and demeanor and was skilled at making the implausible seem true.

Any questioning of her would be extremely difficult because as I had seen in her interviews and phone calls, she could seamlessly meld the truth with her untruths making her statements seem consistent.

Getting at the truth in court would be especially difficult because there were just two people present in Travis' bedroom on June 4, 2008, and only one of them, Jodi Arias, was alive to tell *her* story. The challenge was all the more daunting because it included discrediting her assertion that Travis was a cad who hit her at times and spoke to her in a demeaning tone, as illustrated by some of the text messages and instant messenger conversations now available. The clanging of his "3 hole wonder" comment, in particular, reverberated loudly, as it provided support for her allegation that Travis was abusive, making for what appeared to be an almost insurmountable hurdle. Given the damning electronic conversation, I had to admit that Arias' self-defense claim seemed to have a chance of succeeding.

Providence seemed to have miraculously come to her aid through these ten letters allegedly written by Travis, and it was no coincidence that her claim of self-defense arose shortly after her defense counsel received Bob White's e-mail containing the prejudicial letters. If they could be authenticated and the acts described within them proven to be true, I knew they would present a nearly impossible hurdle to clear at trial. Jurors might even acquit Arias in reaching their verdict if they believed Travis was a reprehensible individual who had been abusing her.

CHAPTER 9

People would be amazed at the stories I hear in this job, everything from situational amnesia, where the accused claims he or she cannot remember anything about the crime, to denying his or her presence at the crime scene when there are pictures or video to prove otherwise. It is never easy to ascertain when a person is telling the truth, and the task becomes even more difficult when the individual has nothing to lose and everything to gain by being deceitful.

Jodi Arias' filing with the court announcing her new strategy left me with little recourse but to go back and reexamine the police investigation more closely, as well as review any other information I might not have previously read. I had already amassed a voluminous amount of material, more than in any other case I could remember. Nearly a dozen three-ring binders full of investigative materials, file folders stuffed with photographs and documents, and stacks of miscellaneous papers crowded the bookcases that spanned nearly an entire wall of my small office.

A quick reexamination of the police materials yielded no evidence of any claim of domestic abuse. Other than her expressed disappointment to Detective Flores at learning that Travis had been communicating with other women during their relationship, she had offered nothing but compliments and praise for the man she was now claiming had abused and terrorized her. While it contradicted her current claims, this alone would not be enough to discount her assertions. I needed to find some concrete proof that I could hold up in front of a jury to repudiate her allegations.

Everything the Mesa Police Department had done in their investigation had focused on placing Arias at the scene of the crime and proving *she* had been the one who killed Travis. With her change in strategy, she was effectively sticking her tongue out at them, negating the importance of the evidence they had already collected and presenting me with a wholly different task. Nothing in the photographs, police reports or countless other documents addressed the issue of self-defense, so much of the investigative material was now of little use to me.

A sense of alarm began to take hold, if only for just a minute. It felt as though I were standing on a lunar landscape, pockmarked with gaping craters having been shipwrecked there with no way of returning back to Earth. As I looked at the bookcases in my office, I slowly recited the labels of some of the black binders lining the shelves: *Photographs, Cell Phone Records, Text Messages, Arias' Statements.*

My concern over the state of the case was compounded by my knowledge of how well Arias had handled herself when faced with incontrovertible facts and pointed questions. I had spent hours watching the interviews she had done with Detective Flores at police headquarters in Yreka, and I had reviewed the raw footage of her stellar performances during her two jailhouse interviews with *48 Hours.* Even though the story she was now telling was different from the one she'd told on those previous occasions, she was quite good at coming across as the victim.

I started by revisiting everything the police had done, trying to identify avenues that could possibly have been explored had the investigation not been so duly focused on proving that Arias was the killer. I knew this was counterproductive, so I took a few hours out of the office, hoping that something

I hadn't yet thought of would crystallize. Upon my return, I found myself back in front of the bookcases once again.

Placing some of the binders I had already skimmed back onto the bookcase, I noticed a large manila envelope inside an accordion folder on the second shelf. Inside were more than three hundred pages of background material that had been provided to me by Arias' first defense team months earlier as part of the discovery process. Because these reports were intended as an argument for why Arias should be shown leniency if faced with the death penalty, I hadn't reviewed them in detail, but had merely browsed them. Typically, I don't review in-depth the items meant for the sentencing phase of the trial this early in the proceedings while I'm preparing for the guilt phase. But the vulnerability of the case as it currently stood compelled me to take a closer look at these documents.

The materials included Arias' work and educational histories, dozens of photographs, and interviews with family members, a friend, and two ex-boyfriends. All of the interviews had been conducted between October 23, 2008, and April 26, 2009, by an investigator working on Arias' behalf and were sent to me in summary form, so I couldn't read the actual text of the discussions. If the interviews had been recorded, I hadn't been provided with any of the audiotapes.

As this material had been assembled to illustrate why Arias didn't deserve the death penalty, I was aware that it was meant to present her in the best possible light, so I didn't expect to find much that would be helpful in discrediting her self-defense allegation. Probably because there was nowhere else to look, I decided to wade through the pages and started reading the contents whenever I could find time. Because I was carrying a caseload that included other prosecutions, I had to carve out reading time in between my court appearances, witness interviews, phone calls, and filing of responsive pleadings.

I am methodical when it comes to reading case materials,

and I have acquired habits that help me with this tedious process. I closed the door to my office to avoid the need to constantly look up every time someone walks by and to muffle the noises from the copy machine just outside my door. I turned off the ringer on my cell phone, so I could devote my full attention to the materials, and with a black rollerball pen in hand, I began to read.

I started my review by looking at Arias' employment history, which showed that she had worked mostly as a food server in various restaurants in Arizona as well as California. It struck me that she was probably doing a job she did not enjoy, as she had floated from restaurant to restaurant, only staying for several months at each. Her more recent employment records included documented disciplinary actions that, in at least one case, had resulted in her termination.

Mimi's Café in Mesa had fired her for "unpleasantness and services issues." As she acknowledged in one of her journals, "I got two complaints in 3 days. They said I wasn't smiling enough & that I didn't seem happy. That's probably the case." Employment records from P.F. Chang's China Bistro, also in Mesa, showed that her "lack of attentiveness towards her tables has lead [sic] to refills being missed." The owner at the Purple Plum in Yreka, one of the two places Arias had been employed just prior to Travis' death, told the defense investigator that "she [Arias] was not attentive and wouldn't take care of her customers—except for males." He also complained of having to "redirect her to wait on customers to do her job," as well as her refusal to work on Sundays.

While her inconsistent work history did not touch on the issue of her self-defense claim, it did offer a small window into Arias' life away from Travis. She approached her work unenthusiastically, not caring about the quality of her service, perhaps because she knew the next server job was just an application away.

I then turned my attention to reading about Arias' educational history. According to her academic transcripts, she had dropped out of Yreka High School after her junior year, and there was no record that she had ever returned to obtain her diploma or that she had earned a GED. Looking closely at her transcripts revealed that she had been achieving top grades and accolades from all of her teachers during her freshman and sophomore years, and was enrolled in honors English courses for both years. But her academic performance dropped dramatically in the eleventh grade, which she completed with mostly Fs and a few Ds.

During her junior year, Arias had moved in with her grandparents because of tension at home with her mother. In an interview with the defense investigator, Arias' maternal grandmother, Caroline Allen, recalled waking her granddaughter up in the mornings and believing that once she left the house, she was heading for school. Only later did she learn that Jodi was ditching classes to hang out with a young man named Bobby Juarez, who family members described as a high school boyfriend.

Like her employment record, Arias' educational history, while interesting background, really didn't touch on the self-defense claim in any way, so I turned my attention to the conversations that the investigator had summarized with other members of Arias' family, which included her parents, Bill and Sandy; her three siblings, Carl, Joey, and Angela; her half sister, Julie; her maternal grandfather, Carlton "Sonny" Allen; a cousin; and two aunts.

I was surprised to read that nearly everyone that the investigator spoke with echoed what Arias' parents had told Detective Flores in their initial interview with him— that Jodi could be hurtful and unkind, especially to her mother. She would regularly call the house and out of nowhere berate her mother for the strangest of reasons, before suddenly slamming down the phone. As the family members told it, one time Jodi called her mother to say she had just gotten a haircut; when Sandy said it probably looked nice, Jodi became upset and started screaming at her.

Her parents also said that on at least two occasions there were incidents that had turned physical. Bill Arias recalled one time when Jodi hit her mother for no apparent reason, and he smacked his daughter in response. Arias' half sister, Julie, recounted another incident when Jodi and Sandy were sitting side by side, Sandy lightly touched Jodi, and Jodi kicked her mother in response.

Arias' childhood friend Zeyna Corronzo also told the investigator of a trouble-filled relationship between Arias and her mother. She informed the investigator that she and Arias first met at Los Padres Elementary School in Salinas, California, and they remained close even after Arias moved to Santa Maria, and then to Yreka. While Zeyna expressed great fondness for her childhood pal, whom she described as "very bright," "hilarious," and "like a sister" to her, she admitted that when Arias got angry, she "really laid into" her mother, who tried to control and calm her, but Arias "wouldn't listen" and was grounded "a lot" because she was so "defiant." Even when she knew the consequences, Arias just didn't care, Zeyna said, telling the investigator that of Bill and Sandy's four children, Jodi was the most "unruly." "She would say to Sandy, 'I hate you, I wish you weren't my mother,'" Zeyna recounted, remembering one time when Arias kicked a hole in the wall because her mother was angry with her.

Reading through this, it was not lost on me that Zeyna was the only friend who had been interviewed by the defense investigator, leading me to suspect that Arias was a person who had difficulty bonding with and keeping friends, especially women. Thinking back, this point emphasized why the police's decision to send Siskiyou County Detective Rachel Blaney into the interview room with Arias had not yielded the desired results. Arias' troubled relationship with her mother and the glaring absence of any interviews with female friends other than Zeyna illustrated her inability to relate to women in the same effortless way she had of connecting with men.

Other family members' interviews further complicated the portrait of Arias' relationship with her family. Her brother Carl described his sister as someone who tended to live above her means and wondered if her extravagant spending habits, such as driving an expensive car when she had no money, coupled with her tendency to overreact and blow up at people for no reason, pointed to mental illness, such as bipolar disorder. He cited as an example her "out-of-the-blue" phone calls to her parents' house, during which she would yell and shriek and then hang up. More interesting was the disturbance Carl described between Arias and her father after her recent move back to Yreka. Carl explained that at his sister's request, their father had rented a storage shed for her, but said she grew belligerent when she saw the unit, yelling and calling her father "stupid" for choosing the wrong size.

Arias' cousin Aimee Lantz said Jodi would be "snide" at family functions and speak sarcastically to others. Aimee's assessment was that Jodi could be a total "bitch." This sentiment was echoed by Jodi's maternal grandparents, the Allens, who said their granddaughter would correct the way people spoke. They mentioned that if you talked to her "you had to use perfect grammar and speech."

These descriptions were in line with what her parents had told Detective Flores, and it struck me just how out of step this collective illustration was with the idyllic childhood Arias had described to Flores. The woman detailed in these records was a huge departure from the demure, soft-spoken one who had presented herself during her conversations after her arrest in Yreka and her jailhouse interviews with the national media. As I read on, a different composite began to emerge, one of a churlish grammar tyrant who was mean to her mother and seemed to derive pleasure from belittling and correcting others.

Her family perceived Jodi as someone who would react in

unpredictable ways, even when people were being kind to her. This theme kept arising in these statements—usually as it pertained to her mother. While having a nasty temper did not prove her a murderer, it did demonstrate a pattern of behavior when it came to how she interacted with people about whom she purported to care. She could clearly be cruel, volatile, and impulsive when the mood struck her.

Perhaps the most striking thing about these interviews was how replete they were with negative tales of her background. After all, this was a composite that was prepared by her defense team and meant to portray her in a positive light. Instead the picture of her that emerged was anything but positive. Even when speaking to someone who was sympathetic to Jodi's cause and trying to help her defense, it seemed her family could not help but show the true nature of Jodi Arias.

As I let all of this sink in, I spent a few moments preparing some notes about what I had just read before putting the folder back on the shelf and heading out for my next appointment. It was several days before I was able to get back to the materials provided by defense counsel, but I decided to shift my attention. This time, I concentrated on some of the peculiar behaviors Arias' family described around the time of Travis' memorial service in Mesa. Detective Flores had told me that Arias had traveled to Arizona to attend the memorial service, which took place a couple of weeks after police had discovered Travis' body, and that Travis' family and friends had found her presence there both strange and disturbing. What I hadn't heard was how she had behaved after the service, which was part of the interview summary from Arias' half sister, Julie.

In particular, what caught my attention was Julie's recollection of a phone call she received from Jodi on her way home from the airport following her return from Mesa. Jodi wanted to stop by and asked what time dinner would be served. She told Julie she would be at the house in a few minutes, but more than an hour passed before she finally arrived.

Julie was "shocked" and "upset" when Jodi told her that she had been out shopping for bikinis and lost track of time, finding her indifference to Travis' death especially disturbing in light of the fact that she had just attended his memorial service. Even more strange was Jodi's admission that she had exchanged phone numbers with a man named Nick, who was seated next to her on the flight from Phoenix to Sacramento. Julie said she was bewildered that her sister would so freely give her contact information to a stranger and mortified when she heard them talking on the phone later that evening. Even more puzzling was that Julie never saw Jodi cry after Travis' memorial service. Instead, she appeared "agitated" and "nervous" and was "always" on the phone.

That Arias chose to go bikini shopping on her way home from Travis' memorial service raised obvious questions about what she was thinking and how she was reacting. If she had killed Travis in self-defense, it appeared she had not been upset or fazed by it, and had moved on in more ways than one.

Arias' younger sister, Angela, also provided some insight. Because she was a minor, she spoke to the defense investigator in the company of her parents. Angela proudly described herself as "just like Jodi," explaining that they both liked to sing, they were both very musical, and they both preferred to be alone rather than with people. But there was one important detail that caught my attention, as it related to Ryan Burns, the man Arias claimed to have been meeting in Utah on the day of Travis' death. Though Arias had only met Ryan once, Angela recalled Jodi telling her how much she liked him, that he was her "soul mate," and that she was convinced the two would get married.

Arias' strange behavior following Travis' death didn't end there. Even after her arrest in Yreka, Julie found her half sister's demeanor peculiar for someone who was facing murder charges. She said Jodi was always "upbeat" and "happy," beginning all of their jailhouse calls with a cheerful "What's up?" She next described a postcard she received from her sister in April 2009, thanking her for "saying a few kind words to *The Californian,*" referring to an article that had appeared in a Salinas newspaper. "Everyone else in the family stands by and lets me get slaughtered by ignorant, hateful judgmental people," Arias wrote.

Bill and Sandy Arias also referenced their daughter's strange contentment when they had first visited with her at the Siskiyou County Jail. "She was happy as hell," Bill recalled. Bill recounted a phone call he received from his daughter when she was told that a psychiatrist would be evaluating her in jail as part of her defense claim. He related Jodi's excitement at learning that she would undergo an IQ test as part of the examination and was eager to see how close her IQ was to Albert Einstein's. "She thinks she is close to his IQ," Bill told the investigator.

Her father's comment reminded me of Arias' bravado in the days after Travis' body had been discovered, when she thought she could outwit the police by offering to help with the investigation. She'd clearly had a lot of faith in her intelligence, but comparing herself to Einstein showed just how much faith she really had.

Looking back over the statements of her family, it seemed clear that Arias reveled in her newfound celebrity status and seemed to enjoy being the center of attention, even if it was behind bars. She acted as if the television interviews and newspaper stories were a just reward for a major accomplishment, even if that accomplishment was killing Travis.

Four hours had passed since I'd started reading and I had missed lunch, so I was beginning to feel hungry. I have never fallen into the habit of eating or drinking at my desk when reviewing paperwork, not even a sip of water, as I have seen too many attorneys spill liquids or leave food smudges on shirts, ties, and important documents that then can't be wiped clean.

I always eat away from my desk, whether it be at our office lunchroom, downstairs at the tables outside the Change of Venue café on the second floor or at one of the restaurants near my office in downtown Phoenix, depending on how pressed I am for time.

It was already past 4:00 P.M. when I decided to give myself a break. My body was beginning to cramp from sitting hunched over the desk, so I took the stairs down two levels to get the blood circulating. I was still feeling frustrated when I reached the vending machines on the second floor and bought a snack. While the information I had read thus far had been enlightening in terms of presenting another side of Arias, none of it would be useful in disproving her allegation of self-defense, and I was nearly halfway through with my read.

When I got back to my desk, I moved on to the conversations the investigator had summarized with two of Arias' former boyfriends. Based on what I had already read, it was clear that her family members knew very little about her life in the eleven years since she had left home, so I looked to her boyfriends to provide the best window into what happened to her during that time.

In reading these interview summaries, I learned that Arias had been involved in three significant relationships before Travis. The first was with Bobby Juarez, the young man she had met in the eleventh grade. Her parents told the investigator that Jodi stayed with her grandparents until her eighteenth birthday, when she moved in with Bobby and his parents in a neighboring town. There was no interview with Bobby included in the materials provided by Arias' defense counsel, and by all accounts, Arias appeared to have lost touch with Bobby after that.

Also according to the summaries, Arias' brother Carl told the investigator that his sister's next relationship was with Matthew McCartney, an individual he described as "strange," with "long black hair" who had an interest in the martial arts. He remembered their relationship as volatile, with the two constantly fighting, breaking up, and getting back together.

The investigator followed up by speaking with McCartney, who was living in Big Sur, California, and working as a waiter at the Ventana Inn & Spa, an upscale resort where Arias had once been employed. He told the investigator that Arias had been hired to work at the Ventana Inn before he followed and was also hired. He said they lived together in a tent on the resort's campground for a short period of time.

McCartney said he met Arias through her ex-boyfriend, Bobby Juarez. He and Bobby were roommates, sharing an apartment in Medford, California, when she showed up there one afternoon. He saw her as "perfect," "perfect body, very creative, very intelligent." Apparently the fact that McCartney and Juarez were roommates did not bother Arias, as she and McCartney subsequently went on to date for about two and a half years. The two remained friends after the breakup. He described her as having "two different sides," "a serious side" and an "innocent, fun, and sweet side," acknowledging that she could be emotionally volatile and had high expectations of others.

McCartney told the investigator that Arias had a lack of grammatical tolerance. He explained that she couldn't accept the way he communicated and directed him to be "impeccable" with his words, because she needed "exact communication" to understand him. He corroborated this to me later when he told me during an interview in Seaside, California, in July 2011, that Arias was "a grammar Nazi" who would constantly correct him.

McCartney admitted that he would always love Arias, but said they could never be more than friends. He explained that toward the end of their relationship, he felt they needed to spend time apart, so he moved to Crater Lake in Oregon. He

broke off sexual relations before he moved out. Although he
tried to end the relationship, Arias was very resistant to breaking up, even going behind his back and confronting Bianca, a
woman with whom he already had a nascent relationship.

McCartney knew Arias' next boyfriend, Darryl Brewer, because Brewer was his supervisor at the Ventana Inn. Brewer
was also the food and beverage manager who interviewed and
hired Arias in 2002. He was twenty years older than Arias
and had a young son from a first marriage that had ended in
divorce.

Even though it was getting late, I pulled out the interview
summaries with Darryl Brewer. It was already after 8:00 P.M.,
and from what I could tell, I was the only person still in the
office, as not even the janitorial staff are permitted to be in the
building after hours. Staying late was something I had grown
accustomed to over the years. The stillness of the rooms and
hallways is almost meditative and provides a tranquil backdrop
that enables me to concentrate more fully. But I had an early
court hearing the next day, and I was pretty much at the end of
my energy stores, so I promised myself I would skim only the
first few pages of the interview summaries with Darryl Brewer
before calling it a night.

The defense investigator documented three separate conversations with Brewer. During their initial phone call, which had
been brief, Brewer indicated that he was still in touch with
Arias, and revealed that he had advised her not to speak to
anyone, particularly the media. But he said she does "what she
likes," and she was encouraging friends and family to sit down
with producers from *48 Hours* on her behalf.

Brewer's second conversation with the investigator provided
a little more insight into his relationship with Arias. He admitted being impressed with her during her job interview in 2002.
"She carried herself well, had great presence, dressed well, was
very well spoken and respectful," he recalled.

Brewer recounted that he and Arias began dating about a year after her arrival at Ventana Inn, when he was no longer her manager. But after dating for some time, he decided that he couldn't get too involved with her. He had previously been married and didn't want to be exclusive because of a son from a previous marriage. Although they decided to pull back for a while, Arias kept showing up and calling him. He described her as "needy at times and whiny" and sometimes "she was clingy." He eventually capitulated, and the couple moved in together. They left their jobs in Northern California and bought a three-bedroom, twenty-five-hundred-square-foot house in Palm Desert complete with in-ground pool, for $360,000. The mortgage was $2,800 per month, which they agreed to split evenly. Arias began working two jobs and according to Brewer faithfully paid her half until September 2006, when Brewer said she suddenly "just stopped working." "I saw her change in front of my eyes," he recalled.

Brewer complained that Arias started to spend all her time going to Pre-Paid Legal Services motivational seminars and meetings, leaving her no time for her restaurant jobs at California Pizza Kitchen and another restaurant, Cuistot. Soon, she had maxed out all her credit cards on car payments and cash advances.

That September, according to Brewer, she went to a Pre-Paid Legal convention in Las Vegas, where she met Travis. "She drove in the middle of the night to get there, just like she was in high school," he said, recalling that upon her return, she cut off all sexual contact with him, claiming she was now going to save herself for marriage.

Arias evidently still felt comfortable enough to call him and ask for a favor less than two years later, in May 2008. Her favor was related to a trip that she planned to take to Mesa in June.

I sat up in my chair.

This statement was at odds with what she had told everybody else—including Detective Flores. As tired as I was, a surge of excitement coursed through me.

According to the summary, during that phone call in May, Arias told Brewer that she was driving to Mesa, Arizona, and she wanted to borrow two gas cans for the trip. Arias got "testy" with him when he asked why she needed them. Her irritation with his inquisitiveness did not stop Arias from calling him a second time during the last week of May, when she repeated her request to borrow the gas cans for her trip to Mesa.

As I read this description, I wasn't thinking about her asking for a favor or the gas cans; I was too focused on the fact that as early as May she knew she intended to go to Mesa in June. I remembered that in her second interview with Detective Flores, Arias had mentioned that before she and Travis had sex for a second time on June 4, they had attempted to look at photographs from their recent travels that were on a CD that *she* had brought with her to show him. She had the CD with her in the car, which meant she'd planned this trip. All at once, I realized her trip wasn't a spur-of-the-moment jaunt. The whole thing had been preplanned. The fact that she'd brought the CD to show Travis *and* told Darryl Brewer about the trip spoke to premeditation and called into question her self-defense claim.

I wanted to continue reading, but my excitement, coupled with the exhaustion I was feeling from my long day of reading, called for me to make my way home. For the first time in months, I would be able to drive home leisurely and enjoy the sounds of traffic as I merged from one freeway to another.

But as I walked to my car, in the back of my mind, I kept thinking about the gas cans. At first, I hadn't thought much of them because her request to borrow them seemed innocuous, and I wasn't sure what to do with the information. The more I focused on them, though, the more significance they seemed to hold. As I pulled my car out of the parking garage, I was already trying to figure out how I was going to fit in more reading time when I returned to the office the following day. I had a court appearance in the morning and knew that I wouldn't get back to my desk until around eleven. I was anxious to look into why Arias had asked to borrow two gas cans for her trip to Mesa. After all, there were countless gas stations dotting the route from California to Arizona, so I could think of no reason why Arias would even need gas cans in the first place.

CHAPTER 10

T he following morning, I swiped my security badge past the card reader and the barrier arm rose slowly as it granted me access into the parking garage at around 7:15. It's not that I was keeping track of the time, but I reflexively looked at my watch because I was surprised to find a space not too far from the walkway leading into our office building. I was not accustomed to seeing the garage half empty, because I normally arrive about an hour later, when the only place to park is usually on the roof, where every spot is exposed to sun.

Though I was looking forward to continuing the review to see how far the Darryl Brewer summary might go, I wasn't starting the day early because of that. It was more the fitful night of sleep I'd just had, brought on by my hesitation about what to do. I wanted to tell Detective Flores that Darryl Brewer had said in an interview that Jodi Arias had planned on traveling to Mesa, but I was concerned that if I shared my findings with him, he might prepare a police report detailing my impressions that would then have to be disclosed to Arias through her counsel. Because of everything I'd seen of Arias' skill at bending the truth to fit her needs, I feared that once she saw my line of inquiry she would have time to formulate an explanation. Even if her explanation wasn't totally plausible, it wouldn't matter; all she needed was an opening and she would be able to give a reason that would diminish the value of my discovery.

Withholding this information from Detective Flores would

not be easy. Since the beginning of the case, he and I had been
in almost constant contact, sharing ideas and comparing notes,
and in that time, I'd come to rely on his judgments of Arias and
the case. It would be a struggle to keep this information to
myself, and as I sat down to read the rest of Brewer's summary,
I felt uncomfortable about not sharing it.

I returned directly to page 357 of the defense materials,
where Brewer described how Arias had initially called him
sometime in May to let him know that she was intending to
drive to Mesa and wanted to borrow the two gas cans for her
trip. He said she got "testy" when he asked why she needed
them, and she didn't call him later in the week as she promised
she would, but her testiness did not stop her from phoning him
a second time, in the last week of May, to again inquire about
borrowing the cans. During that call, she told Brewer she
needed the gas cans because she was going on "a long trip,"
and she didn't want to run out of gas.

Brewer recalled that a few days later, on June 3, Arias
showed up at his house in Pacific Grove, California, near Monterey, at around 7:30 P.M. After joining him and his young
son for breakfast, she asked to use his computer to check her
e-mail. I wondered if she was expecting to receive a communication from someone, perhaps Travis.

After a very short visit, she was on her way by 9 P.M., with
two of Brewer's five-gallon plastic gas cans in tow.

After about forty-five minutes, I realized it was time for me
to go to court on a different case, even though I wanted to
continue reading to see where the story went. Grabbing my
monthly planner and the case file, an orange folder containing
the relevant documents and minute entries, I left my office.
As I sat waiting for my matter to be heard by the court, I paid
no attention to the other cases that were also on the morning
calendar, because my mind was back at my desk with the materials I had just been reading.

I knew police had not found the gas cans during the execution of the search warrants in Yreka, so I wondered where they were. I also found myself wondering about Arias' motivation for bringing the cans on the trip. Although the cans would have allowed her to fill up at stations in Nevada and Utah where gas was cheaper, I was pretty certain that saving money was not the true motive for taking them on the trip. Arias would still have to pay the higher price in California and gas cans are heavy and cumbersome and can leak if not properly secured. At most she would get a few cents a gallon in savings, which hardly seemed like a good reason justifying the inconvenience and danger of using them.

"State of Arizona vs. . . ." The judge's voice announcing my case jolted me out of my ruminations and brought me back to the matter at hand. After a discussion of procedural matters with the judge, which only took a couple of minutes, I immediately left the courtroom and walked back to my office.

Although I returned expecting to get right back to my reading, other matters and repeated phone calls kept pulling me away, and it was already noon before I was finally able to return to the story about the gas cans. The summary of Brewer's interview continued on for another three pages, which I read slowly and carefully, but after finding nothing else related to the topic of the gas cans, I decided to take lunch.

As I prepared to leave the office, a black binder labeled *Police* caught my attention, and I remembered that when detectives had executed the search warrant on Arias' grandparents' house in Yreka following her arrest, they had found an Airwalk brand shoebox containing some personal papers of hers, including receipts. I wondered if there were any receipts that showed the places she might have stopped for gas while on her trip to Mesa and Utah, so I called Detective Flores and asked if he could provide me with copies of everything they had found in the box.

When he asked me what I was looking into, it struck me that normally I would have readily shared what I was thinking, but I wanted to protect my thoughts about what I had just read in Brewer's summary. So, I trotted out an excuse, telling him I just wanted to see how long it had taken Arias to drive from Northern to Southern California, which was actually part of the reason I wanted to see the receipts.

Flores provided me copies of the contents of the box within the week. Among other papers there were about fifteen receipts in the box. Arias had a single Washington Mutual card that could be used either as a debit card tied to her bank account or as a MasterCard credit card. I spread out a map of California on my desk, so that I could visualize Arias' movements based on the story the receipts told. I recorded each receipt on a legal pad in chronological order. To help keep track of Arias' various stops, I added a running list of each destination mentioned in the receipts, starting with Redding, where she rented the car.

The first receipt was for Budget Rent A Car System, Inc., indicating that Arias had rented a white Ford Focus in Redding, California, on Monday, June 2, 2008, at 8:04 P.M. The detailed receipt included the rental contract, which called for the car to be returned after four days on Friday, June 6, by 8:15 A.M. The same receipt indicated that she returned the car a day late, on Saturday, June 7, at 1:08 P.M., after having driven it 2,834 miles.

A second receipt, stamped June 2, 2008, at 8:41 P.M., indicated that Arias purchased gas at a Valero gas station in Santa Nella, a small hamlet of less than two thousand people. She used her bank card to pay $20.14 for 4.751 gallons of gasoline. On the map, I noted that Santa Nella was approximately 272 miles south of Redding, and circled both locations on the map.

According to the next receipt, dated the following morning, June 3, Arias visited a branch of Washington Mutual Bank in Monterey, California, just after 10:00 P.M., where she made three transactions. Writing "Monterey" down on my legal pad and circling it on my map, I could see it was right down the road from Pacific Grove, where Darryl Brewer lived. Apparently, the bank was her first destination after she left his house.

From there Arias headed southeast to Salinas, the city where she had lived for part of her childhood. Salinas is around twenty miles, approximately a thirty-minute drive, from Monterey. While in Salinas, she stopped at a Walmart that Tuesday afternoon around 3 P.M. and purchased five items, as shown by the receipt. I noticed that she paid cash for her items rather than using the bank card, as she had for other purchases she'd made along the trip, and spent a total of $43.90.

The receipt showed that she bought two packages of Noxzema face pads and two tubes of Neutrogena SPF-85 sunscreen. The last item on her receipt was labeled "5G KERO CARB" for $12.96, and by that description it was impossible for me to tell what it was, so I called a Phoenix-area Walmart store to find out. The manager I spoke to told me that the last item on that receipt was a five-gallon gas container. He made it clear that, although "KERO" seemed to be an abbreviation for kerosene, manufacturers of those containers use the label "kero" on containers designed to carry gasoline. He told me that the "CARB" notation was added to give notice that the container met the EPA carbon-emission standards.

I now had confirmation that Arias had bought another gas can to add to the two she'd borrowed earlier in the day, but I remained unsure of what it meant. The cash transaction suggested that there was an ulterior motive for the gas cans, one that was surreptitious in nature. It was the first time I had evidence that I could use at trial to show that Arias had engaged in some sort of activity that she wanted to go undetected.

I wanted to follow the path she'd left behind as far as it would take me, so I scrutinized the remaining receipts to see if there was any other anomaly about her trip. Arias' next destination was Pasadena, a city about three hundred miles south of Salinas. According to the store receipt, her initial stop in that city was at a CVS pharmacy, where she checked out at 8:31 P.M. after buying over-the-counter medications and water—all with her bank card, no cash. Approximately ten minutes later, she bought an egg salad sandwich at Starbucks, also using her bank card.

But with the next string of receipts, the paper trail created even more questions. After Starbucks, Arias drove to a nearby ARCO gas station, where she made three separate gasoline purchases from the same station. With the first purchase, Arias used her bank card, choosing not to go inside, but rather to use the Payment Island Cashier (PIC), the machine where the gas pumps are located that will take either cash or debit and credit cards. Arias dispensed 8.301 gallons and paid a total of $35.06, completing that transaction at 8:42 P.M. Interestingly, there was a transaction fee of 45 cents assessed because she chose to use her bank card. If the point of using gas cans was to save money, then this fee would have largely negated any savings that she might have hoped to gain.

From there, things only got more strange. The next receipt was for a purchase at the same ARCO and same pump, time-stamped approximately four minutes after the first. The receipt showed that she initiated this transaction at 8:46 P.M., but unlike the first transaction, she walked inside and paid the clerk forty dollars in cash for 9.594 gallons of gas, instead of continuing to use the PIC, where she had just used her bank card. This was enough to fill two gas cans.

After the Walmart purchase, this was now the second time that she had paid for something involving the gas cans with cash. Seeing the pattern, I began to suspect that anything associated with the gas cans was going to be a cash sale. I couldn't imagine what her motivation was, but I hoped a review of the rest of the receipts would make it clear to me.

I looked through the rest of the receipts and found a third purchase at that same ARCO only seven minutes later, at 8:53 P.M. It involved the same clerk as the previous purchase and was also a prepaid transaction for $20.00 in cash, which bought the equivalent of approximately five gallons of gas. She ended up only buying 2.774 gallons, costing $11.56, so I immediately surmised that this final gas can probably still had some gas in it, which could have come from either an earlier stop or from there being some gas in the can when Darryl Brewer gave it to her.

In all three instances, she used the same pump, Number 2, which left me visualizing Arias going back and forth between the pump and the minimart, like wipers on a car windshield. The difference was that I knew the purpose of the windshield wipers was to wipe away the rain. With Arias, shuttling between the pump and the clerk made no sense and seemed random. Although her behavior seemed odd, without more information it didn't prove anything. At this point all I had were some receipts from California and a map with circles around the cities—I had no idea if Arias had taken the gas cans any farther than Pasadena.

While I didn't find any more receipts from gasoline purchases in California, or any at all from Arizona, there were two gas receipts from transactions made in the early morning hours of June 6, at a Tesoro gas station in Salt Lake City, Utah. These purchases took place three days after Arias' June 3 stop at the ARCO station in Pasadena. Since I knew that she traveled to Arizona in that time, this left me with two possibilities for the lack of receipts between June 3 and June 6; either she had purchased gasoline elsewhere and had thrown the receipts away, or she had used the gasoline in the cans from the ARCO in Pasadena rather than stop at another gas station along the way.

Her gas purchases at the Tesoro gas station in Salt Lake City on Friday, June 6, started at 3:57 P.M. The first receipt was for a pay-at-the-pump transaction of $41.18 for 10.672 gallons. Arias then walked inside and paid at the counter for another purchase of gasoline seven minutes later, at 4:05 P.M., as shown by the second receipt. This time she pumped 9.583

gallons for $36.98. In both instances she used her bank card to pay.

I was convinced that she still had the third gas can with her at this point in her trip, but the amount of gas purchased in Salt Lake was consistent with having only filled two gas cans. I reviewed all the receipts one more time to make sure I had not missed one, but there was nothing there indicating any more purchases in Salt Lake City. By all appearances it looked like she hadn't used the third gas can during that stop, and I had no way of knowing whether it was in her possession for the remainder of the trip. The rest of the shoebox receipts were miscellaneous purchases, including for food, and added nothing to further advance the inquiry.

As I reviewed the copies of last few documents found in the box, I came across something I hadn't seen before, an undated letter that had been written by Travis Alexander to Arias.

"Dear Jodi, a note a note, a note! blah, blah, blah," it began.

Maybe it's ego and pride then that constrain me from being so personal. I am very a [sic] matter of fact with you. Towing the line sort of speak [sic]. I know at times it makes me seem without soul. Who knows? I think sometimes I am. Let me just be short and uncharmingly sincere. You are a person of great worth and potential. There's (sic) difference to be made in the world by you. All of us (most of us our entire lives) walk the earth shrouded in heavy locks and chains of of [sic] self doubt, limitation and despair. Holding tightly and unconsciously in our hand the key to the locks and chains. It only drops from our hand with death or when it is has finally been used to free us from those binding self limitations. . . . I hope you will take this interregnum from who you have been and who you really are and never look back. To be ruled by your best self, to yield your best results. Remember everything is perfect and there is a road in front of you that leads to an exceptional life. I love you! Sincerely yours, Travis

The letter itself didn't add much to the investigation, but its inclusion with the receipts in the shoebox sitting on the bed appeared to give it significance. It was as if Arias had prepared the items in the shoebox for police to find in the event she were arrested. The letter would show that she had no motive to kill Travis because its content and tone seemed to indicate they had a wonderful relationship. The receipts supported her story that she had not been in Arizona at the time of the murder. As she had told her mother when Sandy had asked her if she had gone to Arizona, she was "nowhere near Arizona" and she had the "gas receipts and everything else to prove it."

I spent the next several weeks trying to figure out other ways to see whether or not the third gas can Arias bought in Salinas had actually made the trip with her. It wasn't until a couple of weeks later when I opened the file cabinet to put away a copy of a motion from Arias' defense attorneys that I noticed a purple folder. It caught my attention because I don't normally use purple folders for my cases. The tab on the folder was labeled *Washington Mutual,* and the handwriting belonged to my legal assistant. The folder appeared to have been misfiled, so I figured I would put it away in its rightful place. When I looked inside to see where it belonged, I noticed they were Washington Mutual bank statements for Jodi Arias.

I browsed through the statements until I came to one, which covered the period from 6/01/08 to 6/30/08, the time of Arias' trip. But it didn't show any transactions for June 6, the day Arias bought gas at the Tesoro station in Salt Lake City. I was momentarily disappointed until I noticed three transactions identified as *MC-Tesoro 62097 Q39 Salt Lake Cty UT* that had been logged in on June 9.

Because of the rental car records, I knew that Arias was already back in Yreka by then, so I wondered if the date on the statement was incorrect. I called Washington Mutual, now part of JPMorgan Chase, to get more information about those entries, and a bank employee informed me that because they did not typically record transactions over weekends, they were left as pending until the following Monday. This meant that transactions that may have occurred on Friday, June 6, would not have been recorded until the following Monday, June 9, as indicated by the bank records. I then called Tesoro Corporation, and a representative named Chelsey Young confirmed that all three transactions had been on June 6.

Young told me that the first charge was for $41.18, for 10.672 gallons of gas; the second charge was in the amount of $19.65, for 5.091 gallons of gas; and the last transaction was for $36.98, representing 9.583 gallons. I recognized the first and third transactions from the Tesoro receipts, but the second transaction for $19.65 was new to me. An expletive escaped from my lips as I took in that number—$19.65, the cost of filling the third gas can in Salt Lake City. I now knew she had carried the third gas can with her for the entire trip and realized that Arias had used the cans to avoid having to put gas in the car in Arizona, so that she could drive through the state undetected and no one would know that she had killed Travis.

In order to back up this theory, I decided to mathematically compute the gas usage to see if the extra fifteen gallons would have allowed her to make it through Arizona without stopping for gas. My research indicated that the 2008 Ford Focus had a fuel tank capacity of 13.5 gallons, with a U.S. Department of Energy fuel economy rating of twenty-four city miles per gallon and thirty-five miles per gallon on the highway. This meant that the car had a minimum range of 324 miles and a maximum range of 472.5 miles to its tank, depending on whether it was city or highway driving. Arias' three gas cans represented an extra fifteen gallons, which increased the car's minimum driving range an additional 360 miles to 684 miles.

Between the gas tank in the car and the cans, Arias had at least 25.868 gallons of gasoline when she left the ARCO station in Pasadena, meaning she could drive between a minimum of 620.83 city miles and a maximum of 905.38 highway miles without stopping to buy fuel. The approximate distance between Pasadena and Mesa is four hundred miles of mostly highway driving. Interstate 10 eastbound through the Sonoran desert is mostly flat, with no city driving. There is a checkpoint just east of the California/Arizona border, but it is only for trucks and passenger vehicles are not required to stop there.

The distance from Mesa to Las Vegas, Nevada, is approximately three hundred miles, and Highway 93 North is the shortest route. It includes minimal city driving through Wickenburg and Kingman, both cities in Arizona. The total distance from Pasadena to Las Vegas via this circuitous route through Mesa is roughly seven hundred miles, well within the fuel range of Arias' Ford Focus and the extra fifteen gallons in her three gas cans. There was no doubt in my mind that Arias had gone through a similar computation, and that's why she made the stop in Salinas to buy the third five-gallon gas can.

The cans were not in the rental car when she returned it a day late, on June 7, 2008. The agent who originally rented the car to her conducted a walk-around inspection, documenting that the car had been driven 2,834 miles, which surprised him because he remembered Arias telling him that she was only renting the car to drive around town.

The extra gallons had assured that she would drive undetected through the Arizona darkness.

Arias appeared to have thought of everything, but one thing that she could not have foreseen was that her defense counsel would turn over these interview summaries. The detail that Darryl Brewer had lent her two gas cans turned out to be the key in unraveling her plan to travel to Arizona undetected, and it exposed that she planned the murder of Travis Alexander.

Premeditation refers to a person's thoughts before they act on them. It is characterized by planning prior to carrying out an objective, such as murder.

Buying the third gas can was not the only step Arias would take to achieve her ultimate goal of ending Travis' life. But as helpful as those containers were in carrying out her plan, they would be her undoing when she took the witness stand at trial.

———————————

CHAPTER 11

Although my discovery of the three gas cans went a long way toward disproving Jodi Arias' self-defense claim, I still faced an uphill battle with Travis' offensive instant messages and the ten highly inflammatory "Bob White" letters.

The risk with each of these was palpable. Circumstances like these can be challenging for the prosecution in a jury trial, because jurors can be forgiving if they view the accused as the one who has been victimized. Juries have been known to show compassion, even to someone accused of first-degree murder, when presented with evidence that paints the deceased victim in a bad light. Sometimes this compassion can motivate them to return a guilty verdict on a lesser charge such as manslaughter or, in an extreme case, even an acquittal.

The materials that showed an unflattering side of Travis' character hung like a dense fog, making it difficult to discern Arias' conduct through the haze. But instead of rushing forward and blindly defending Travis' reputation by saying "he wasn't like that" or arguing "this behavior wasn't in line with who he was," I decided to focus my attention on the materials themselves, rather than get drawn into the specific allegations they contained.

I started with the Bob White letters. When I sat down to read them again, my task was made more difficult because they were second-generation copies, and the writing was faint in many places. Experience had taught me that any item appearing under such dubious provenance needed to be viewed with suspicion. I wanted to give these letters a closer read on the off chance that I might identify any irregularities.

It didn't take long to see that there were numerous problems with the letters. For one thing, the misdeeds detailed in them seemed to be described too specifically, and the prose seemed unusually stilted. What also caught my eye was that none of the letters, which had been written on unlined 8½-by-11-inch paper, had creases, which surely would have been present had they been folded and put in an envelope for mailing.

Thinking back to the letter from Travis to Arias that had been found by police in the Airwalk shoebox, I noticed that these ten letters were all dated in the upper right-hand corner, whereas the one from the Airwalk shoebox was undated. I also observed that the language and word choices in these letters did not seem consistent with the language of that Airwalk shoebox letter—or, for that matter, with the entries I had read in Travis' journal.

I decided to put the letters in chronological order by date to see if anything else of note stood out for me. As I examined the dates and the content of the letters, I immediately realized there was a major error in the date of the most damaging one. This mistake added to my suspicion that all ten of the letters were forgeries.

Comforted by that discovery, along with all the other inconsistencies I'd found, I decided to follow up with a more scientific approach and see if the Bob White letters could be discredited by handwriting analysis. I set out to locate anything original that Travis had written and signed, so that a handwriting analyst at the Arizona Department of Public Safety, which is contracted to handle all handwriting analyses for the Mesa Police Department, could make a comparison to the Bob White letters. I began my search by calling Travis' family and friends to see if anybody had kept any of the letters he may have sent to them.

After a bit of calling around, I soon learned that one of

Travis' old girlfriends, Deanna Reid, had saved all the letters Travis had written to her while she was on an LDS church mission to Costa Rica from June 2001 to November 2001. At the time, Deanna was twenty and Travis was twenty-one, and they had broken up by letter in the summer of 2001. They had been apart for a while, and Travis was thinking of dating someone else. After Deanna returned from her mission about six months later, they rekindled their relationship and dated exclusively until 2005, when Deanna expressed a desire to get married and Travis told her he wasn't ready. The breakup was amicable, and the two remained close friends.

I'd never spoken to Deanna myself, but I knew from police reports that she had been close to Travis. Of all his friends, she was the one who ended up caring for his pug, Napoleon, after his death. The police had already met with her and determined she had no useful information about the killing.

When I called Deanna to schedule a time to meet and collect the letters, she had other news to share. Some weeks earlier, Arias' two attorneys and their investigator had shown up unannounced at her house in Riverside, California. According to Deanna, they failed to identify themselves as Arias' counsel and were vague about their motivation, telling her only that they wanted to speak with her because they were somehow "involved" in the Jodi Arias case. They wanted to ask questions about Travis.

Deanna recounted that the three of them assured her that their conversations would not be on the record. She also remembered that the female defense attorney was being very "chummy," seeming to imply that their discussion would be just between "us girls."

Deanna explained that during the visit, defense counsel had allowed her to read one of the Bob White letters, and Deanna recalled initially becoming upset at the reproachful things it said about her. But, as Deanna kept reading, she noticed word choices and phrasing that Travis would never use. Although the handwriting resembled Travis', she believed the letter to be a forgery.

It appeared that this surprise visit did little to assist Arias' defense team. Even after reading the unflattering things Travis had supposedly written about her, Deanna had nothing disparaging to say about him. That the defense team had presented themselves to Deanna in this ambush-type fashion told me they didn't have anyone to corroborate the allegations in the Bob White letters.

As I listened to Deanna's story over the phone, it became clear just how important the genuine letters in Deanna's possession were. With seemingly no one on Arias' side to verify the truth of the White letters, a handwriting comparison showing they were forgeries could be enough to have them excluded as evidence. Deanna's letters were so crucial that I decided to make the five-hour trip to Riverside that very day to pick them up, because I didn't want to chance their getting lost in the mail. Deanna agreed to see me that afternoon, so I began the drive to Southern California within minutes of hanging up the phone.

Deanna came out to greet me before I could knock on the front door of the house she shared with her parents. I had not met her before, so I had no idea what she looked like and I didn't know what to expect. She was dressed casually in jeans and a blouse, her straight black hair falling past her shoulders, and she immediately put me at ease with a welcoming smile. Deanna seemed to be the opposite of Arias—warm, genuine, and sincere.

After inviting me in, she directed me to the breakfast nook off the kitchen, where we sat down at a table. Travis' dog Napoleon had been outside when I arrived, and as soon as he saw me through the sliding glass door, he started to bark, so Deanna let him in to meet me. His tail was wagging as he sniffed at my hands, snorting. He looked old but appeared to be well taken care of and in good spirits. I found myself thinking back to that first walk-through at Travis' home, when it was still a crime scene, and how Flores and I wondered whether the dog had been cared for during the days that Travis had been upstairs lying dead on the shower floor. Napoleon had been in the house during Travis' murder, a four-legged witness to the identity of the killer.

Deanna had twenty-one handwritten letters on the table ready for me to take back to Arizona. All but one was still in its original envelope. I chose not to read them in front of her, as I understood they were private in nature. When I later reviewed them, I saw that they were the kind of letters a boyfriend would write to a girlfriend with whom he is in love. Deanna agreed to let me keep the original letters for our investigation but requested that I mail her back copies, as the sentiments they contained were very meaningful to her.

As soon I arrived back in Phoenix, I turned the letters Deanna had given me over to the Arizona Department of Public Safety for a handwriting analysis by Alan Kreitl, an experienced document examiner.

Not long after, I spoke with another of Travis' friends, a young woman named Sky Hughes, who told me she had also been contacted by defense counsel Laurence Nurmi in regard to one of the Bob White letters. Sky and her husband, Chris, were among Travis' closest friends. The Hugheses were members of the Church of Latter-Day Saints, and Chris was Travis' colleague and mentor at PPL. I spoke with Sky over the telephone to learn the circumstances under which she had been contacted.

After introducing myself as the prosecutor in the Arias case, I asked if she would be willing to speak to me about her interactions with defense counsel, and she was happy to cooperate. She told me that Nurmi had contacted her in early June 2010 to alert her to the existence of a letter that he claimed contained offensive information about Travis. Nurmi also informed her that the letter had been "100 percent verified" by a handwriting analysis as having been penned by Travis. Sky explained that Nurmi had followed up his call with an e-mail, to which he attached a copy of that one letter.

"To relieve your initial concern it contains no graphic images but I suspect you will find the contents disturbing," Nurmi wrote as part of the accompanying e-mail, in which he also provided his reason for sharing the letter with Sky instead of waiting to show it to her at a pretrial interview he had scheduled. "By providing it to you now you won't have to see it for the first time in the view of strangers."

Sky admitted to being upset when she first read the letter, believing it to be authentic. But like Deanna Reid, upon further review, she became certain that Travis could not have written it, nor could he have done the things the letter alleged. Once again, a defense attempt to enlist the help of one of Travis' friends came up empty.

A few days later, I received a call from Kreitl informing me that the signatures on the ten Bob White letters had probably not been executed by Travis Alexander. He explained that because all ten were copies and not the originals, he was unable to reach a definite conclusion. The poor quality of the second-generation copies prevented him from going forward with a more complete examination.

Kreitl's expert determination that the letters were likely forgeries bolstered my belief that they had been created for the sole purpose of supporting Arias' self-defense claim, but I wanted more definitive proof that I could use to discredit them. I knew that the Maricopa County Sheriff's Office conducted random searches of all inmates' cells, including Jodi Arias', so I called the office's intelligence unit asking whether they had seized any contraband items from her cell. My interest was piqued when one of the intelligence officers told me that they had confiscated a number of postcards from her cell and that I could view them.

I put aside my other work and drove to the Estrella Jail,

about seven miles from my office. When I arrived, the intelligence officer was waiting for me and escorted me to a room in the office adjacent to the security desk, where about fifty postcards that had been sent to Arias during her stay at the jail were waiting for me to review. They had been seized as contraband because Arias had evidently peeled the top layer of paper—the layer with writing on it—off the back of each one so that she could reuse them, which was a violation of jail policy.

I had been sifting through the pile for a few minutes when I came upon a number of blank three-by-five index cards. One of them caught my eye because it had writing on one side. A while back, Travis' sister Samantha had shown me similar cards on which Travis had written out daily to-do lists. I had also seen one of these three-by-five cards pictured in a crime scene photograph taken by police in Travis' office. The upper right-hand corner of each card was dated, and one side of the card was lined, with Travis' numbered lists on the unlined backside. These lists were a mixture of aphorisms and encouragement— "Visualize," "Prayer," "Finish goals"—with practical tasks and chores—"Water grass," "Workout," "Yoga," "Fold clothes," "Wash linens," "Dust," "Mop floor." The lists were often numbered up to fifteen or sixteen and were always written in this concise style.

I was somewhat familiar with Travis' handwriting, having read his journal and the Deanna Reid letters, and the handwriting on the three-by-five card from the jail looked very similar. It seemed an odd coincidence, because the subject matter being addressed on this card could not have been more different from Travis' to-do lists. In blue ink, it said, "Just so you know I followed you so don't try to play 'stupid' later when I ask you where you were and with whom. And if you don't answer your phone tonight I'll know your [sic] just a whore. P.S. Anyone who takes you to that dive is a loser."

As soon as I read that message, I began to doubt that this

card had been written by Travis. The tone of the message was different from all of the index card lists I'd seen. Travis' lists were always fragments, never complete sentences, and never angry or emotional—this message was clearly addressed to someone else, unlike the "to do" lists that he had on his index cards.

When I brought the index cards to the attention of the Maricopa County Sheriff's Office, they were unable to determine how they had been smuggled into the jail or how Arias came into their possession. After I prepared and served a subpoena, the cards were released at my request to Detective Flores, who picked them up and submitted them to Alan Kreitl, so that he could review the handwriting in one of them alongside the letters.

While waiting to hear from Kreitl, I filled my weeks with work on other cases as well as continuing to review selected portions of the Arias investigation in depth. At times, my attention to the case bordered on the obsessive, to the point that I couldn't get it out of my mind—I was now fixated on the three-by-five card and wanted to know how Arias was using it. Concerned that perhaps I had missed something, I arranged to return to the jail and review the pack of postcards again.

My follow-up visit to the jail, which took place on August 4, 2011, did not turn up anything that I hadn't already seen, but as I lingered in the waiting area talking with the intelligence officer, I saw a woman with short-cropped hair and rimmed glasses entering the facility. I recognized her as a friend of Jodi Arias' named Anne Campbell, who had attended a number of Arias' court hearings. I watched as she went to the window to fill out the paperwork requesting an inmate visit with Arias. I was surprised when she turned and fixed her gaze on me before breaking into a grin.

"They're up to something, and I know it, and there is nothing we can do about it," I said to the intelligence officer. She didn't say anything, just nodded. All we could do was stand there and watch as Campbell was allowed inside to visit Arias. Not long after, I headed for the parking lot to return to the office.

Perhaps my comment struck a chord, because I'd only been on the road for about five minutes when I got a call on my cell phone from the intelligence officer, directing me to come back to the jail. She had something to show me, and the urgency in her voice suggested that it couldn't wait.

Upon my return, I was led to the same office adjacent to the security desk, where I was shown two magazines. One was an issue of *Star,* dated July 25, 2011, the other an August 2011 edition of *Digital Photo Pro.*

"Arias requested that these magazines be turned over to Anne Campbell," the officer told me, directing me to have a look at them.

Nothing of note jumped out at me as I leafed through the pages of *Digital Photo Pro.* "I don't see anything," I said.

"Are you sure? Turn to page 20," the officer instructed.

I slowly scanned the page and noticed the words "you testify so" written in pencil along the right edge, next to the magazine's spine.

"Okay, now go to page 37."

Flipping ahead seventeen pages, the words "we can fix this" jumped out at me.

"Well, I'll be . . ." I remarked. "Give me another."

"Page 43." The officer smiled.

"You fucked up. What you told my attorney the next day," I said, reciting aloud the words scrawled across the top of this page.

"How did you find these?" I asked, awestruck at Arias' attempt to clandestinely communicate with someone outside the jail.

The officer explained that she hadn't noticed the concealed messages when she first skimmed the magazines, and neither had her sergeant, who had also perused them in the dim light of their office. But a gnawing feeling prompted the officer to further scrutinize the magazines, first by raising the lights in the room, which yielded no results, and then by taking them to another room, with brighter lighting, to comb through them one last time. It was then that she noticed some writing on one of the pages in *Digital Photo Pro*. Grabbing both publications, she returned to the office adjacent to the security desk, where she enlisted the help of another officer to make sure they found all the messages hidden on the pages.

Grabbing a sheet of paper, the two officers pored over the pages of *Digital Photo Pro,* writing down the page numbers and the cryptic message associated with each page:

20: you testify so
37: we can fix this
40: directly contradicts what I have been saying for over a
    year
43: You fucked up. What you told my attorney the next
    day
54: Interview was excellent! Must talk asap!
56: get down here asap and see me before you talk to them
    again and before

When they were done, they knew they had a message intended for somebody outside the jail, but they couldn't understand its meaning. They then turned their attention to *Star* magazine, featuring a smiling Casey Anthony on the upper left-hand corner of its cover. They looked slowly through every page, finding nothing until they reached page 82, the last page of the magazine. There, along the bottom border of the page, also written in pencil, they found the following numbers, in this order: 43, 40, 56, 20, 37, 54. When they rearranged the messages on those particular pages of *Digital Photo Pro* in that order, they realized they had decoded what were obviously instructions to someone outside of jail to do Arias' bidding:

43: You fucked up. What you told my attorney next day
40: contradicts what I've been saying for over a year
56: get down here asap and see me before you talk to them
again and before
20: you testify so
37: we can fix this
54: Interview was excellent! Must talk asap!

If I had any doubts that Arias would stop at nothing, including changing a witness's story, they evaporated as I read this attempted communication, in which she even cursed, in violation of her Mormon faith, which prohibited profanity. After preparing and serving another subpoena duces tecum, I immediately called Detective Flores, who agreed to drive to the Estrella Jail to pick up the publications and take them to the Mesa Police Department so they could be held securely should they be needed in any future court proceedings.

When Flores arrived, we discussed the implications and consequences of what the Maricopa County Jail officers had just found, and I was tempted to tell him about Darryl Brewer's interview summary where he had revealed to the defense investigator that Arias had told him she intended to travel to Mesa before she took her trip in early June. This was the closest I came to disclosing the existence of the gas cans to him, although as the trial neared there would be other times where I thought about it.

But while the intelligence officer had managed to foil the delivery of Arias' outgoing message, I still didn't know who the magazines were intended for or how they were going to be used. Driving back to the office from the jail, I started to think more about the timing of the attempted secret communication.

As I focused on both the date and the message itself it became clear there was nothing coincidental about the timing.

The court had scheduled a hearing in four days, on August 8, where I would challenge the credibility of the Bob White letters and attempt to preclude them from being introduced as evidence at trial. It appeared that the cryptic messages in the magazines were somehow linked to the upcoming hearing. Arias was clearly trying to communicate with someone regarding his or her potential testimony. Whoever the intended recipient of the magazines was, he or she was most likely planning to give testimony that would support Arias' claim about the authenticity of the White letters.

The problem that Arias was attempting to remedy, according to the note in the magazines, was that the story this person had told to Arias' lawyers didn't line up with what Arias herself had been saying for over a year. Because all phone calls are recorded, she couldn't risk conveying that message via the telephone, so she had to resort to the magazine route instead. With the coded message, it appeared that Arias was trying to influence the person to testify to her version of the truth, tampering with someone who would likely be a witness on her behalf.

In the days before the August 8 hearing, I disclosed the existence of the magazines to the defense. I also disclosed the results of Kreitl's analysis of the writing on the index card found in Arias' cell. He had concluded that the writings on that card were an attempt by the writer to "simulate" Travis' handwriting. He reached this conclusion after comparing the writing on the index card to the handwriting samples that were known to have been written by Travis, including his two journals and the letters to Deanna Reid.

This final detail about the three-by-five card brought everything about the White letters into sharp focus. It was obvious that the ten letters disclosed by defense counsel to the State were forged, and it seemed that Jodi Arias had forged them, as it appeared she had practiced simulating Travis' handwriting on the three-by five card while she was at the Maricopa County Jail.

When August 8 arrived, I presented my case, calling four witnesses, beginning with Deanna Reid and Alan Kreitl to prove that the White letters should be precluded from any part of the trial. The witnesses' testimony combined to paint a clear picture that the letters were forged, with Kreitl's handwriting analysis making the most compelling argument.

Under direct examination, Kreitl cited several differences he had found when comparing the content of the ten White letters with those provided by Deanna Reid. For one, the spacing in the White letters was much tighter than in Travis' letters. The letters known to have been written by Travis also didn't contain dates, while the questioned ones all had dates in the upper right-hand corner of the page.

In comparing the signatures on the two sets of letters, Kreitl found that the size of the signatures on the known letters was much larger than the signatures on the questioned ones. He also observed that the height relationship between the letter *r* and the letter *a* in the name *Travis* on the questioned documents was different than on the authentic ones.

But my presentation did not end with Kreitl and the other witnesses I had called to testify that day. I also planned to call additional witnesses, including the deputy from the jail who had discovered the coded messages in the magazines. By bringing the magazines into the discussion, my plan was to show that the coded messages were connected to the Bob White letters, indicating that Arias was trying to tamper with a witness who she was asking to testify as to the letters authenticity.

Only it didn't work out quite that way.

The following day, August 9, the court allowed the defense to call a witness preemptively to challenge the prosecution's account of the magazines before I'd had a chance to show their connection to this hearing. The witness was Heather Nitterauer, a fellow inmate of Arias', who testified that she had been the one who had written the messages in the magazines as a way to communicate with her codefendant in an impending case.

As implausible as her testimony was, what was even more strange was that the person interrogating Nitterauer was not Nurmi or Washington, but Jodi Arias herself, who had elected to proceed "propria persona," or "pro per"—acting as her own lawyer for the purposes of these proceedings. The result was that for the first time, Arias and I were on opposite sides of the debate, addressing each other directly, without an intermediary. The seating arrangements in the courtroom also changed, with Arias now sitting in the lead counsel's chair, just two feet away from me. This shift in roles moved Arias from quiet spectator to active participant, meaning that she could now make objections, question witnesses, and introduce or object to any evidence.

Even though she had taken over the first counsel's chair, both figuratively and literally, she was still in her jail garb, a two-piece pantsuit of black and white stripes from top to bottom. And instead of the ballpoint pen commonly used by lawyers to take notes, she was allowed only a three-inch yellow golf pencil, which required her to continuously sharpen its point throughout the proceedings.

If her lack of legal experience intimidated Arias, she didn't show it. But in her eagerness to begin the questioning of her witness, she started her examination before Nitterauer had even been sworn in, a fact that was not lost on the courtroom clerk, who interrupted Arias by indicating to the judge, "She hasn't been sworn," referring to the witness.

Judge Sherry Stephens said to Nitterauer, "Yes, you need to stand and be sworn."

Arias waited as Nitterauer stated her name and recited her

legal oath, before jumping back in with her questions. "You have already stated your name," she began. "Can you just tell us why you're here?"

"I'm here to testify that I wrote something in a book," Nitterauer replied, seeming to misstate her answer.

"Okay. Do you remember what—you said a book?" Arias said, in an attempt to coach Nitterauer to correct her blunder.

Apparently the witness picked up Arias' cue to modify her answer, because she gave the desired response, "Magazine."

As Arias continued with the direct examination, it appeared her focus was no longer on the witness as she turned her eyes to the back of the courtroom. "Okay. So did you—you wrote something in a magazine? Okay . . . I'm sorry, Your Honor, I'd like to remind the Court the rule has been invoked. We have a witness in the room," she told Judge Stephens, referring to Deanna Reid, who was sitting in the gallery listening to the testimony.

Arias' comment to the judge was referencing Rule 615 of the Arizona Rules of Evidence, which requires the Court to "exclude" witnesses from the courtroom who will be called to testify, so they cannot hear the testimony of others.

When I pointed out that Deanna Reid had already testified at this hearing and was no longer a witness in these proceedings, Arias responded, "She's still a trial witness."

"Is she going to be a trial witness?" Judge Stephens asked, directing her question at me.

"Not for the State at this point," I replied.

The judge next asked Arias, "Are you planning on calling her?"

Arias avowed that she would be calling Reid as a witness at trial, and therefore the judge had no choice but to exclude Deanna from the proceedings.

Three years had passed since her arrest, and it appeared Arias still harbored resentment toward Deanna for the place that she held in Travis' life, and her request that Deanna be excused appeared to be merely a ploy to prove that *she* was in control.

With Deanna now out of the courtroom, Arias refocused her attention on Nitterauer. "Okay, so what about the magazine brings you here today?" she asked.

"I wrote something to—a message for my boyfriend [to] give to a codefendant of mine."

"And do you remember which magazine you wrote the message in?"

"*Digital Camera* magazine," Nitterauer replied, citing the name incorrectly.

"And what about the other magazine?"

"The other was the *Star* magazine, and it had the pages circled . . ." she replied.

This too was an erroneous fact, as I knew the numbers found on the page of *Star* had not been circled, and I intended to assertively point that out to Nitterauer during my cross-examination.

"So, in the *Star* magazine, you indicated certain pages in reference to the *Digital Pro* magazine?" Arias continued, perhaps hoping to remind her witness of the correct name of the magazine that had contained the cryptic messages.

"Yes" was Nitterauer's one-word response.

"And so that would contain the message in the *Digital*—"

"Objection, leading," I interjected.

"Sustained," Judge Stephens ruled.

"Sorry. So the message was for whom? Sorry," Arias continued, seeming slightly taken aback by my opposition to her question and apologizing not once but twice.

When Nitterauer provided the name of the supposed intended recipient of the magazines, Arias asked her final question. "Your codefendant?" to which Nitterauer replied in the affirmative, "Yes, ma'am."

"Well, I think that's it," Arias said before returning to her chair at the defense table. She had posed just ten questions and she was done.

I waited for her to sit down before starting with my first question. "Ma'am, one of the things you indicated to us just now was that the pages were circled, right?" I began.

The witness offered up a more specific reply, which was equally incorrect. "The numbers for the pages were circled . . . on the third page in the back."

"On the back of it, you circled the page numbers?" I asked, confirming her response.

"Yes."

"And with regard to the other magazine that contained messages, you indicated that you were the one that wrote whatever messages were on there, right?"

"Yes."

"And you wrote them on the left margins, right?"

"I put them all different places, like in the seam of the book, on top of the book, in the little areas where there's clean pieces of paper on the magazine."

". . . And that was on the photo magazine, correct? . . . And then the *Star* magazine is the one with the page numbers? Those are the ones that are circled?"

Nitterauer again affirmed that the numbers in *Star* magazine were circled, which was problematic because when she was shown the magazine, she couldn't even find the page on which the numbers were written. She also claimed to know that the issue of *Star* she had wanted Anne Campbell to deliver to her codefendant had a photo of Casey Anthony on the cover, but when I asked her to describe where on the cover Ms. Anthony's photo was located, she could not provide an answer, seeming not to actually know who Anthony was or what she looked like.

"Where would Casey Anthony's picture be?" I asked, holding up the issue in question.

"On the cover," she replied.

"What part of the cover?"

"I don't know" was Nitterauer's reply.

"Even looking at it, you don't know where it is?"

"No."

Nitterauer also testified that she had gotten the issue of *Star* at the end of June or beginning of July, which was impossible, as the weekly magazine was dated July 25, 2011.

"I don't know, maybe I have the wrong date," the witness conceded.

"Or maybe you are not telling the truth?" I retorted.

At the close of my cross-examination, Arias stood and performed her redirect examination.

Through a series of simply worded questions, Arias worked to reestablish that Nitterauer had indeed been the one who had written the messages in *Digital Photo Pro* and the corresponding page numbers in *Star,* but after failing in her attempt to rehabilitate her witness she tried to place the blame on me for Nitterauer's erroneous statement that she had circled those numbers. "So, I don't recall you saying that you circled the pages in the interview. Juan said that."

I was prepared for the fight, and before Arias could even finish her sentence, I stood to voice my objection. "I am going to object to the defendant testifying," I declared. "The record speaks for itself."

"Okay," Arias acknowledged, shrinking back on that accusation to put forth another, equally improbable excuse. "Is it possible you're mixed up?"

"Yes," Nitterauer said, grabbing the bait.

"You don't remember exactly when you wrote in the magazine?" Arias coached, prompting me to object once again.

"Sustained," Judge Stephens ruled, and directed Arias to rephrase her question.

This was the first hearing at which I cross-examined a witness presented by Arias and in her presence, so she hadn't known how to prepare Nitterauer for my manner of questioning.

Nitterauer's account did not hold up under scrutiny, and the testimony ended up assisting the prosecution. More than that, the experience proved useful in other ways. After years of seeing how Arias manipulated situations and people to her advantage, it was instructive to watch as she floundered in a courtroom, where rules are nonnegotiable.

After Nitterauer stepped down from the witness stand, the hearing was continued until August 15, when I was expected to call the remaining witnesses and Arias would question them, continuing to act as her own lawyer. But when we arrived on August 15 to resume the hearing, there was a change in the proceedings. Arias had chosen to stop representing herself, and after the reappointment of Nurmi and Washington as defense counsel, I was surprised when they withdrew their objection to my request that the letters be excluded from use during the trial.

And with that, the letters were gone from the case.

Even though Nurmi had claimed to Sky Hughes that the authenticity of the letter he showed her had been verified by a handwriting expert, this claim had fallen apart under closer scrutiny. It was an abrupt reversal, and defense counsel never gave a reason to the court for their decision agreeing to withdraw the letters.

Whatever the defense counsel's rationale for withdrawing them, the case had a new reality. Without the Bob White letters to aid her, Arias' claim of self-defense was weakened substantially, because it was based solely on her uncorroborated word. She had painted herself into a corner with her different stories and now had no choice but to stay the course with her latest one.

——————————

CHAPTER 12

Though I'd successfully dealt with the Bob White letters, they were only part of the problem. I still had to contend with the instant messages and various electronic communications that portrayed Travis as someone who was quick to anger and used sexually offensive language toward Arias. These messages and words were probably going to be admissible, and they seemed to support Arias' claim that Travis could be verbally and physically abusive and, at times, sexually inappropriate.

I needed to find a way to counter this interpretation of the messages. Rather than challenging Travis' written words, I chose to focus on what might have provoked his angry missives, which meant looking more closely at his constant antagonist, Jodi Arias. There had to be a reason, even a bad one, to help explain his harsh written outbursts.

In Arias' telling, Travis was the sexual aggressor of the two, while she was the more passive one, a self-characterization that helped form the foundation of her self-defense argument.

The electronic correspondence showed them both to be sexually aggressive in their own ways, and a different story of what was going on between them appeared to unfold. Travis may have had his moments of harsh words for Arias, but his messages like "3 hole wonder" did not seem indicative of his behavior throughout their relationship. Those harsh moments were just that—moments. They showed all too clearly that there were times when Arias could push Travis too far, and like anyone pushed so hard, he got angry. Combined with the shame and guilt that he was already feeling toward himself as a religious person in this highly sexual relationship, there were times when her antagonism resulted in words that he couldn't take back. This didn't make his lashing out acceptable on any level, but viewed through this lens, it was clear that these charged moments of anger were the exceptions, not the rule.

In order to counter the idea that Arias was simply a passive figure and Travis a constant sexual aggressor, I needed to move beyond the instant messages and e-mails, which would always be open to interpretation from either side, depending on who was discussing them. I began to think back to what I knew of her previous relationships.

I remembered reading something which spoke to Arias' demeanor in an intimate setting during the interview that the defense investigator had done with Darryl Brewer back on October 6, 2008—the interview that had first put me on the trail of the gas cans—so I pulled out the binder with his summary to verify my recollection. When the investigator had asked Brewer about his intimate relationship with Arias, Brewer had talked about when they first met. "The first time, she was pretty aggressive," he recalled when speaking to the investigator, describing Arias as "enthusiastic" and always "comfortable" sexually and with intimacy. Turning this information over anew, it was intriguing how different Brewer's characterization of Arias was from the way she was portraying herself now that she was claiming she had killed Travis in self-defense.

I wanted to find out if Arias had been as sexually forward with Ryan Burns as she had been with Darryl Brewer. She had visited him in Utah less than twenty-four hours after she'd been intimate with Travis before she killed him, so I wanted to find out how sexually appropriate she had been with Burns, especially after having rolled around in Travis' bed a day before.

To prepare for my call to Burns, I decided to review the telephonic interview police had conducted with him on June 25, 2008. The information he had provided to them was silent with regard to any sexual interplay that he and Arias may have had, but my review was not in vain, as I did find another discrepancy in the story Arias had told Burns about why her cell phone hadn't been working during the drive from California to Utah.

Burns told police that Arias called him on Tuesday, June 3, 2008, at around 11:00 P.M., to let him know she had just left the Monterey area and would be arriving in Utah the following day. He didn't hear from her again until approximately twenty hours later, when she phoned him the evening of June 4, claiming to have driven in the wrong direction, gotten lost, and run out of gas. She told Burns she had just passed a highway sign that read 100 MILES TO LAS VEGAS, which would put her on Highway 93 North passing through Kingman, Arizona. Her stated reason for not contacting Burns sooner was that she had forgotten her cell phone charger and turned off her phone to save the battery.

This was in stark contrast to what she had told Detective Flores on July 15, 2008, just after her arrest in Yreka. During that conversation, Arias claimed that her cell phone had powered off on its own just east of Pasadena, California, and it wasn't until she found her cell phone charger, which had lodged itself under the passenger-side seat, that she was able to power it on north of Kingman.

That Arias had told two different stories about the cell phone charger, one to Burns and the other to law enforcement during an official police interview, convinced me even more that she had deliberately powered off her cell phone to avoid being detected in Arizona. This certainly spoke to her planning of the murder, because it was another step she took knowing it would be impossible for police to electronically track her movements if her phone was powered off. This became one more point I didn't want to forget to discuss with Burns on the phone.

It was midmorning when I reached Burns on his cell phone, and from the outset he sounded eager to cooperate. I explained that I had some questions for him that had not been covered during his interview with police, assuring him that I was not recording our conversation or taking notes. I avoid using a recorder when I speak with witnesses because I want them to be comfortable knowing there is no recording device, and I don't take notes because I don't want to stop the flow of the conversation by asking the person to repeat something to enable me to write it down.

"I am happy to tell you what I know," Burns said.

I didn't want to initiate the conversation with questions about his intimate relationship with Arias, so I began by asking him about his living situation. He explained that back in June 2008 he had resided with his parents in West Jordan, a suburb of Salt Lake City, but that his quarters were private and separated from the rest of the house.

Next, I asked him about Arias' failure to arrive in Utah on the morning of June 4, as she had promised, and he indicated that he'd started to worry when she didn't turn up as scheduled. As the hours passed without hearing from her, he grew increasingly concerned and called around to mutual acquaintances in the Salt Lake City area, hoping that they had heard something. It struck me that his community was close-knit and he felt comfortable calling others to share his concern. When he learned that no one had heard from her, there was nothing he could do but wait and hope she was okay.

Burns told me that it wasn't until later that evening, while out to dinner with two friends at the Cheesecake Factory, that he finally received a call from Arias, claiming she had gotten lost and would be in Utah some time the following morning.

Burns recalled that she was in good spirits and was looking forward to seeing him.

When she finally arrived the next day and greeted him outside his front door, he told me he was surprised to see that she was now a brunette, since she'd been a blonde when he first met her.

"You're a lucky guy that girls come to see you," I said, trying to move the conversation to the more pertinent topic of their physical relationship. I knew that Ryan Burns was Mormon, and I wanted to be respectful, but I needed to find out what had happened during their brief time together.

When I asked if they had kissed, he revealed that Arias was more than a willing participant, as she kissed him first. Burns described the kiss as "passionate," so I asked him if anything else had happened. He admitted that the two had engaged in sexual behavior the only night she was in Utah. He explained that after attending a PPL meeting in Salt Lake City, the two went to dinner with friends and then back to his house, where they watched a movie together. He recalled that Arias was tired, so the two lay down on his bed for a nap, so she could get a few hours of sleep before starting her drive back to California. Upon waking, according to Burns, they engaged in romantic kissing and grinding of their pelvic areas, with Arias straddling him while the two were fully clothed.

Listening to Burns' narrative, it was surprising to hear that Arias would be so intimate and aggressive with him given what, according to her, she'd just been through with Travis. After all, if her version of events was to be believed, less than two days earlier, she'd slept with Travis, who had caused her to fear for her life to the point that she'd killed him. And yet, in spite of all this apparent emotional trauma that she'd experienced, here she was with Burns, carrying on in a sexual manner as though nothing had happened.

"Did anything unusual happen while you guys were together?" I asked.

It was then that Burns told me something that had not been mentioned in the police report. Shortly after Arias arrived at his house on June 5, the two drove in separate cars to a restaurant, where they were meeting friends for lunch before going to the PPL seminar. It was around noon, and he was driving in front of her, when he looked in his rearview mirror and noticed that she had been pulled over by a member of the West Jordan City Police Department. He watched as Arias spoke briefly with the police officer and was allowed to drive on without being cited.

Once they arrived at the restaurant, Burns asked her what had happened with the cop, and she explained that he'd pulled her over because her rear license plate was affixed upside down. She claimed that some kids had been goofing around near the front of her car while she'd been inside a restaurant while driving through California. She added that when she came out to the parking lot the kids saw her approaching, dropped the front license plate, and took off laughing. She'd picked up the plate and put it in the backseat of her car, telling Burns those kids were the ones responsible for removing the back license plate and replacing it upside down.

At the end of my call with Burns, I was anxious to know more about what had happened with the traffic stop, so I attempted to get a copy of the police report detailing the events. I phoned the police station in West Jordan and was told that a report of the traffic stop had not been generated because Arias had not been cited. I know that each dispatch operator also generates another, less detailed report, and I immediately called the dispatch center and requested the event log for the traffic stop. The log did not include much information, but it did indicate the name of the police officer, Michael Galieti, and the time of 12:03 P.M. when he had pulled Arias over on June 5.

After leaving a message for him, officer Galieti returned my call, and I asked about the traffic stop hoping he remembered pulling Arias over. As it turned out, he remembered the stop quite well, saying it was the only time in his career where he had seen a car being driven with a rear license plate affixed upside down. He also said that there was no front license plate on the car when he stopped it that day and remembered that the driver was a woman whom he identified as Jodi Arias. When I asked if she had provided an explanation, he told me that during traffic stops he hears a lot of stories, and hers was that her friends—not strangers—must be "playing a joke on me."

It was impressive that Arias was able to spin a spur-of-the-moment tale so convincingly that she was able to talk a police officer out of giving her a ticket for the infraction. And once again, just like with her story about the cell phone charger, she'd told Ryan Burns one thing and law enforcement another.

With these two competing versions revealing her untruthfulness, it seemed evident that Arias had removed both license plates before she arrived at Travis' house in Mesa in the early morning hours of June 4. This would have made it difficult for anyone to identify the vehicle should it have been seen at or near Travis' house. She had apparently never put the front license plate back on the car and had remounted the back one upside down, leading to the stop by Officer Galieti.

After my conversations with Burns and Galieti, I made the decision that I was going to call both of them to testify, and as required by the rules, I filed a notice letting defense counsel know of my intention. As with every other potential prosecution witness, defense counsel indicated that they wished to speak to Burns and Galieti, so that they could ask them questions and tape-record their answers. Rather than inconvenience the two individuals with a trip to Arizona, I informed defense counsel Laurence Nurmi that the interviews would take place in Utah, and as is my normal practice, I would also be present during the interviews—not to interrupt or question, but simply to observe.

The conversation Nurmi had with Ryan Burns was conducted in an interview room at the West Jordan City Police Department. Nurmi was a hulking man with close-cropped hair and rimmed glasses. He was dressed casually in contrast to my dress shirt and tie, and he had a legal pad in front of him that he would refer to while asking questions, along with a tape recorder. Burns was in his late twenties, approximately six feet tall, with red hair and green eyes. We all sat at the table, and I began the dialogue by thanking Burns for coming. I let him know that Mr. Nurmi was one of the lawyers for Jodi Arias and wanted to ask him some questions.

During these kinds of interviews, my attention is always focused on the witness, not defense counsel, as I am looking to see their demeanor and style in answering questions, as well as their level of composure. Burns had an air of confidence, and I sensed that he would tell the story as he remembered it without being unduly influenced by the question. Nothing emerged from Burns' interview that was of a surprising nature, except I realized that he was three years younger than Arias.

I wasn't timing the interview, but it seemed like about thirty minutes had passed when Nurmi indicated that he had no more questions, and I let Burns know the interview was over and again thanked him for making himself available.

That same morning, Nurmi also interviewed four other potential witnesses who either were acquaintances of Arias' or had interacted with her on June 5, 2008, when she traveled to Utah. Among those interviewed was a woman named Leslie Udy.

Udy lived in the Salt Lake City area and had met Arias through Pre-Paid Legal. On the evening of June 5, 2008, Udy, Arias, Burns, and a few others had dined at Chili's. Arias had driven her to the restaurant that night and told Udy that she and Travis weren't together anymore, but said she could imagine them both married to other people someday and socializing at PPL events, where their kids would play together.

Our next interview was at the Cottonwood Heights Police

Department, about ten miles away, where Officer Michael Galieti now worked. Nurmi and I drove in separate cars, and he apparently got lost on the way, because he was approximately thirty minutes late. When he finally arrived, Nurmi apologized to Officer Galieti, who ushered us into a room just inside the lobby. Nurmi and I sat down, turned on our tape recorders, and the interview began. This interview was also short, just about thirty minutes, with Nurmi asking Galieti about the circumstances of the traffic stop.

Officer Galieti was in uniform and appeared to be in his late fifties. He was poised in his responses and confident of his information. He came across as someone who was observant and paid close attention to details, and could still remember what happened when he made a traffic stop of the car driven by Jodi Arias.

I'd initially called Ryan Burns to talk about his sexual interaction with Arias and ended up learning something about the traffic stop. But that's how cases are—there is always a dash of luck in every one of them, and this one was proving no different. I'd found something compelling—another part of the plan in Arias' scheme to kill Travis. Taken with everything else I'd learned, it was clear that this was not a crime of passion where Arias just reacted or the situation got out of control. This was a killing that had been well thought out to include such fine details as removing license plates to avoid being detected. This was premeditation, down to the last gallon of gas.

———

CHAPTER 13

I had almost missed the signposts on Jodi Arias' road to Mesa. But I was now beginning to understand what fueled her motivation for the road trip to Arizona.

Her overnight journey across the desert that June 4 wasn't to enjoy the weather. The high in Pasadena was around 70 degrees while in Mesa it was slightly over 100. Arias wasn't coming to visit friends either. She hid her itinerary from others. It most certainly wasn't a religious pilgrimage. She didn't even stop at the Mormon temple. It went beyond hiding a visit to enjoy a sexual tryst, no matter how much premarital sex was forbidden by her religion.

The trip was a journey that would bring permanent closure to her relationship with Travis. She was going to end it by ending his life. Bringing three gas cans was just one part of her elaborate plan.

To avoid missing any of her steps, I took a synergistic approach and detailed on my legal pad all the key elements leading to the killing. I had familiarized myself with this case to the point where I was intimate with the details of the investigation and could rely on that memory to formulate a timeline of Arias' preparations to carry out the murder.

The trial was still a few months away, but preparation on this scale doesn't happen overnight. I started working on evenings and weekends when everyone was out of the office and I didn't have to worry about being interrupted. The office was hushed in a way that only happens after hours, and as I sat down at my desk, I turned around and looked out the window at the Fourth Avenue Jail, with its visitors streaming in to see the inmates. Looking outside was only a momentary distraction before turning my attention to the blank legal pad in front of me to begin summarizing the steps Arias had taken in premeditating Travis' murder.

Arias' planning for the trip to Arizona had started in mid-to-late May, with the call to her ex-boyfriend Darryl Brewer requesting to borrow gas cans. This was the call that ended with her becoming frustrated with him for asking why she needed the cans. Even though she'd hung up without giving him a definitive schedule to pick up the containers, this call marked the first outward sign that Arias' plan had been put into motion.

From there, she moved on to obtaining the gun. On Wednesday, May 28, 2008, she found that she had the house to herself for approximately five hours, and she used this opportunity to stage the break-in at her grandparents' house on Pine Street in Yreka, where she was living. Her objective was to take the .25 caliber handgun that belonged to her grandfather. This handgun would never be recovered, but the bullet casing found in Travis' bathroom matched the caliber of her grandfather's gun. During the investigation, Arias would confirm to Detective Flores that Travis did not own a gun, .25 caliber or otherwise, which showed that Arias had brought the gun "stolen" from her grandparents' house to kill Travis, disposing of it after the crime.

Around the same time as the "break-in," Arias followed up with Darryl Brewer and called him again asking to borrow the two gas cans for her trip to Mesa. In a few days' time, she would show up at Brewer's house and take the containers with her.

Her desire to travel in early June 2008 was not borne out of a need to take time off from a job following months of hard work. She had only been employed for one week before her road trip. As she wrote in her journal, "speaking of Casa Ramos, last night [Monday, May 26, 2008] was my first night. It was cool. Everybody seems nice. I think I'll like it there."

Arias came up with a cover story for taking the trip. She was going to visit Ryan Burns, a man she barely knew in West Jordan, Utah, a suburb of Salt Lake City. She mentioned Burns in a journal entry of May 27, 2008. "He's fun to flirt w/ through text messaging. . . . But hey, I like this guy, well so far, what I know about him, I like."

Three days later on May 30, Arias' journal entry spoke of her decision to travel to Utah to see Burns in the coming days. But according to her, "He doesn't seem overly interested in me, although he seems happy that I am coming out to see him."

It was perplexing that Arias had told her younger sister Angela that she saw Burns as her soul mate and future husband, yet apparently she wasn't even sure if he was interested in her in a romantic way.

Burns told police that the two agreed that he would wait for her to arrive at his place sometime in the morning on Wednesday, June 4.

Arias rented a car for her supposed trip to Utah on June 2, 2008, at the airport in Redding, a city approximately ninety miles south of Yreka. The person renting her the car remembered the transaction and after identifying Arias in a photographic line-up mentioned that her hair was blonde when he first met her. The picture in the line-up was Arias' mug shot taken after her arrest when her hair was brown.

During her interaction with the rental car agent, she made up a story and told him that she was just going to be using the car for driving around locally. The first car offered to her had been red, but she had refused it because it might be "more noticeable" to law enforcement, deciding instead on a white Ford Focus. Obviously any encounter with Arizona police would prove fatal to her plan of driving into and out of the state undetected.

According to the only undated entry in any of her journals, Arias spent that evening, the first night of the trip, going out to dinner with one of her ex-boyfriends, Matthew McCartney, singing karaoke after meeting him at the Red Room in Santa Cruz. She wrote that McCartney bullied her into singing a duet to the song "Cruisin'." She complained in the journal, "Not that I'm any better, but I totally carried him through that song."

Even though Arias had told Detective Flores during her interview in Yreka that she was ambidextrous, I had come to understand that she only issued left-handed compliments, such as her pointing out that although saying McCartney could sing, it was *her* performance that carried the day.

The next morning, June 3, Arias showed up at Darryl Brewer's house in Pacific Grove, near Monterey, at approximately 7:30 in the morning. She had breakfast with Brewer and his young son. Once they were done eating, Arias used Brewer's computer to check her e-mail. She then took the two five-gallon gas cans and left.

Arias stopped at the Washington Mutual branch office in Monterey and engaged in three bank transactions, the last one at 10:15 P.M. There was an approximately four-hour gap between that transaction and the next time police were able to pick up her movements, based on a few time-stamped selfies she took en route to Salinas. Those photographs were found by police on her cell phone after her arrest.

Because of the changing scenery outside her car window, it appears she was sitting behind the wheel of her rental car and driving while she took these selfies, the first of which was snapped at 2:12 P.M. What made them so significant was that they showed Arias as a brunette, which meant that at some time after she rented the car at the airport in Redding she had dyed her hair from blonde to brown. A half smile is evident in two of the three pictures, while the last displays Arias' more serious side, but all three show her brown hair spilling past her neck and shoulders.

Arias' next documented stop on June 3 was Salinas, where she visited the Walmart at around 3:25 P.M. She purchased five items that afternoon, including another five-gallon gas can to add to the two she had borrowed from Darryl Brewer.

Her trip then took her to Pasadena, where she stopped at the ARCO station shortly after 8:30 P.M. and filled both her gas tank and the three gas cans.

Arias had ensured that the three containers would hold enough gasoline to guarantee she would not have to stop for gas in Arizona, so the police would not be able to place her in the state. She had also saved those gasoline receipts which, according to her, would support her claim that she had traveled directly from California to Utah.

Making sure that her alibi was still in place, Arias called Ryan Burns some time around 9:00 P.M. She assured him that she was on her way to Utah to see him and would be there in the late morning of the following day, June 4, as previously discussed. What she didn't tell him was that she was going to drive through the night to visit Travis. She placed the call to this boyfriend-in-waiting shortly before she headed east on Interstate 10 toward Mesa.

Not long after, on the night of June 3, Arias powered off her cell phone. She did not turn it back on until approximately twenty-four hours later, in northern Arizona near the Nevada border, which ensured that police would not be able to electronically trace her detour.

Arias' plan of driving through Arizona undetected was successful. No one remembered seeing either a brown-haired woman entering the house in Mesa in the early-morning hours of June 4 or a white Ford Focus parked in Travis' driveway. Tired from a long night of driving, Arias went to bed with Travis, waking up at around 1:00 P.M.

I knew from the time stamps on the nude photographs that they began taking sexually explicit pictures at around 1:30 P.M. After this initial bedroom session in the midafternoon, Arias and Travis went downstairs, where they tried to look through the CDs of photos that she had brought with her of their travels, CDs whose very presence demonstrated that she had planned to visit Travis. Sometime shortly before 5:30 P.M., Travis decided to take a shower, with Arias documenting his final moments on his Sanyo camera.

The first stab wound ushering him to his death came while Travis was seated on the shower floor, followed by more stab wounds, which caused Travis to raise his hands to defend himself. He stood up and struggled to the sink, where Arias continued to stab him repeatedly on his shoulders. In an attempt to get away from the onslaught, Travis made his way down the hall, where Arias caught up with him and slit his throat as he was about to go into the bedroom. She continued the attack by dragging his body down the hallway to the bloodstained sink, where she shot him once in the head. She then continued to drag his body, finally stuffing Travis into the shower.

It was at this point that Arias began the cleanup at the scene. She turned the shower on to wash away any biological evidence from Travis' body that could be tested later by DNA analysis. She took a plastic tumbler out from under the sink and used it to pour water on the floor in an attempt to clean some of the blood in the hallway. She then used one of the gold-brown bath towels in the bathroom to soak up some of the watered-down mixture.

Retreating from the bathroom, she took the bloody towel and went downstairs to put it into the washing machine. She also placed the camera into the washer, after having deleted the pictures of their sexual activity, those of Travis in the shower, and the inadvertent photos showing her dragging him down the hallway. After dumping in some bleach, she began the wash cycle.

Before she left Travis' house, she removed her bloodstained socks, which she is seen wearing in one of the inadvertent photographs retrieved from the camera's memory card, and left with the knife and the gun. Neither of those weapons has been found.

She walked out of the house and resumed her trip to Utah, using the gasoline stored in the three gas cans to fill her car along the way. It wasn't until she was near the Nevada border that she powered her phone back on and called Ryan Burns to tell him that she'd gotten lost and would be arriving one day later.

Her explanation for not arriving in Utah until June 5, was not questioned by Burns or her other acquaintances. She told them that she had taken the wrong freeway and driven for many hours. She also claimed to have stopped and slept for a long time. Arias was self-deprecating, blaming herself for getting lost, and even called herself an airhead. That same day, almost immediately after arriving at Ryan Burns' home in West Jordan, she was stopped for a traffic violation because her back license plate was upside down.

Arias' meticulous approach extended to the cleanup of the rental car before returning it to the rental car agency in Redding. She removed the front and back floor mats before turning the car in, presumably because they might have had blood or other evidence on them that could have linked her to the crime. She also disposed of the three gas cans. Neither the mats nor the gas cans have ever been found.

I also intended to call the jury's attention to the three communications Arias made to Travis—the June 4 voice message she left on his cell phone, the June 6 text message, and the June 7 e-mail—showing that she'd tried to cover up her involvement in the murder by making it seem as though she and Travis hadn't seen each other in a while.

For almost four years, I had endured Arias changing her story as she shifted her version of events. I had always known that I would need something concrete to confront her with at trial that she could not explain away. In this high-stakes game of poker that she was playing, I had found my ace in the hole with the gas cans. And the best part was that she would not hear about them until she was on the witness stand when it would be too late for her to again change her story in an attempt to explain them away.

━━━ ━ ━ ━ ━ ━━━

CHAPTER 14

Trial strategy isn't a matter of simply calling a witness to the stand, asking questions, and showing pictures to the jury— it's about making difficult decisions regarding who will be called as a witness and what evidence to present, along with the order in which each will be introduced. Choosing when to present a piece of evidence to a jury is almost more important than the evidence itself, as the timing can affect the way a jury may treat it. Introducing a fact too soon can cause them to miss its importance, while introducing it too late runs the risk of having jurors disregard it, as their minds may already be made up. This is the fine line I had to walk in the Jodi Arias case.

The trial had already been rescheduled a number of times before the judge set a firm date of December 10, 2012, for the start of jury selection. I'd been preparing for this since my walk-through of the crime scene on June 10, 2008. Preparation isn't something that I do all at once, but rather it's a gradual and ongoing process, as I refine my thinking about each witness and decide the best approach to maximize the impact of their testimony.

In this case, my most important decision was deciding when I was going to introduce the information that Arias had utilized three gas cans to hide her trip into Arizona. Prosecutors are trained to present their most compelling evidence as part of their opening remarks, as a way to signal to the jury the most significant aspects of their case. Under normal circumstances, I would have included the information about the gas cans in my opening statement and made it a part of my case in chief. But I did not want to give Arias time to formulate a story explaining why it was necessary for her to take three gas cans on her trip. My plan was to wait until the opportune time to reveal that I knew of their existence. That would be when the defense was presenting its case and called Darryl Brewer to the stand.

Arizona law does not limit cross-examination of a witness to questions about issues raised during the direct examination. Once the defense called Brewer to testify, my intention on cross-examination was to have him confirm that he lent Arias the two five-gallon gas cans for use during her trip. Having this information come from Brewer would make it harder for Arias to deny that she had made the request and that she had told Brewer her intended destination was Mesa.

This approach was extremely risky. I was relying on defense counsel to call a witness, but there was always a chance that they would choose not to have Brewer testify, even though his name was on their witness list. He was merely an ex-boyfriend who had lived with Arias and could only speak about how well she got along with him and his young son, which didn't make him crucial to Arias' self-defense claim.

To ensure that defense counsel, and Jodi Arias herself, did not know of my desire to have Brewer take the stand, I went out of my way to appear uninterested in him as a witness. Just as defense counsel has the right to interview all potential witnesses to be called by the prosecution, I have the same right with any of the defense's potential witnesses. I made a conscious decision not to request an interview with Brewer prior to trial, although I conducted interviews with every other person on the defense's list of potential witnesses.

If the defense ultimately decided not to call Brewer, I knew I could still raise the issue of the gas cans in my cross-examination of Jodi Arias, but relying on that as a backup strategy was even riskier. Without Brewer's testimony framing the story, it would be easy for her to deny borrowing them, leaving me worse off than if I had never broached the subject. My decision would be further complicated if I then wanted to call Brewer as a witness to rebut her denial. Brewer lived in California, and the subpoena power of an Arizona court to compel his appearance as a witness extends only as far as the state border. I could request that a California court order him to travel to Arizona and give testimony, but that would take time. There would be no way to guarantee that he would be forced to appear pursuant to an out of state court order before the trial ended. And even if I could get Arias to admit that she bought a gas can at the Walmart in Salinas by showing her the receipt, that admission alone would prove nothing, because one five-gallon can of gasoline was not enough to get her through Arizona without stopping and filling up.

There was another drawback to my strategy, which was that the defense could choose to call Brewer *after* calling Arias. Usually defendants taking the stand in their defense go on last, but that isn't always the case. My strategy regarding the gas cans would be more powerful if Brewer testified before Arias. If the order were reversed and Arias went on before Brewer, I'd be forced to ask her about the gas cans first, which would not be as impactful as having Brewer lay out a story that she could not refute.

Hoping the defense would call Brewer to the stand before Arias was a gamble, but it was one I was willing to take, because it was my best chance of showing Arias had planned the trip to Mesa thereby exposing her self-defense claim as a sham.

Another decision I needed to make was when to introduce the three "attempts" Arias made to contact Travis *after* she killed him. Their existence had already been disclosed to defense counsel, and while presumably Arias was aware of them, she didn't know when I was going to use them.

Because I anticipated that Arias was going to testify in her own defense, I decided that asking her about the text, voice message, and e-mail on cross-examination would be much more powerful than introducing them during the presentation of my case. Waiting until Arias was on the stand to ask about these three communications would force her to explain why she sent them if she knew that Travis was already dead.

The other important decision I had to make was how forcefully I would approach Arias when she took the stand. Long before the trial started, I had decided that I was going to question her aggressively if she made good on her promise to *48 Hours* that she would testify. From my close viewing of Arias' interviews with Detective Flores, I'd seen what could happen if she was given space to get comfortable. In the span of two interviews with him, she'd told two different stories about Travis' murder. If that weren't reason enough to be cautious, the forgery of the "Bob White" letters was a strong indication of the lengths that she would go if unchecked. I could not afford to give her any room to believe she could manipulate the truth on the stand by taking advantage of an easy-going questioning style.

Even when backed into a corner, she still seemed comfortable, so my intent was to keep her off balance and under pressure. I knew from experience that there are a couple of ways to do this—one comes from the pace of the questions, the other from the tone of voice. I'd planned to use both.

Although the use of this aggressive approach would make it harder for Arias to come up with answers on the spot and keep them consistent with the many stories she had told, there was also the chance that this style could backfire with the jury. Arias' position was that she had been victimized by Travis, so a harsh approach could be seen as another instance of a man in her life mistreating her. But, in the end, I had no doubt that my approach was the right one, and under the circumstances, it was a risk I had to take.

Arizona is one of the few states that permits jurors to submit questions in writing, which may be asked of a witness after the lawyers have completed their questioning. The procedure for asking jurors' questions differs in that the judge is the person who reads the questions to the witness. After the judge finishes reading the questions, the party calling the witness may follow up on issues raised by the jurors' questions. The opposing party is then afforded the last opportunity to question the witness which is significant because the final thing the jury will hear will be answers to the opposing counsel's questions.

This meant that when Arias testified, as I anticipated she would, I would have the last word, potentially providing me the opportunity to have the third gas can issue be the last thing the jury would hear discussed with Arias before she left the witness stand.

With the presentation of my case, my aim was to keep the jury's attention focused on the horrific nature of the killing. This would be a challenge because the defendant was a woman, some would even think she was attractive, and juries historically associate brutality as endemic to a man. So, I needed to have them look past the stereotype and just consider the evidence.

Similarly, I wanted the jury to see beyond Travis' faults, to make them focus on what she had done to him, not on the way he had spoken and written to her. I was not going to hide that he was human and had his shortcomings, but I wasn't going to linger on them either. If I was not careful, and became too focused on protecting Travis' character, I might turn the trial into a rehabilitative exercise, rather than proving that Arias had planned and carried out his murder. While it would have been easy to try to focus on Travis' Mormon faith, his work history at PPL, or his relative youth, none of those things were what this case was about. It was about a scorned woman who exacted revenge for Travis' failure to choose her.

But taking his life had not been enough. She was now claiming he was a pedophile, alleging that she had walked in on him on January 21, 2008, while he was masturbating to pictures of young children. She recounted that the pictures were on the bed while Travis was touching himself. Arias' uncorroborated accusation that Travis was a pedophile appeared to be gratuitous character assassination that raised the already inflammatory tone of her defense to a higher level. According to her, he had always been verbally abusive, but after she caught him that day, he became physically abusive as well.

Arias described three occasions when she claimed that Travis had struck her. She said the first occurred in October 2007 when they were arguing and he pushed her down on the ground to prevent her from leaving the bedroom. The second supposedly happened at Travis' house, where he threw her down on the floor and kicked her, breaking a finger on her left hand. The last incidence of alleged violence was when he struck her while she was staying at his house immediately before her move to Yreka. According to Arias, he threw her down on the ground, got on top of her, and choked her until she passed out.

The introduction of these latest allegations smacked of desperation because she now apparently realized there was nothing other than her word to support her self defense claim that he had attacked her. But I was not going to be anticipatory in my presentation in an attempt to discredit these claims as part of my case and would instead wait until cross examination to dispute these allegations while Arias was on the witness stand.

Proving the first-degree murder charge required that I show that Arias was the one who killed Travis and that she had premeditated his killing, and the place to start was by showing what had happened in the master bedroom suite on June 4, 2008. I had a choice of whom I was going to call to set the crime scene, which involved explaining to the jury the date, time, and circumstances under which Travis' body was found.

This is usually done through the testimony of either a police officer who had responded to the emergency call or detectives responding to the scene, but I wanted to start my presentation of evidence with a more impactful witness.

I could have called Travis' roommate Zachary Billings to offer testimony about his role in the discovery of his friend's body, but I wanted a broader picture painted through my first witness and instead chose to call Mimi Hall. Mimi was a Mormon woman and Travis' friend, someone he had dated for a brief time. She was also the person he had invited to accompany him on a trip to Cancún, Mexico, which appeared to be the motive that spurred Arias to kill Travis. He had never asked Arias to go with him on that trip, and she had tried to act as if not being chosen to accompany him hadn't bothered her, to the point that she had gone to the other extreme of telling Detective Flores that she was planning to ask Travis if she could stay at his house during the time he was in Mexico.

Mimi Hall would be able to describe the circumstances that led her to Travis' house the night his body was eventually found. She was also knowledgeable about the Mormon religion and would discuss aspects of the faith, including the prohibition against premarital sex, which applies equally to all members regardless of gender.

Continuing the crime scene story would be witnesses from the Mesa Police Department, because they had carried out the investigation and could speak to the specifics of how Travis was killed. Officer Sterling Williams was the first officer on the scene and would describe the signs of decomposition he observed on the body when he found it. His observations would support the notion that the killing had occurred days before the body was discovered.

Of course, I would also call Detective Flores to testify. He was the lead investigator in the case, who was familiar with every aspect of the investigation. He kept track of the roles of other officers involved in the case, submitted items for testing, such as DNA and fingerprint analysis, and would sit next to me at the prosecution table throughout the trial. His time on the stand was going to be broken down into segments rather than having him complete his testimony in one sitting. I planned to call him to provide testimony about such things as Arias' in-person and telephone statements to him over the course of the investigation, her appearance on *Inside Edition,* and details about Arias' arrest and the search of Travis' home. I would not be presenting all of her statements at one time, as I had found that video or audio statements played one right after the other have a tendency to run together and be confusing to the jury, which could lessen their impact.

The other reason for truncating Flores' appearances on the witness stand was that he could fill gaps of time that normally occur during trial because of witness-scheduling conflicts. Juries do not appreciate when their time is wasted waiting for a witness to appear, or when the court day ends early because the next witness is not available until the next day. As case agent, Detective Flores would be present in court and available to testify at a moment's notice, so it wouldn't be an inconvenience or waste of time for him, and there would be no dead time for the jury.

Another member of the Mesa Police Department who would testify was Heather Conner, a technician experienced in finding latent prints at a scene and comparing them to a suspect's prints. Conner had collected a left palm print in blood from the west wall of the bathroom hallway and determined that the latent palm print was Arias', establishing that Arias had been at Travis' house. That her palm print was on the west wall, where one of the retrieved inadvertent photographs showed Arias' foot at Travis' head as blood runs down his right shoulder, would go far in removing any doubt that the jury might have that someone other than Arias had killed Travis.

Heather Conner had also been present when the hundreds of photographs were taken of the crime scene, documenting the body, bathroom, and master bedroom from every angle. It would have been counterproductive to show every one of those photographs to the jury, so I spent days narrowing the number that I would introduce down to 140. The photographs I selected showed the entirety of the scene, which would help the jury understand how the killing occurred and also help them appreciate the pain and anguish inflicted by Arias on Travis.

Although photographs accurately depict the size and relationship between items, they are not a life-size representation, which is why I like to bring in the actual object or documents whenever possible. I had spent a great deal of time going through the items that had been collected as part of the investigation. In looking at the piece of carpet that had been cut from the master bedroom showing the ovoid blood stain, I was surprised to see how much larger the pattern was than I remembered it from my walk-through. Because the carpet swatch had been cut from the floor, I was able to look underneath it and noticed that the blood on the underside appeared diluted, just like the blood on the side of the cardboard box sitting on the floor of the bathroom linen closet. It was obvious that Arias had used the plastic tumbler to apply water to that area of the carpet in an attempt to clean up the scene by pouring water on the blood.

I realized that the actual section of carpet would be far more impactful to the jury than an 8½-by-11-inch photograph, giving them an understanding of how profusely Travis was bleeding as Arias chased him down and slit his throat at the end of the hallway.

Another item from the house that caught my eye was the goldish-brown bath towel that police had found in the washing machine. It was the mate to the one I had seen hanging in Travis' bathroom, although this one was now discolored in spots from having gone through the wash cycle with bleach. It seemed clear that Arias had been the one to put it in the washing machine with the bleach to remove any biological material she may have left behind, so if a DNA test were done, there would be no evidence to show she was there. This would be significant for the jury to consider when assessing Arias' claim that she was confused and could not remember much about the attack or her actions after she killed Travis.

Also important was that one of the goldish-brown towels had been found in the washing machine next to the camera, showing that Arias appeared to believe that adding bleach would destroy the photographs linking her to the crime, which would help answer for the jury the question of why she had failed to take the camera with her when she left Travis' house that day.

Once the police photographer finished taking pictures, investigators from the Maricopa County Office of the Medical Examiner had come in and placed the body in a bag to remove it from the crime scene for examination by Kevin Horn, M.D., a doctor with that office. As Dr. Horn would describe, Arias first stabbed Travis in the chest, then slashed his throat, finally ending her attack with a shot to Travis' right temple. He would also tell the jury that Travis was conscious for the first part of the attack and tried to protect himself from the knife, as indicated by the defensive wounds on his hands.

To avoid any confusion about the caliber of the casing found near the sink area, I intended to call Elizabeth Northcutt, a forensic firearms examiner with the Mesa Police Department. She examined the casing found in the blood in front of the sink and determined it was .25 caliber. She also examined the bullet fragment recovered by Dr. Horn from Travis' head and found that it was consistent in weight with a .25 caliber round. Northcutt would also speak to the difference between a revolver, which does not eject the casings after the bullet is fired, and a semiautomatic handgun, which extracts and ejects the casings, and is the kind of gun that was used to shoot Travis in the face.

I knew that Detective Flores would be grilled about an assertion he made at a court hearing very early in the case that was at odds with Dr. Kevin Horn's findings. That hearing was to determine whether there was probable cause to believe that the killing was especially cruel, addressing whether Travis suffered emotionally or physically as a result of being stabbed and shot. I had called Flores to testify and reprise Dr. Horn's opinion as to the sequence of the fatal injuries leading to Travis' death. My decision to call Flores instead of Horn was an acknowledgment of how busy Horn's schedule was at the time. There was a shortage of doctors at the Maricopa County Office of the Medical Examiner, and I knew that the rules allowed for Flores to testify based on what Horn might have told him. Detective Flores does not have any medical experience, and his knowledge of the sequence of events was predicated on a very brief phone conversation with Dr. Horn that took place a couple of days before the hearing. It was unclear whether Horn understood what Flores was asking, but the end result was that Flores interpreted what he heard to mean the shot to Travis' temple happened before the stab wounds.

The defense had raised this inconsistency in prior pleadings, so I was sure they would raise it again at trial. It was a point of little consequence, because no one could dispute that Travis suffered extreme physical pain and emotional distress as shown by the defensive wounds on his hands. I hoped defense counsel would continue to focus on this "inconsistency" rather than spend time on the self-defense claim.

Corroborating the testimony of Dr. Horn would be forensic chemist Lisa Perry of the Mesa Police Department, a blood spatter expert who could detail Travis' movements during the attack based on the blood patterns in the bathroom. Her opinion was that the attack began in the shower, where Travis' blood was first shed, and moved to the sink area, where Arias repeatedly stabbed him in the back as he stood over the vanity. Somehow Travis made his way down the hall toward the master bedroom until collapsing at the doorway, where his throat was slashed. Arias dragged him back down the hall-way to the sink area, where she shot him in the face, with the ejected casing landing on blood already pooling on the floor. Perry's testimony would be offered to help fill the gaps left by the thick "fog" that prevented Arias from remembering most of what happened during the attack.

Testimony from Jodi Legg, a forensic chemist with the Mesa Police Department, would be another scientific piece in prov-ing that Arias was the person who murdered Travis. Legg had examined the biological evidence collected at the scene and found a mixture of Travis' and Arias' blood on the hair and the bloody palm print found on the wall in the hallway. The significance of this was that it placed Arias at the scene at the time of the killing, when blood was being shed.

Perhaps the most important pieces of evidence during my case were the deleted photographs that Mesa Police detective Michael Melendez retrieved from the memory card of Travis' camera. The photographs helped prove that Arias was the person who killed Travis on the afternoon of June 4, 2008, and at least two of those pictures showed how she dragged his limp body down the hallway after she rendered him uncon-scious. If there was any doubt as to her identity, the photos of their afternoon sexual foray showed not only her private parts but her face as well. Melendez would also discuss the photos of Travis in the shower, which established that he and Arias were still together in the late afternoon, at 5:30 P.M., minutes before Travis was killed, as shown in the three inadvertent photographs.

Once Arias was shown to be the killer, the emphasis of my presentation would shift to proving that she premeditated the murder. Though I would only bring up the gas cans and the three messages she sent to Travis after his death during my cross-examination of Arias, I still had several pieces of evidence that I was going to introduce during my case in chief to demonstrate her planning of the murder. I would call witnesses to testify to the change of Arias' hair color, her selection of a rental car location that was far away from Yreka, her removal of the floor mats from the rental car, her theft of the gun from her grandparents' home, turning off her phone to avoid being tracked, and her removal of the license plates from the rental car.

The testimony of Detective Nathan Mendes of the Siskiyou County Sheriff's Office would serve to point out other steps Arias had taken in furtherance of her plan to kill Travis. Detective Mendes held one of the keys to establishing the foundation for my theory about the gas cans, and through his testimony I intended to introduce a photograph of the Airwalk shoebox found in Arias' bedroom at her grandparents' house and the twenty-two receipts from Arias' trip that had been found inside. He had been one of the officers who assisted the Mesa Police Department in the execution of the search warrant on the Pine Street home on July 15, 2008, and could speak to the items that had been found. My plan was to ask him about the receipts while he was on the stand in an expeditious fashion, almost as if they were an afterthought, so once they were in evidence, I could come back to them later, after I had introduced the borrowing of the gas cans through my cross-examination of Darryl Brewer.

Through Detective Mendes' testimony, I also wanted to show that Arias' decision to rent a car at the Budget counter at the airport in Redding, located ninety minutes from Yreka, instead of from one of two local rental agencies, Hertz and Enterprise, was a deliberate act to avoid being recognized. Officer Mendes was the detective who had assembled the photo lineup that included the booking photo of Arias. He had shown it

to the Budget rental agency employee Ralphael Colombo on
July 17, 2008, and would testify to Colombo's positive identification of Arias and to his statement that she was a blonde
when she rented the car from him on June 2, 2008.

Like Mendes, Colombo would travel from California to
testify about his interactions with Arias when she rented the
vehicle and when she returned it to the counter at the Redding
airport. He would confirm his immediate selection of Arias
from the photo lineup and that her hair was blonde when she
rented the car. Colombo would also testify about his observations when Arias returned the car on June 7, with four missing floor mats and an unanticipated number of miles on the
odometer.

Officer Kevin Friedman of the Yreka Police Department
would speak to his role in the investigation of the purported
burglary of Arias' grandparents' house on May 28, 2008,
during which her grandfather's .25-caliber semiautomatic
handgun was reportedly taken.

Arias' traffic stop in West Jordan, Utah, would be introduced through the testimony of Officer Michael Galieti, who
would describe how he pulled her over after observing that her
rear license plate was upside down.

Ryan Burns stood out as an example of Arias' pattern of
chasing love from state to state, and was illustrative of her
tendency to jump into a relationship and imagine it being more
than it was. Burns would testify that Arias was calm when
she arrived in Utah after the murder. And he could speak to
her aggressive pursuit of sexual intimacy almost immediately
upon her arrival in Utah. This emerging picture of Arias was
at odds with her self-portrayal as a woman who submitted
herself sexually to the whims of men.

Burns would also indicate that he was familiar with the
route between Los Angeles and Salt Lake City, which was a
straight drive north on Interstate 15 all the way to Utah, with

no need to exit the freeway. Burns could also refute any claim that Arias was either on the road to Utah or with him at the time of the killing. He was the person who initially informed me about the traffic stop by Officer Galieti of the West Jordan Police Department. He also saw a cut on Arias' hand when she arrived in Utah, when he also immediately noticed that she had changed her hair color to brunette.

Detective Larry Gladysh of the Mesa Police Department would testify that powering off a cell phone would make it impossible for police to trace its movements. He would also tell jurors that Arias' cell phone was powered off just west of the Arizona border and turned on just south of the Nevada border. I would also call the custodians of records for the cell phone companies Verizon and Sprint to introduce the phone records should there be any question about the calls that were made.

I don't normally script the order in which I call witnesses to the stand. It is almost impossible to adhere to it, because testimony may be longer or shorter than anticipated and scheduling conflicts usually arise, making it impossible to pinpoint an exact date and time the next person will be called. I made an exception in this prosecution for the testimony of Arias' friend Leslie Udy, because I wanted her to be last person the jury would hear before turning the case over to defense counsel.

After Arias was "notified" of Travis' death, she called Udy on the morning of June 10. Udy would recall that Arias was distraught and crying, asking how somebody could do that to Travis. As she sobbed, she told Udy that Travis was such a wonderful person, and she couldn't imagine why anyone would do that to him. Udy received a second call from Arias around 2 P.M. on June 11, during which Arias was hysterically crying, explaining that this was the time of day that she would talk to Travis and now he was dead. She said she had lost her best friend and didn't know what to do.

As Arias sobbed about losing her "best friend," she knew
she was the sole cause of her supposed anguish, because she
was the one who had ended Travis' life. This juxtaposition
spoke volumes, and it would be a powerful image on which to
end the presentation of my case, because it demonstrated how
deceitful Arias could be when it was to her benefit.

━━━━━━━━━━

CHAPTER 15

When jury selection in the trial of Jodi Arias for the murder of Travis Alexander began on December 10, 2012, it had been 1,646 days since his body was found and the investigation into his death had gotten under way. In that time, I had looked at this case from every angle and in every light. I'd spent nights and weekends at the office and nearly memorized every item related to the investigation. After four and a half years of preparation, I could say that I felt ready to prosecute the state's case.

It is always hard to know how a trial will go at the start. A trial is a drama that unfolds around you, and even as a key player I recognize that I can only control my piece of it. All I can do is prepare as completely as possible and hope that my legal skills and mastery of the facts are enough so that justice will prevail. At the same time, I always try to recognize that things will happen around me that are unpredictable, and I need to be ready for whatever comes up. That's one of the reasons I like working alone—it allows me to think on my feet and react accordingly, without consulting anyone, as the case develops.

In the weeks leading up to jury selection, I'd heard talk that the media intended to follow the Arias case closely, so I anticipated there would be a fair number of reporters in the courtroom for the start of jury selection. As it turned out, there weren't. In spite of the media's early interest in Arias and the requests for cameras to be in the courtroom to cover the proceedings gavel to gavel, only Grace Wong, a field producer from TruTV, was present in the gallery to cover the proceedings on that first day of jury selection. I had seen this before with the media expressing an interest during the early stages of a case, only to turn their attention to more current news events when the trial date arrived. A lot of time had passed, and apparently the interest had gone with it.

Jury selection in capital cases is a burdensome process that requires people to show up in court and detail private aspects of their lives in a public forum, as a court reporter writes down their every word. So it is understandable that some are reluctant to share the intimate details of their life in front of a roomful of strangers and request to provide their answers in private, which calls for the other jurors to step out of the room while the judge, staff, and litigants remain behind to hear their responses. This is as private as the process gets.

During my first interaction with potential jurors, I am always mindful that they are regular people and that even the subtlest gesture or facial expression may be misinterpreted, resulting in hard feelings towards me even before my first word has been spoken about the facts. I am careful not to show emotion by laughing, smiling, or continually speaking to the detective sitting next to me at prosecution table. The courtroom is no place to be amiably chatting or chuckling.

After each group of jurors filed into the courtroom of the Honorable Sherry K. Stephens and at the judge's request I would stand up and identify myself as the prosecutor in the case, taking that opportunity to also introduce Detective Flores, by telling the prospective panel that the detective would sit with me throughout the trial. My introduction was followed by that of defense counsel and their client. Laurence Nurmi was still lead counsel, but he was now assisted by Jennifer Willmott, who had been assigned to the case in January 2012, replacing Victoria Washington. As was the case with Nurmi, I had never tried a case against Willmott, and our interactions in the Arias case had been limited to our status conferences.

In most cases, the selection process eliminates around fifty of the prospective jurors from each group of the approximately one hundred who make the trek from the first-floor office of the jury commissioner to Judge Stephens' courtroom on the fifth floor. Those whom the court determines to have a hardship that precludes them from serving are dismissed, with those remaining instructed to return downstairs to the jury commissioner's area on the first floor to complete a lengthy questionnaire. Before those individuals are allowed to leave the courtroom, they are ordered to return the following week to be questioned further based on the answers they provide on the questionnaire.

Copies of the completed questionnaires are provided to the prosecutor and defense counsel for review so that each side can be prepared to question the potential jurors based on their answers. Reading the questionnaires is a tedious and time-consuming undertaking, and while I can ask a paralegal or another prosecutor to assist me, by doing so I risk missing information that may affect my decision as to whether that person should serve on the panel. As a result of this approach I spend what seems like endless hours reviewing the thirty-page questionnaires to make sure I don't miss anything important.

The juror questionnaires address many areas, including the person's views on the death penalty and whether they would always vote for or against the death penalty without regard to the evidence presented at trial. In a capital case like Arias', this is always an important point for both sides, as both the prosecution and the defense screen out people who are strongly biased in one direction or another.

There are also questions about the jurors' exposure to media coverage of the case, and jurors may be excused if it seems that they might not be able to remain fair and impartial based on what they may have read or heard about the case. Arias' early television appearances on *Inside Edition* and *48 Hours* did not present a problem in picking a jury for the trial, as most jurors did not remember seeing her on television.

Jury selection in the Arias case was completed on December 20, 2012, after six days, with eighteen jurors empaneled—eleven men and seven women—who were given preliminary instructions by Judge Stephens that same day. With the date so close to Christmas, the court scheduled opening remarks for January 2, 2013.

For most people, New Year's Day is a holiday celebrating a new beginning by making resolutions, but as the year 2013 got under way, for me it was a culmination of many years of work on this case. I don't usually go out on New Year's Eve, so I spent the next day at the office going over the case one last time to make last-minute preparations.

Immediately before I went to court on Wednesday morning, January 2, I did what I always do before every court appearance and trial. I checked my hair in the small mirror I keep on the back of my office door to make sure it is neatly combed. I had been given the mirror as a joke at a Christmas office party some years back, and I have used it ever since, even though initially it was a source of teasing from my coworkers.

For the first day of the trial, I wore a blue suit, white dress shirt, and peach-colored tie, not because the ensemble held any significance, but because it was the next suit and tie in line to be worn. I see it as a cliché to choose a power tie and suit for occasions such as delivering an opening statement.

Before I left my office, I repeated the first few lines of my opening statement so that I had them on my tongue ready to deliver to the jury. After that, it was all about getting to court.

I don't remember stepping onto the elevator and hitting the button for the fifth floor, but when the doors opened, I noticed a large crowd of people mingling in the hallway outside of courtroom 5C. Immediately I knew that the quiet of jury selection had been an anomaly. The ID cards hanging from lanyards around their necks told me these people were members of the press corps, confirmed by the thick black wires running down the hallway to a satellite dish. The hallway looked as if it had been taken over, and the hum of voices bounced off the walls. *So, there is going to be gavel-to-gavel coverage,* I thought.

The scene outside the courtroom continued inside as well. I had no idea how many journalists were in the courtroom, but I could see as I entered that every seat in the five rows of the gallery was taken. Court officials had even added extra chairs, which still didn't accommodate all the people wanting to see the opening remarks. The other prosecutors from my office who had come to watch the opening remarks were forced to view the proceedings on a television in the victim's room. This was the biggest media event I'd ever seen at the Maricopa County Courthouse.

As I walked to the prosecution table, I paused to acknowledge Travis' siblings Samantha, Tanisha, and Steven, who were seated in the front row of the gallery, behind the table where Detective Flores and I would be sitting for the trial. Also in the gallery, on the other side of the aisle, was Arias' mother, Sandy, whom I recognized on sight from her July 2008 interview with Detective Flores. She had sobbed through most of their conversation, so I hoped she wouldn't cry through these proceedings as she had back then. Catching a quick glimpse of Arias, I noticed that she appeared demure, quite different from the person jurors would soon see in the photographs of her lying naked and splayed out on Travis' bed.

Arias is permitted to wear street clothes for trial, and her librarian look, which included a modest black top, a face free of makeup, and her straight brown hair cut with wispy bangs, was not lost on me. I believed her "look," which would soon include glasses, was a deliberate attempt to inspire the jury's sympathy. She sat impassively at the defense table, with Willmott, who was dressed conservatively in a royal blue skirt suit, to her immediate left. Nurmi sat in the lead counsel chair next to Willmott, dressed in a tan suit, green shirt, and green patterned tie.

Not long after Judge Stephens entered the courtroom, the proceedings got under way. But when the judge asked if I was ready to proceed with my opening statement, Nurmi stood up and took the opportunity to make an oral motion for discovery, which was denied by the judge after I explained that I had already turned over what he was seeking. As I stood up for a second time and started to speak, the judge stopped me and asked the court clerk to read the indictment to the jury setting out the first-degree murder charge. The third time was the charm, and at last I strode to the front of the jury box to deliver my opening statement.

"Good morning again," I began, referring to the other two unsuccessful tries at starting my presentation. "This is not a case of who done it. The person who done it, the person who committed this killing, sits in court today. It's the defendant, Jodi Ann Arias," I said, turning and pointing in her direction. "And the person that she done it to is an individual by the name of Travis Victor Alexander, a former boyfriend of hers, an individual that she was in love with, an individual that was a good man, an individual that was one of the greatest blessings in her life. And this love, well, she rewarded that love for Travis Victor Alexander by sticking a knife in his chest. And you know, he was a good man according to her, and with regard to being a good man, well, she slit his throat as a reward for being a good man. And in terms of these blessings, well, she knocked the blessings out of him by putting a bullet in his head during one event that occurred on June 4 of 2008," I continued, pacing the floor and gesturing with my hands to emphasize the three mortal wounds.

I had chosen my words deliberately based on what Arias had written on a card at Travis' memorial service: "Travis, you're beautiful on the inside *and* out. You always told me that. I never stopped believing in you, and I know that you always believed in me. Thank you for sharing so much. Thank you for all of your generosity. This world has been blessed because you have been here. I love you.♥"

Arias had written she loved Travis and called him a good man, a blessing in her life. So it was only fitting that I employ her words in my message to the jury.

My presentation lasted approximately one hour and twenty minutes and included a chronology of Arias' and Travis' relationship, from their meeting and courtship to Travis' gift of the Book of Mormon, which the two read together, Arias' conversion to Mormonism, and their sexual relationship.

To dramatize the brutality of the killing, I asked Detective Flores to hold up an enlarged diagram of the crime scene for jurors as I described the details of June 4, 2008. My back was to the gallery for much of my presentation, so I had no idea how people were reacting to my remarks, although I learned later that Travis' sister Tanisha had cried quietly, as did her sister Samantha.

I was told that Arias cried, too, while I was describing how she had attacked Travis as he sat naked on the floor of the shower and how, after the killing, she had dragged his body back to the shower stall. My intention was to tell the story with words rather than through pictures, because my description could be more three-dimensional, and the jury would see the disturbing photos soon enough.

"As he sat there, she took the knife and began to stab him when he was in that defenseless sitting position . . . stuck the knife in his chest. He struggled. . . . The slitting ear to ear took place. . . . And by the time she was dragging him down, pulling him down towards this area right here," I said, pointing to the blowup of the crime scene diagram, "he didn't need that shot to the head. But she had a gun somewhere. . . . She put that bullet right in his temple."

In recounting Arias' many stories, I began with her initial statement that she was not in Arizona at the time of the killing, followed by her story about the two masked intruders who killed Travis but spared her life, and finally her latest version, that she had killed Travis, but only after he attacked her and she was fighting for her life.

"It was her," I affirmed. "She is the person who actually did this. . . . She is the one who did the stabbing. She's the one that slit his throat. And she is the one that shot him."

To dramatize my concluding remarks, I showed a clip from Arias' interview with *Inside Edition*. "No jury will ever convict me, and you can mark my words on that," a much younger-looking Arias tells the interviewer with an air of confidence as she appears to suppress a smile. "No jury will convict me."

With her face frozen on the three monitors around the courtroom, I delivered my closing comment, "I also ask that you mark her words, the words that no jury will convict her, even though she has admitted that she's the person that did this after giving many different stories of what happened. And as you mark her words, I ask you while you are doing that in your final deliberations—that you remember that while you're marking the guilty verdict for her premeditated killing of Travis Alexander. Thank you."

There was no time for me to reflect on my opening statement. Even before I sat down next to Flores at the prosecution table, I was already thinking about my first witness, Mimi Hall, who was outside the courtroom and ready to testify. I was also wondering what Arias' counsel would say on her behalf. Through the years of wrangling at our status hearings, I certainly had my ideas about what direction they would take, but I was curious to see if my instincts were correct.

After a ten-minute break, it was Jennifer Willmott's turn to make her opening remarks.

"Jodi Arias killed Travis Alexander," she told the jurors.

"There is no question about it. The million-dollar question is what would have forced her to do it?"

This strident admission relieved me in a practical sense from having to prove that the petite woman sitting quietly at the defense table had done all of this, stabbing a man who was bigger than she was, dragging his body down a hallway, and stuffing it in the shower.

When I heard Willmott tell the jury of Arias' decision to take a detour to Arizona on her way to Utah, I wanted to nudge Detective Flores to signal him to listen closely.

"Travis knew that Jodi was planning a trip to Utah, 'cause they had talked about it," she informed the jurors. "He knew that she was going to stop along the way and see friends of hers. He kept asking her to stop and see him. And at the last minute, Jodi decided that she would veer off and take a short trip to Mesa to come and see Travis at his beckoning."

When I heard Willmott say that Arias' visit to Travis was a last minute decision, I thought that defense counsel must have assumed that I hadn't taken note of what had been said in the interview summaries that Arias' previous defense counsel had disclosed to me. But I had certainly given them my full attention, and I was going to wait for the opportune time to use what I knew during the trial.

Willmott continued her remarks, employing a strategy I had expected, painting Arias as a victim, a person to take pity on, someone to protect. "And through this trial you will hear that Jodi was indeed forced," she explained, putting up several of the photographs that had been retrieved from Travis' camera. "In just under two minutes we go from the last picture taken of Travis in the shower, in just under two minutes to the picture of Travis' body. You can see the foot in the front, with his head and his shoulders and blood clearly on his shoulders. In just those two minutes, Jodi had to make a choice, she would either live or she would die."

Willmott described a number of lurid sexual encounters that had allegedly occurred between the two, portraying Arias as a sexual servant, who was only doing her job by submitting to Travis' desires—and none of this was her fault. Willmott was setting up a characterization of Travis as an abuser, someone who bullied Arias into having sex with him.

"As Travis would explain to Jodi, oral sex really isn't as much of a sin for him as vaginal sex. And so he was able to convince her to give him oral sex. And later in their relationship, Travis would tell her that anal sex really isn't much of a sin compared to vaginal sex. And so he was able to persuade her to allow him to have anal sex with her."

It was a graphic start to the defense's case, and as much as I'd known that this sexualized commentary would be a part of their argument, it was still striking to hear those words said aloud in open court for the judge, jury, and spectators to hear. Ever since she'd changed her plea to self-defense, I'd assumed that tainting Travis' character would be central to her case; after all, Arias had been willing to accuse him of pedophilia, so nothing Willmott was saying was truly shocking. What I hadn't known was how they would choose to deploy these sexual details for the jury, and with these words at the start of what was sure to be a long trial, they sent a strong signal that they were going to press this point at every turn.

After hearing the sexually explicit leadoff, I felt a bit reassured, mostly because I didn't see it as the best strategy. Each of the extreme images that Willmott's words conjured up held shock value for a jury, but I'd always found that for maximum effect, you had to be careful when using extremes. Just as with showing a crime scene photo too many times, a jury can get desensitized to graphic language. I'd seen it happen before— when strong words become a refrain, sometimes they can have the opposite effect, callousing the jurors instead of persuading them.

The other risk here, which was both more subtle and more

dangerous to the defense case, was that the use of overly sex-ualized language and images could potentially overshadow the other aspect of their case, which was that Arias was sup-posedly a victim. By going so quickly and so visually to the role that sex was going to play in this case, defense counsel didn't give jurors a chance to know Arias as a person and as a woman. They allowed these supposed acts to define her, and it is always harder to be the victim when the jury can't see who you really are.

But there was no denying that this opening sent a strong signal, a shot across the bow, not just to me, but to everyone in the courtroom. Nothing would be off limits. Looking around the room at the sea of journalists, I found myself no longer surprised that the subdued atmosphere from jury selection had been abandoned. The media had come for a juicy story, and it seemed like that was exactly what the defense was going to give them. They appeared to be producing a story tailor-made for the media, and while it might play well on TV, I wasn't sure if it would do the same for the jury.

Listening to Willmott's opening statement, it confirmed my belief that Arias was going to take the stand, because now she had to tell her story. It would be impossible for Willmott to make an argument about Arias' sexual relationship with Travis in her opening remarks without Arias' testimony to back it up. Defense counsel's case would hinge on the success of Arias' appearance on the stand. It appeared they wanted to portray her as the victim, and she'd even dressed for the part.

CHAPTER 16

There was about a twenty-minute recess between Jennifer Willmott's opening statement and when I would call my first witness, Mimi Hall. Mimi had been waiting in the prosecutor's work office outside the courtroom since about lunchtime, so during the break I went to tell her that she would be testifying shortly.

When I found her, she indicated that she was nervous about taking the witness stand. I told her I understood her trepidation and suggested that we walk together to the courtroom, so she could acclimate to the setting before all of the parties returned from break. Providing testimony in court can make people anxious, and in this case the number of media in attendance and the fact that the proceedings were being broadcast to a national audience added another layer of apprehension.

Mimi reminded me of a young Sigourney Weaver. She was slight of build, with curly, shoulder-length brown hair and horn-rimmed glasses. Her anxiety seemed to ease a bit once she saw the layout of the courtroom and I explained how things would go once the proceedings resumed that afternoon.

It was just after 3:00 P.M. when Judge Stephens returned to the bench, and I called Mimi to the witness stand. I had called Mimi as my first witness because I wanted her to set the tone for my case by describing her interactions with Travis and providing the circumstances under which she had discovered his body. Through Mimi, the jury would also hear that Travis had invited her, not Arias, to accompany him on his trip to Cancún—the event that I considered the trigger for Arias' rage and what led her to make the trip to Mesa to kill him.

To dispel Arias' portrayal of Travis as sexually aggressive, I asked Mimi about his behavior on their three dates, which included hot chocolate at Barnes & Noble, a few hours of painting pottery at a local ceramics center, and an afternoon of rock climbing at an indoor facility. Mimi recounted that Travis was a "total gentleman," explaining that the only physical contact the two had was an "awkward hug" at the end of each date.

I also wanted to demonstrate Arias' pattern of confronting women she viewed as rivals. I thought back to Matthew McCartney's story of how Arias had driven hours to challenge a woman who she viewed as a threat to her relationship with McCartney, and how similar it sounded to the way she had approached Mimi at Travis' memorial service.

"Where was this service held?" I asked Mimi.

"This was at the church building where he went to church every Sunday in Mesa. It's off Guadalupe and the 202 area."

". . . And were there a lot of people there, yes or no?"

"Yes, there were a lot of people."

"And of all the people that were there, was there somebody by the name of Jodi Arias?"

"Yes."

"And is the person that you knew as Jodi Arias, is she in court today?"

"Yes . . . she is seated over there at the end of the table, and I can't see her clearly, but she's wearing black and has dark hair." Mimi pointed to Arias, who was seated at the far end of the defense table.

I asked the judge to have the record reflect that Mimi had identified the defendant as Jodi Arias. "So, you see the defendant there and do you go up to her, or does she go up to you?"

"She came up to me and she introduced herself to me."

"What did she say?"

"She said are you Mimi Hall? . . . And I said yes, and she introduced herself as Jodi Arias."

"And did she say anything else?"

"I asked her how she was doing, and she said she was upset. That was about it, though."

"Did at any time she say, 'I'm the person who killed him?' Anything like that?"

"No."

"Did she ever tell you why she was there [at the memorial service]?"

"No."

"I don't have anything else. Thank you."

As I returned to my seat, Nurmi stood and walked to the podium in the center of the courtroom to begin his cross-examination. Based on his questions, it appeared his objective was to show that Mimi's standing in the LDS Church—which included having been born into the faith and attending Brigham Young University, an institution supported by the church—commanded a certain level of respect and dictated the way that Travis viewed and treated her.

"Did he [Travis] tell you that he was having sexual relations with Jodi Arias?" he asked Mimi.

"No," she replied, appearing to grow uncomfortable.

"I'm not going to ask exactly what he said, but it was during a camping trip, if I recall correctly, that he told you he had a stalker . . . ?" Nurmi inquired.

"Yeah, he didn't say a name at all. But he was having break-fast with a couple of friends around and he told me at that point that he had a stalker. And that she had actually followed us on a date and that she knew who I was. And I told him that was really scary and that he should get a restraining order."

This line of questioning caught my attention and I wondered how far Nurmi would go into this area, which was highly in-flammatory and could hurt his client. During my initial ex-amination, I did not ask Mimi about whether she knew Arias to be a stalker or what she might have heard in that regard, because I didn't want to create any issues leading to a mistrial or being raised on appeal. Had I broached the subject first, the argument almost certainly would be that the prosecution had been unfair because these were unproven acts of domestic violence that were unrelated to the murder. But now that Nurmi was discussing Arias' stalking behavior with the witness, defense counsel was opening the door to the topic, allowing me to walk in and explore the details on my redirect examination.

"And you say that he didn't tell you—he didn't say that this was Jodi, right?" Nurmi continued.

"No, he didn't say who it was," Mimi responded. She looked frail and vulnerable, and I felt sorry that she had to be up there on the witness stand and be asked about her friend's relationship with another woman.

Nurmi showed her a page from a transcript to refresh her recollection of what she had said in an earlier interview where both he and I had been present. "You said you gave him the advice that he seek a restraining order against this stalker, right?" he asked.

"Yeah."

"Okay, and you expressed to him that you were scared of this stalker, right?"

"Scared of any stalker. It's not something you want to deal with."

"And to your knowledge, did he ever seek out a restraining order?"

"Not that I knew of, no. He told me not to be afraid."

"And your testimony is that he never said to you, Jodi Arias was his stalker, that's your testimony?"

"That's from what I can remember. I don't remember him ever saying at the time. I remember hearing the name 'Jodi.' It could have been then, but I don't actually recall," Mimi replied, adding, "The name 'Jodi' was [mentioned] the night that we found him at his house."

"Okay, thank you, Miss Hall," Nurmi said as he concluded his cross-examination.

My first question to Mimi on redirect examination continued the line of questioning that defense counsel had started when he asked her whether Travis had identified Arias as his stalker.

". . . You indicated that part of what he [Travis] told you was that this stalker was a female, right?"

"Yes."

"And what had this female done that he was warning you about?"

Before Mimi could respond, Nurmi broke in with an objection. "Beyond the scope," he told Judge Stephens.

Nurmi's objection was overruled because he had questioned Mimi about Travis' stalker.

". . . He had dated someone earlier that year," Mimi replied, referring to Travis' ex-girlfriend Lisa Andrews. "She slashed her [Andrews'] tires. She had sent threatening e-mails to both Travis and his girlfriend at the time. She had followed us on one of the first dates that we went on, and she sounded dangerous. She had broken into his e-mail account, his bank accounts. She would break into his house through the doggy door, and sleep on his couch at night without him knowing that she was there."

Having this portrait of Arias out there so early in the case enabled me to cast doubt on her portrayal as a victim. This testimony showed Arias to be a woman who not only was obsessed with Travis but would act on that obsession.

The following day, I called Detective Flores to the stand. The first area I intended to cover with him was his initial telephone conversation with Arias on June 10, 2008, the one he had with her after leaving the crime scene to return her call. The jury would be hearing Arias' voice for the first time, and I wanted them to hear how engaging she could be, playing the part of the grieving ex-girlfriend.

To ensure the jury understood that Arias had brought the gun with her to Mesa, a significant step in her premeditation of the murder, I played the portion of the telephone conversation with Flores during which Arias had admitted to the detective that Travis did not have a gun in his home and did not have any other weapons. Since Willmott had admitted in her opening statement that Arias had killed Travis, this meant that Arias must have brought a gun and a knife with her when she paid him the early-morning visit on June 4, 2008.

Jurors sat impassively as I cued up the recording and Detective Flores' voice came over the sound system: "Um, do you know if he had any weapons in the house?"

To which jurors heard Arias reply, "Uh, his two fists."

"That's it? No handguns or rifles?"

"No, he wasn't one to keep any of that. . . . No, only his two fists. . . . No, he was more into like wrestling and UFC and he had a, you know . . . he said he just bought a punching bag and he's like . . . 'I love beating the crap out of the punching bag,' you know."

For the most part, Nurmi's cross-examination of Flores centered on Arias' comment about Travis' "two fists" as being his only weapon and Travis "beating the crap out of the punching bag" as a way to illustrate why Arias was scared of him. But the fact remained that Arias had admitted to Flores that there was no gun in Travis' house, which could only mean one thing—that she had brought the gun with her with the intention of killing him.

Nurmi's strategy of soiling Travis' character was evident in his final set of questions to Detective Flores, when he asked about an agreement Arias had with Travis to clean his house. "Do you remember whether or not she had to do it in a French maid outfit?" Nurmi asked, referring to the photograph of the French maid outfit that Arias discussed with Detective Flores during their July 15, 2008, interview in Yreka.

Pausing as if to search his memory, the detective responded, "That doesn't sound familiar to me."

Later in the questioning, immediately before ending his cross-examination, Nurmi asked about an instant messenger conversation between Travis and Arias. Although the conversation he was referencing had occurred via instant messenger, Nurmi referred to it as an e-mail communication when he asked, "Okay, do you remember seeing the e-mails in which Mr. Alexander referred to Miss Arias as a three-hole wonder?"

"Yes," Flores replied matter-of-factly.

"As a slut?"

"Yes."

"As a whore?"

"Yes."

"Thank you, Detective."

It was clear that Nurmi's objective was to pick up where Willmott's opening remarks had left off in painting Travis as a bad person, but introducing Travis' derogatory statements to Arias so early in the proceedings seemed a poor strategic decision, because as the trial progressed, Nurmi would do it so often that it became something he appeared to like repeating for its own sake, which lessened its shock value as well as its impact.

When court reconvened that afternoon to continue with my redirect examination of Detective Flores, I was eager to give jurors some insight into what had motivated Travis' offensive missives to Arias, by providing the context in which they were written. While I knew that there was nothing I could do to eliminate those words from playing a part in the trial, I hoped that offering a sense of what was driving Travis' emotions would soften their harshness.

(*Above*) Travis Alexander's house in Mesa, Arizona, cordoned off with crime scene tape as police investigators execute a search warrant on June 10, 2008.

(*Below*) The garage through which Mimi Hall and her friends gained entry into Travis' house on the evening on June 9, 2008.

(*Above*) Travis' journal found by police inside his black Toyota Prius parked inside the garage of his home.

(*Below*) Travis' Bible was found by police on the passenger seat of his car.

(*Above*) The sliding glass door in the back of Travis' house that Arias used at times to enter the home, showing the "doggy insert."

(*Below*) Crime scene photo of the first floor of Travis' house, with Napoleon's "doggy" gates blocking entry to the living/dining room area and the upright steam cleaner visible in the background.

(*Above*) The CDs of photographs of Arias' and Travis' travels that Arias brought with her on June 4, 2008, to view with Travis, indicating that she had planned to visit him that day.

(*Below*) A check for $200 that Jodi Arias wrote to Travis as partial payment for his BMW, which police found in a drawer of Travis' desk in his home office on the first floor of the house.

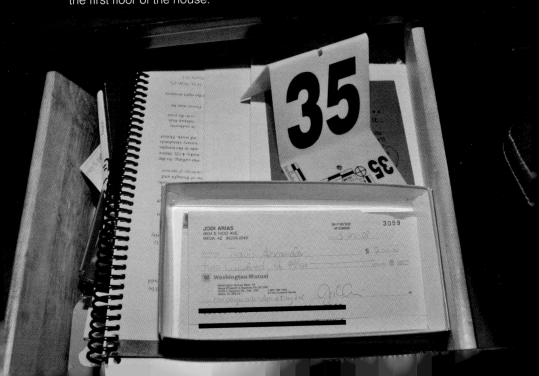

(*Above*) The screening room on the second floor, where Travis would hold parties, showing the double doors leading to his bedroom.

(*Below*) The view upon entering Travis' bedroom during my walk-through on June 10, 2008, with the bed stripped of its sheets and comforter.

(*Above*) Crime scene photo of Travis' bedroom, showing the door to the walk-through closet, and the bloody ovoid stain on the carpet near the breech to the tile hallway.

(*Right*) The blood-streaked hallway connecting the master bedroom to the bathroom.

(*Above*) Crime scene photo of the vanity and sink area of Travis' master bathroom streaked with blood patterns showing that Travis stood at the sink while Arias continued her attack.

(*Below*) A close-up of the sink area with various bloodstain patterns.

(*Above*) The .25 caliber casing found resting on top of blood on the bathroom floor near the sink area.

(*Below*) The shower stall after Travis' body was removed, showing the plastic tumbler Arias used to clean the scene.

(*Above*) Police found Travis' Sanyo camera amid wet laundry in the washing machine of the pantry on the first floor.

(*Below*) A close-up of the camera in the washing machine.

(*Above*) One of the photographs Arias took of Travis in the shower minutes before she killed him.

(*Below*) The first inadvertent photograph showing the ceiling above the shower snapped at the inception of Arias' attack on Travis.

(*Left*) The second inadvertent photograph snapped as Jodi Arias stands in the hallway at Travis' head, after she has slit his throat. Her pants with the stripe down the leg and her stocking foot can be seen in the foreground.

(*Left*) The third inadvertent photo shows Arias dragging Travis' body down the hallway as blood flows down his back.

(*Above*) The house on Pine Street where Arias lived with her grandparents. The home was the scene of a burglary staged by Arias on May 28, 2008, during which she took a .25 caliber gun that she used to shoot Travis.

(*Below*) Police found an Airwalk shoebox filled with receipts from her trip to Arizona in Arias' Pine Street apartment. The box included gas receipts and a receipt from the Walmart store in Salinas, California, where Arias bought a third gas can.

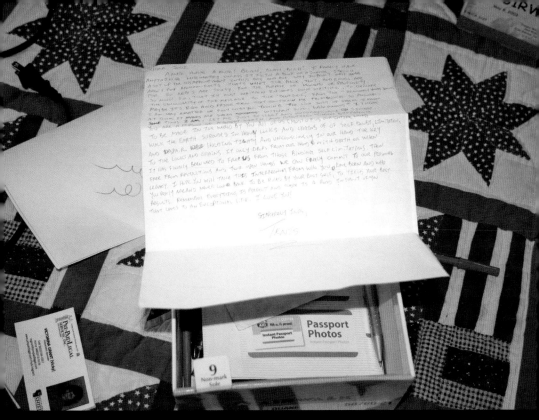

(*Above*) A letter written by Travis that Arias kept in the Airwalk shoebox along with the receipts.

(*Below*) The flyer from Travis' memorial service that Arias kept in her bedroom.

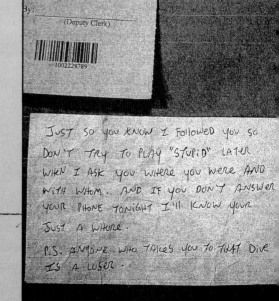

(*Above left*) The receipt from the Walmart in Salinas showing that Arias bought a third gas can for her trip to Arizona.

(*Above right*) The 3" x 5" card confiscated by intelligence officers during a search of Jodi Arias' cell at the Maricopa County Jail.

(*Right*) Jodi Arias smiles in her booking photo at the Siskiyou County Sheriff's Office on July 15, 2008.

(*Above left*) Mesa Police Detective Michael Melendez, who recovered the photographs from the memory card of the camera found in the washing machine.

(*Above right*) Siskiyou County Sheriff's Detective Nathan Mendes, the lead investigator assisting the Mesa Police Department in the execution of the search warrant on Arias' home.

(*Right*) Mesa Police Detective Esteban Flores, who was the case agent in the investigation, and his fifteen-year-old son Tony, who was killed in a zip line accident during Arias' second trial. Detective Flores continued to participate in the trial even after the tragic death of his son.

(*Right*) Jodi Arias looking at the family of Travis Alexander as the jury is seated during the aggravation phase of the trial on May 15, 2013.
(AP Photo/ The Arizona Republic, David Wallace, Pool)

(*Below*) Returning to the prosecution table after one of the many bench conferences with Judge Stephens.
(AP Photo/ The Arizona Republic, Rob Schumacher, File)

I showed Flores a copy of the transcript of the instant messages the two had exchanged, and I asked him, "Why was the comment made as indicated in that document?"

After an objection by Nurmi, I directed Flores' attention to the bottom of page 8 of the instant messenger conversation I had marked as an exhibit and handed it to him for his review.

Flores spent a few seconds reading the passage before responding. "He [Travis] references being used by Arias," he replied.

"What is he saying?" I asked, directing Flores to read aloud from the conversation.

" 'I think that I was little more than a dildo with a heartbeat to you,' " he recited from the instant message.

"And that is what he is saying to her?"

"Yes."

"And the previous pages, pages one and two and three, is there—do they talk about whether or not to tell the truth?"

"Yes."

Before I could make my point, Nurmi interjected with another objection, which the judge overruled.

"And in terms of the reference to the three-hole wonder . . . what is the context of that comment?" I asked Flores.

"Travis is complaining about her lying to him."

And with that, I ended this first portion of Flores' testimony.

Over the next several days, I called a number of witnesses to introduce the evidence that had been collected at the crime scene to show it had been Arias who had killed Travis, among them was the expert who discussed the blood-spatter patterns that helped explain Travis' movements during the attack, the fingerprint technician who identified the palm print on the west wall as belonging to Arias, and a DNA expert who analyzed the hair and blood on the palm print and matched them to Arias.

My next witness was Mesa Police Detective Michael Melendez. I began my direct examination of Melendez by asking
about the incriminating photographs he had retrieved from
Travis' Sanyo camera. I also asked Melendez to explain the five
steps that Arias had taken to erase pictures from the camera,
as well as the process he had used to retrieve those photos from
the unallocated space on the camera's memory card—no small
feat in light of the fact that Arias had put the camera through
the wash cycle with bleach. Another point I made through
Melendez's testimony was that Arias had not deleted all the
photos on the camera's memory card, only those that were
taken on June 4, 2008, which implicated her in the murder.

It was unavoidable that the explicit nature of some of the
photographs caused a stir in the courtroom, especially the
ones of the afternoon sex session, which included close-ups of
Arias' breasts and vaginal area, along with photos of Travis
and Arias posing nude on Travis' bed with a tube of K-Y jelly
in the foreground. By introducing all the photos—including
those of a sexual nature, the first of which was time-stamped
at 1:44:52 P.M.—I wanted to establish that Travis and Arias
had spent a substantial amount of time together that day. And
during that whole time, Arias had the gun and knife stashed
somewhere nearby, ready to access them when the moment
was right.

I followed up that first set of photographs with the introduction of the pictures of Travis in the shower, with the first one
bearing a time-stamp of 5:22:24. Travis appeared very much
at ease and altogether defenseless, without so much as a layer
of clothing to protect him as he poses nude in the shower for
what the defendant had described to Detective Flores during
their interview on July 16, 2008, as a "classy photo shoot." The
last photograph in that series, which was taken approximately
eight minutes later at 5:30:30, does not show Travis' face, only
his torso and buttocks as he sits on the shower floor. Just forty-
four seconds later, the next photograph was snapped, which

was the first of a set of three inadvertent pictures that capture
parts of Arias' attack at three separate moments.

In displaying this final set of photos, I wanted to show that
less than a minute had elapsed between the time Arias admitted holding the camera to when the initial inadvertent photograph was snapped.

As I showed him the first of the three inadvertent photographs, I asked Detective Melendez, "What do you see there?"

"It's the ceiling area and the upper wall portion of the bathroom."

"And the time?" I asked, making sure to establish that it
had been forty-four seconds since the last posed picture of
Travis in the shower was taken.

"5:31:14," he replied, confirming the time gap.

I went from the photo of the bathroom ceiling to discussing
the second inadvertent photograph, which showed a stocking
foot in front of Travis' head, blood spilling from his neck onto
his right shoulder, as he lay lengthwise along the hallway with
his feet toward the bathroom. I asked, "When you recovered
this photograph, were you able to know or tell whether or not
the camera, when it snapped the photograph, was it right side
up or was it upside down?"

"It was upside down."

"And how do you know that?"

"Because when I looked at the original image, it was upside
down." This meant Arias had carried the camera throughout
the attack until she apparently dropped it as she went to drag
his body back down the hallway.

"And this area down here," I asked, pointing to Travis' right
shoulder and the blood streaming to the tile floor. ". . . Can
you tell what this is?"

". . . It's a stain. It looks like blood," he answered, knowing it was blood, but not committing to it because he hadn't
tested it.

When asked about the third and last inadvertent photograph, Detective Melendez explained that this showed Arias continuing to drag the body toward the sink area.

All of these photographs, starting with the ones taken in the early afternoon to those in the early evening, were so incriminating that it was clear why Arias was so concerned with wanting to look at them during her interviews with Detective Flores in Yreka and why she came up with the excuse that she had killed Travis in self-defense. Having these graphic photographs now in front of the jury, I was interested to see how defense counsel would deal with them, since they contradicted Arias' assertion that she had been the victim. She obviously wasn't being forced to pose for the afternoon nude photographs, and she showed her physical strength as she dragged Travis' limp 189-pound body down the hallway.

In her cross-examination of Detective Melendez, Jennifer Willmott focused on questions related to the time gap between the last photograph of Travis in the shower and the first inadvertent photograph of the bathroom ceiling, apparently hoping to signal to the jury that while the pictures placed Arias in the bathroom of the master bedroom, they didn't capture the attack in its entirety, allowing Arias to argue what may have happened during that undocumented period of time. It would have been fruitless for Willmott to challenge any of the photographs, so she resorted to pointing out what she labeled as a "forty-five second gap" between the pictures, because that was the only unaccounted time period that would allow Arias to make her self-defense claim.

Because the case was being televised, I was the subject of media scrutiny almost from the inception of the trial, particularly with regard to my courtroom presentation, which was being described as too animated and at times combative. The criticism was brought to my attention so that I might conform my style to what some in the media thought was a better way to approach the prosecution of the case. I was a little taken aback by the criticism, as this had always been my approach and juries seemed to have appreciated the passion I had displayed during my previous presentations. I was not putting on a show because the media was in the courtroom, but was trying the case as I would any other. I had to follow the style of prosecution that had worked well for me many times before, so I ignored the criticism, always reminding myself that it was the jury's opinion that mattered.

My conduct in the courtroom would come under further scrutiny during my redirect examination of Detective Melendez.

As I was holding Travis' camera in my hand, I suddenly dropped it on the floor, to the surprise of everyone in the courtroom, and asked the detective, "Did that take forty-five seconds, sir?" My dramatic gesture drew a strong objection from Willmott.

"Judge, I am going to object. That's evidence that was just dropped on the floor," Willmott shouted, an objection that the judge immediately overruled.

I hadn't planned to drop the camera. I did it in response to Willmott's implication during her cross-examination that it had been Travis who had initiated a confrontation during the forty-four-second gap. It was a way of illustrating that although Detective Melendez did not know what had happened during those forty-four seconds, whatever had happened occurred unexpectedly, just like the camera hitting the floor. And it showed that just as everyone in the courtroom had been caught by surprise, so had Travis when Arias attacked him with the knife.

CHAPTER 17

The case I had presented thus far was based in large part on the investigation by the Mesa Police Department and left little room for the jurors to conclude that anyone other than Jodi Arias was solely responsible for killing Travis Alexander. But there was still the issue of premeditation for the jury to consider and decide, and with that in mind, I turned to the efforts of other agencies that had assisted in the inquiry, including the Yreka Police Department, the Siskiyou County Sheriff's Office, and the Maricopa County Office of the Medical Examiner.

Dr. Kevin Horn, a graduate of the University of Maryland, had been with the Maricopa County Office of the Medical Examiner since 2001. My objective in calling Dr. Horn was to describe Travis' many injuries, the order in which they occurred, and how these injuries led to Travis' death. Dr. Horn would also be able to address the defense's claim that he had given erroneous information to Detective Flores that contradicted his findings with regard to the sequence of the injuries Travis sustained.

With Dr. Horn on the stand, I moved to introduce forty-one autopsy photos to supplement his testimony. There were photographs showing the injuries to Travis' head and body, as well as photographs of several X-rays that indicated where the bullet had come to rest in his left cheek. I began my presentation by putting the first photo of Travis' face onto the ELMO courtroom system, which projected it onto the three monitors strategically placed around the courtroom. The ELMO was connected to a large movie-style screen that dropped down from the ceiling for jurors to view, as well as to two TV monitors, one behind the witness stand and the other facing the gallery. This first picture was a close-up shot of Travis' face, which appeared purple and splotchy in areas and showed the gunshot wound above his right eyebrow.

I saw Travis' siblings in the first and second rows out of the corner of my eye and realized the presentation was affecting them, as both Samantha and Tanisha had started to silently cry. I know that for family members and friends of the victims in the courtroom listening to the testimony is never easy. Still, I had a responsibility to present the best evidence to support my case, and I focused on that.

Having established Travis' identity by this first photo, I moved to the photographs of the X-rays, which would identify any foreign objects in either his head, neck, or chest, the areas that had sustained the mortal injuries. The most significant of the three was a frontal view of the head, which showed that the bullet had gone through the brain and come to rest just inside Travis' left cheek. According to Dr. Horn's testimony, the path that the bullet traveled was a downward trajectory, indicating that the muzzle of the gun was above the head when the shot was fired. Because she was at least two inches shorter than Travis, this trajectory implied that Arias stood over him as she fired the gun.

Before we talked about the multiple injuries he observed during his visual examination, I asked him to explain how he determines whether a wound has been inflicted before or after death. "If there's hemorrhaging associated with an injury, then it is before death," he said.

"What is it that causes a person to hemorrhage . . . ?"

"If you have a heartbeat, you are going to have blood flow to the area that's injured, and so you have blood flow from an injury. So if the skin is cut or torn, there will be a great deal of blood that will come from an injury in a living person," Dr. Horn clarified. "A deceased person will lose some blood but not a great deal."

"If an individual is dead, and somebody applies some force, hits them, are they going to bruise necessarily or not?" I asked.

"There may be something that would look like a bruise, but it will not be as large and the color will be different in a deceased person, because there is no blood flow to the area."

"Are you familiar with the term 'defensive wound'?" I asked, eager to have Dr. Horn speak to the deep incisions on Travis' left hand as illustrated by the next autopsy photo I put up for the jurors.

"Yes," Dr. Horn replied. "They're based largely on location on the body. If you have injuries to the back of the forearms or to the palms or backs of the hands, you can have gunshot wounds in those locations, or in the case of an assault with a knife or an edged weapon, you can have cuts or incised injuries to the back of the palms or backs of the forearm. And it's consistent with someone trying to either grab the knife or fend off wounds—or fend off injury."

To illustrate the concept of defensive wounds, I pointed Dr. Horn to the photo of Travis' left hand and asked him to explain the injuries in the image. Dr. Horn determined that all the injuries on the left hand were consistent with defensive wounds. Dr. Horn couldn't identify the kind of blade that was used to inflict the injuries, and could only say that it was a "sharp-edged object."

Speaking about all of the wounds on Travis' left hand, I asked, "Are they consistent with defensive wounds?"

"Yes."

"And does that mean that Mr. Alexander was alive at the time these injuries were inflicted?"

"I believe he was."

I next displayed a photo of Travis' naked body lying faceup

on the autopsy table showing the areas from the top of the head to just below his genitals. A number of incision-type injuries and stab wounds were visible in this photo, including the ear-to-ear gash to Travis' throat. There was a perceptible reaction in the courtroom, and I could feel the tension as I began asking Dr. Horn to provide details of each one.

He began by describing a one-inch, superficial injury on the right shoulder, before moving on to the three stab wounds to the chest, starting with the one right near the biceps.

"That one goes all the way to the breastbone," he said. "But does not go all the way to the chest cavity. It would not be fatal."

The same could not be said for a second, deeper wound in the middle of the chest area that he described as a "stab wound."

"That one actually penetrates a major vessel coming into the heart," he said as he explained how the vein drains into the heart.

"So what happens when the knife goes in and causes this amount of damage . . . ?" I asked.

"Well, depending on the position of the body, you may have significant internal bleeding. Or, if the person is leaning forward, they may bleed outside the body, because there's a tract leading from that vessel outside. But this was a major vessel. It's not going to bleed as fast as an artery, but it will bleed a considerable amount."

"With regard to this considerable amount of bleeding that's going on, is this a wound that could kill this person?" I continued.

"Yes."

"And do you have an estimate or is there any science out there that tells you, well, this type of wound, given what I know about it, would take x amount of time (for death to ensue)."

"No," Dr. Horn replied. "It depends on so many factors. It depends on the person's health. It depends on the care that they received. It depends on their blood volume to begin with, and the position of their body."

This was an important detail to spell out, because I wanted to establish that Travis had been experiencing mental anguish and excruciating physical pain after the initiation of the attack, proving he was the one who needed to defend himself, not Arias, as she alleged. Dr. Horn went on to describe that while "eventually" unconsciousness would result from the wound, it wouldn't happen right away.

"When you say eventually, do you have an estimate, maybe minutes, seconds, between the time of infliction and the time that he lapsed into unconsciousness?" I asked.

"If that were the only wound, and it's not, probably a few minutes, because we're dealing with a vein and not an artery, so it's a lower-pressure system, so blood loss is slower. . . . With this wound to the heart, he should have been able to get his hands up and attempt to defend himself."

"If he was in a seated position when this wound was inflicted, would he have the ability, even though this was inflicted, to get up and walk somewhere or move quickly somewhere as a matter of fact?"

"Yes."

Dr. Horn's answer, when considered along with the evidence collected at the scene, confirmed the sequence of the mortal wounds. While the stab wound to the chest would eventually be fatal, Travis would still have been conscious at first, giving him the opportunity to grab at the knife, as shown by the defensive wounds on his left hand. He also had time to make his way to the vanity, where he stood bleeding over the sink while Arias stabbed him repeatedly in the back, resulting in the type of blood-spatter patterns identified by Lisa Perry on the mirror and sink.

The large ovoid stain on the carpet at the threshold between the bathroom hallway and the master bedroom confirms that after standing at the sink Travis got as far as the doorway before collapsing to the floor, where Arias slit his throat from ear to ear, causing his neck to bleed profusely. The left palm print swathed in Travis' and Arias' blood on the west wall, along with the inadvertent photographs, detail Arias' next move, which was to drag the body back down the hallway into the bathroom.

She stopped dragging his body in front of the sink long enough to shoot him in the head while he was on the ground, with the downward trajectory of the bullet leaving no doubt that she stood over him when she fired the single shot. The casing from the semiautomatic gun was ejected, landing in a pool of Travis' blood that he had previously shed. She completed her ghastly pilgrimage by dragging the body the rest of the way and shoving it into the shower, where it stayed until it was found five days later.

Dr. Horn discussed other nonlethal wounds, which included a five and three quarter inch puncture by the belly button that he believed had been inflicted from left to right and slightly downward, as well as contusions on the right leg that were consistent with the body having been dragged.

Travis had also sustained a "grouping" of nine injuries to the back, which were visible in the next photograph I displayed. "More likely than not they occurred close in time and they—a lot of them, most of them, have the same orientation," Dr. Horn explained, referring to a cluster of nine wounds on the upper back. "In general, except for one exception I can see at the lower edge, they are oriented exactly the same direction. They are in a diagonal extending from the right shoulder toward the lower left side of the back."

From Dr. Horn's testimony, it was clear that Arias had the knife in her right hand when she inflicted those wounds as he stood facing the sink with his back turned which created the blood-spatter patterns in and around the sink area.

To illustrate this theory, I did a demonstration for the jury, motioning with my right hand as if I were holding a knife and repeatedly stabbing in a downward motion. "And these injuries that we're talking about coming this way like that, could they be consistent with an individual having his back, as I have to you, turned to the attacker and the attacker is stabbing him like that?" I asked Dr. Horn.

"Yes . . . we have nine injuries and they are all clustered together. They're in the center," he explained, indicating their location on Travis' upper back. ". . . They're all about the same depth. They are about an inch and they are going into the back part of the ribs, and the spine, the spinal bone, and stopped there. And none of them . . . entered the chest cavity."

Of the two fatal stab wounds, the most significant one was the gaping slit to Travis' throat, which Dr. Horn described as so deep it "passes through the airway, so the windpipe is cut through."

"Let me stop you," I interjected. "When it passes through the airway, does this individual . . . lose the ability to scream at that point or not?"

"It's below the larynx, below the voice box, so yes," Dr. Horn replied. This was disturbing because it suggested that Arias cut his throat to stop him from calling out for help as he struggled for his life.

"And if this person—well, this person is alive at this point, according to you, right? He's still alive?"

"Yes."

In a literal sense, this left Travis gasping because the air from his lungs was now being pushed through the gash in his throat rather than through his nose and mouth, causing agonal noises as the air was expelled. "Where would the blood start coming out as a result of this wound here?" I asked, still pointing to the throat.

"Well, right next to the windpipe are the major vessels of the neck. You've got the carotid artery, you've got the jugular vein . . . My examination did show that the jugular vein and the carotid artery on the right side were both cut," Dr. Horn said.

It was during this part of Dr. Horn's testimony that I noticed Arias, dressed in a blue top and black cardigan, hiding her face behind thick strands of her long brown hair, as if trying to shield herself from the graphic images being displayed for the jurors. At certain moments, she appeared to be crying behind the thick-framed glasses that she had begun wearing during the trial, raising her left hand up to her eyes as if to wipe away tears. As the presentation continued, she was either turning her face away from the images or staring blankly as they appeared on the monitor, which made me wonder if she was just feeling sorry for herself because she got caught.

I didn't let myself get distracted by her performance, and instead continued my direct examination by asking Dr. Horn to describe the depth of the wound to Travis' neck.

"It goes all the way back to the spine, so it's three inches, four inches," Dr. Horn continued. ". . . It doesn't go through the spinal cord. So it doesn't penetrate that bone. So it's actually the soft tissues in the front of the neck and then stops at the bone."

"Once this was inflicted on Mr. Alexander, is this something that's number one, rapidly fatal and number two, what about lapsing into unconsciousness? If you could talk to us about those two things."

"He has two major vessels in his throat that have been cut. He's going to lose a great deal of blood very quickly. He's going to lose consciousness within seconds likely, and then die a few minutes later."

"In terms of unconsciousness, how much time are we talking about?"

"A few seconds, probably."

We had talked about the two of the three mortal injuries, the stab wound to the chest and the slitting of the throat. Now,

I introduced a photo that depicted the gunshot wound visible just above Travis' right eyebrow.

"And what's the trajectory of this gunshot wound?" I asked Dr. Horn.

"It passes down through the skull, passes through the face and downward, and to the left, and terminates in the left cheek."

Dr. Horn told jurors he didn't know the distance from the muzzle of the gun to the temple where the bullet entered the head, but he was able to determine the trajectory. "The problem in this case is that the brain was decomposed," he explained. "And the brain is a very soft structure to begin with, so it falls apart very rapidly after death. So, I was not able to see a track through the brain. But just because the bullet passes through the front of the skull where the brain normally would be, I have to conclude that the brain was perforated."

"And, if the brain is perforated, what would happen to this individual once he was shot?"

"He would be incapacitated," Dr. Horn replied.

"Went down?"

"Yes."

"Immediately?"

"Rapidly, yes."

The path of the gunshot and whether or not it had perforated Travis' brain would be a sticking point for the defense, as their client was contending that after dropping Travis' camera during their picture-taking session in the shower, Travis had become enraged and chased her to the bedroom and around the closet. It was here that she claimed she found a gun and shot him, a scenario that would be impossible based on Dr. Horn's testimony that the gunshot would have rendered Travis incapacitated and unable to move, much less chase after her. Arias' story would also be impossible because as she told Detective Flores during her June 10, 2008, phone call, Travis didn't have a gun in the house.

"So if that's the scenario in this case, we have the defensive wounds to the hands. What does that tell you about the sequencing of these three injuries?"

"I believe the wounds to the hands must have occurred before the fatal injuries either of the head or of the throat," Dr. Horn explained.

"So what you're saying is that at some point during the stabbing, but before the slashing of the throat, and before the gunshot to the head, this individual grabbed the knife?"

"Attempted to."

It was a powerful image, Travis in the shower trying to grab at the knife as it slashed toward him.

". . . Tell me about the sequencing of events as applied to the two injuries, the one to the head and the slitting of the throat, and when this individual may have grabbed the knife or the knife was applied to his hands."

"With the throat wound and the head wound, I don't think this person could have had a purposeful activity, meaning I don't think they could have raised their arms and attempted to defend themselves. With a chest wound, that's possible, because he would not have been immediately unconscious."

"Which wound would have been first, in your opinion?"

"Well, the stab wound could have occurred and then the defensive injuries could have happened after the wound to the chest occurred."

"And then in terms of the sequence of the injuries involving the throat injury we talked about, what is your opinion?"

"Well, the throat injuries and/or the head wound are going to be immediately incapacitating and he's not going to attempt to defend himself after that. . . ."

"In terms of the shot to the head, do you have an opinion as to whether or not he was alive at the time that that shot was struck?"

"I can't say."

"Do you have an opinion as to the wound to the neck,

whether or not he was alive at the time that that was rendered, if you will?"

"I believe he was. There's a great deal of hemorrhage associated with that."

"And was he alive with regard to the one to the chest that we have been talking about?"

"Yes, I believe he was."

Beyond indicating that the strike to the chest was the first mortal blow, Dr. Horn's testimony was important in highlighting for the jury another aspect of Arias' plan to kill Travis. The mortal blows were inflicted by two separate weapons—a gun and a knife. Arias' preparedness in bringing a backup weapon should the other fail went a long way in proving that she planned the attack. The three mortal wounds, along with the more than twenty nonfatal injuries, speak to overkill and demonstrate Arias' single-minded intent to end Travis' life even if it took repeated knife strikes and switching to a gun to deliver a parting shot.

With the end of my direct examination of Dr. Horn, Jennifer Willmott rose to begin her cross-examination. As I suspected, Willmott spent a good deal of time working to infuse doubt into Horn's testimony by questioning his opinion that the bullet had perforated the brain. If she could have him admit that he was uncertain whether it had gone through the front part of the brain, she could argue in favor of Arias' claim that the bullet was the first injury she inflicted, not the last. Horn did not waver, maintaining that he could determine both the path of the bullet and when it was fired in relation to the other injuries.

". . . You didn't find any evidence of trauma or, like, a bullet track through the brain?" she asked. "Nothing so clearly defined, no hemorrhage, no foreign bodies, no metal fragments, right?"

Dr. Horn repeated his findings: ". . . For the most part, if you have a bullet pass through the brain you're not going to be standing, you're not going to be functional, you're going to fall. . . ."

"Well, just so we're clear, you don't actually have any medical evidence of it passing through the brain, right?" Willmott prodded, attempting to use earlier testimony that he had not been able to determine the bullet's track through the brain because the brain was already decomposed when he conducted his examination. Her apparent goal was to cast doubt on the entirety of Dr. Horn's findings by claiming that he was going beyond what the medical examination had revealed by maintaining that the bullet had passed through the brain.

"It had to have passed through the brain," Dr. Horn replied emphatically.

"You don't have medical evidence of that, do you?"

"I do," Dr. Horn insisted. "The skull is perforated where the brain is, so it had to have passed through the brain. . . ."

"But you have no idea—you have no medical evidence of how far or what part of the brain it exactly would have hit, right?"

"It would have passed through the right frontal lobe," Dr. Horn replied. "I don't have any evidence of hemorrhage now because of the decomposition, but it had to have passed through the brain because of the part of the skull that was injured.

"The brain in a young person especially is flush against that structure. The brain occupies the entire skull, so to have a hole in the skull here"—he indicated the area of Travis' right temple on the autopsy photo—"and then exit in here"—he pointed to Travis' left cheek—"it has to pass through the brain."

Having failed to shake Dr. Horn's testimony about the bullet track through the brain, Wilmott moved on to other topics, including testimony that had been given by Detective Flores at an earlier hearing that appeared to differ from Dr. Horn's. "Isn't it true that at some point you told Detective Flores that you believe the first wound was a shot to the head?"

"I don't remember ever saying that."

"Do you think that you never told Detective Flores that?" Willmott asked.

"I don't think that's consistent with the evidence that I have, and I don't remember ever saying anything like that," Dr. Horn repeated.

"So what your testimony is, I just want to be clear, is that you never told Detective Flores that the gunshot wound was the first wound?"

"I don't believe I ever said that, no."

"And do you remember telling Detective Flores that you knew this because the gunshot wound wouldn't have completely incapacitated somebody?"

"I don't recall saying that, either," Dr. Horn stated.

She continued to press this point, attempting to sow doubt in Dr. Horn's words or at the very least make it appear that he was contradicting himself. Horn was confident in his opinion, and eventually, having failed to shake his testimony, Willmott gave up and ended her cross-examination.

Dr. Horn's testimony that he recovered a bullet from Travis' left cheek that forensic firearms examiner Elizabeth Northcutt found to be consistent with a .25-caliber round made it important for me to bring in Officer Kevin Friedman of the Yreka Police Department. Officer Friedman testified that he responded to a "cold burglary" on May 28, 2008, at around 3:40 P.M. at the Pine Street home that Arias shared with her grandparents Caroline and Carlton Allen. He conducted the investigation, which included looking at the point of entry on the south side of the house, taking fingerprints, and determining what had been taken.

Officer Friedman portrayed the burglary as "unusual," explaining that four items had been taken—a DVD player, a stereo, thirty dollars in bills, and a black-handled .25-caliber gun—just one item from each of the home's four rooms, while "small items worth money" and a large amount of change had been left behind. Officer Friedman also testified that he thought it was strange that only one of the firearms, the black-handled .25-caliber handgun, was stolen from the dresser that had been converted into a gun cabinet, where other handguns of various calibers were also kept. The .25 caliber handgun taken from Arias' grandparents' house was the same caliber as the casing found in Travis' bathroom.

The jury already knew by Arias' own admission to Detective Flores that Travis did not have any guns in his house, leaving no doubt that she had staged the burglary in order to obtain her grandfather's gun to help carry out her plan to end Travis' life.

I continued my case by calling Detective Nathan Mendes, formerly the lead detective of the Siskiyou County Sheriff's Office's major crime unit, and had him testify to Arias' efforts to hide her identity for her trip to Mesa. Detective Mendes and his team had assisted detectives from the Mesa Police Department in locating and arresting Arias at her grandparents' home in Yreka. Detective Mendes, who was now a special agent for the United States Department of the Interior, had also helped execute the search warrant on Arias' grandparents' Pine Street home that same day, so I intended to introduce the receipts from the Airwalk shoebox through his testimony.

I showed the detective a photograph of the small bedroom in which the shoebox had been found during the execution of the search warrant. "Did police have occasion to search this box here?" I asked, pointing to the white box with the red logo that sat atop the twin bed with the patriotic red, white, and blue quilt.

"Yes, sir."

Holding up the bundle of receipts that had been found inside the box, I asked if he recognized them.

"Yes, sir. These are items taken during the service of the search warrant," he replied.

"I move for admission of Exhibits 237.001 through 237.022," I said, knowing there would be no objection because defense counsel would think those receipts actually helped corroborate Arias' story that the detour to Mesa was the result of an impromptu decision after speaking with Travis while she was already on the road.

"No objection, Your Honor," Nurmi said.

One by one, in a serial fashion, almost bordering on the mechanical, I showed each receipt to the jury through the testimony of Detective Mendes, only pausing long enough to identify the various merchants and the dates of each purchase, and sometimes mentioning Jodi Arias as the person who had made the transaction.

The first receipt I showed Detective Mendes was the one from Budget Rent-a-Car System for the Ford Focus that Arias had rented at the Redding airport. I turned my attention to establishing Arias' aim of not being recognized on the day she rented the vehicle.

"Back in June 2008, were there car rental companies in Yreka?" I asked.

"Yes, sir, there are at least two others," the detective said. ". . . There was Hertz and Enterprise."

"But there was Budget there, right?"

"No, sir."

"Are you familiar with Redding, California?" I asked.

"Yes, sir."

"In fact, you live near Redding now, or not?"

"Yes, I do."

"And with regard to Redding as it relates to Yreka, how far apart are they?"

"Just under ninety miles."

"And approximately, what is the driving time between Yreka and Redding, California?" I asked.

"In the summertime, about an hour and a half," Detective Mendes said, explaining that it could be a longer drive in the winter because there's a lot of snow in Siskiyou County.

I next asked Detective Mendes about his visit to the Budget counter at the Redding airport to show the photographic lineup of five pictures, including a mug shot of Jodi Arias labeled as number 5, to rental car agent Ralphael Colombo.

"What did he say when you showed him that in terms of the identification?"

"He said that the person that came in and rented the vehicle was number 5, except that she had blond hair when she came in and got the car," Mendes told the jury.

Moving the questioning back to the items that had been found in the Airwalk shoebox, I showed Detective Mendes the remainder of the receipts for his identification, going through the different stops that Arias had made, including the gas stations, bank, and Walmart. I didn't want to call undue attention to the transactions at the ARCO gas station in Pasadena where Arias made three separate gas purchases, so I purposely did not focus on the amount of gasoline purchased, but instead concentrated on the times those purchases were made.

I wanted the jury to see that there were three receipts associated with the three different sales, so that there would be no confusion later when I questioned Arias about the three separate purchases at ARCO, if she took the stand as I predicted. I wanted to make sure they were not thinking there had only been two sales—a credit and a cash sale—so I asked the question in a way that emphasized that the receipts were not repeats of each other, careful not to go any further. I then ended the direct examination.

From the line of questioning that Nurmi pursued during his short cross-examination, it was apparent the defense was not concerned with any of the purchases Arias made on her trip. Instead, Nurmi focused his questions on the three deposits Arias made at the Washington Mutual Bank in Pasadena. From his questions, it appeared that the source of the money was somehow significant to the defense, although for me it was just a time marker that Arias had stopped at the bank in Pasadena at 10:15 P.M. on her way to Mesa to kill Travis.

To support Detective Mendes' testimony, I called Ralphael Colombo, who told jurors about renting the car to a blond-haired Jodi Arias.

West Jordan Police detective Michael Galieti then testified about the traffic stop in which he observed that Arias' back license plate was upside down and the front one was missing.

Ryan Burns was in court to testify to Arias' late arrival in Utah, the excuses she provided for her tardiness, the traffic stop by police, and the sexual contact the two engaged in during her brief time in West Jordan.

On cross-examination, defense counsel continued along down the same path they had taken with Detective Flores of attacking Travis' character rather than focusing on the evidence that undermined Arias' self-defense claim. Nurmi asked Burns if he had heard from others that Travis was a big flirt, and whether Arias had told him that Travis had cheated on her. The line of questioning seemed out of place, because it didn't address the conflicting stories Arias had told him about her delayed arrival, her phone charger, and the upside-down back license plate. Using this witness to try to establish what they wanted the jury to perceive as Travis' inappropriate interactions with women was misplaced, as Burns had no personal knowledge and could only speak to what Arias and a few others had told him.

On the ninth and final day of my case in chief, I called the last witnesses, among them Detective Flores again. As part of my direct examination of Flores, I played the telephone message Arias had left for the detective on June 21, in which she provided her mobile phone number, setting the stage for the introduction of the phone records through the testimony of the custodian of records for the mobile phone carrier, Sprint.

What I hadn't expected was the line of questioning Nurmi

would pursue during his cross-examination of Flores that in-advertently emphasized Jodi Arias' momentous error in leaving the camera behind in the washing machine on the day she killed Travis.

"Detective, you were present when the photos of Ms. Arias and Mr. Alexander were shown in court?" Nurmi asked Flores.

"Yes."

"And that was a few weeks after the investigation that those photographs were actually recovered, right?"

"Yes."

"Before they obtained those, had you had any other evidence that Ms. Arias was at Mr. Alexander's home on June 4?" Nurmi continued, to which Flores answered, "No . . ."

After nine days of testimony and twenty different witnesses, it was now clear that Arias had implemented a plan to kill Travis that she carried out on June 4, 2008, and it had gone the way she hoped, except for that one fatal slip-up that Flores was able to highlight in his final testimony.

I concluded with Arias' PPL friend Leslie Udy, who testified to several conversations she'd had with Arias, including the two telephone calls Arias made to her after supposedly learning of Travis' death. Udy described Arias' apparent sadness and claims of disbelief. Udy's testimony was meant to remind the jurors that Arias' feigned disbelief at the news of Travis' death was just another part of her cover-up.

Most emblematic of Arias' deception was the hour-long conversation Udy had with Arias on the evening of June 5, 2008, as the two sat in Arias' rental car in the parking lot of Chili's, days before Travis' body would be discovered stuffed in the shower. "We talked about Travis," Udy recalled. ". . . She said they weren't together anymore, which I already knew . . . but that they would always be friends, and that they had joked and laughed about the fact that at some point further on, they would see each other at the Pre-Paid Legal events and their children would play together and be friends. . . . She indicated . . .

that although they were broken up and weren't together anymore, they would always be best friends."

Udy also recounted for the jury the two telephone calls she
received from Arias, the first on the morning of June 10, 2008,
telling her Travis was dead, and the second around two o'clock
the following morning.

"And what was she saying?" I asked, with regard to the
second call.

"She was saying that this was about the time of day that she
would normally talk to Travis . . . they were both night people
and that they talk about that time . . . and that she had lost her
best friend and that she didn't know what to do."

It was then that I asked Udy the final question of my case
in chief. "In any of those three conversations, did she ever tell
you that she killed Travis?"

"No," she replied.

Udy's testimony helped unveil the deceitfulness that was
Jodi Arias, someone who would even manipulate her own
friend in her friend's time of grief.

CHAPTER 18

O n Thursday, January 17, I rested my case, and the court indicated that trial would resume with the beginning of the defense's presentation of evidence on Tuesday, January 29, giving us a twelve-day recess. But while those twelve days offered a break from the trial, there would be no shortage of drama.

The court set an evidentiary hearing for Monday, January 28, to hear evidence of supposed prosecutorial misconduct, one of the many occasions when such an allegation would be made by defense counsel as the trial progressed. Defense counsel refused to inform me what acts they believed constituted the misconduct and which witnesses would testify in support of their latest accusation, giving them an obvious tactical advantage at the upcoming hearing.

Fortunately, their key witness, someone named Gus Searcy, talked to others about the hearing and his upcoming testimony, claiming it would change the course of the trial. Searcy, an executive director at Pre-Paid Legal Services, now called LegalShield, held himself out as the paradigm of success at the network marketing company. He had met Arias at a PPL business briefing in Arizona when she approached him to help her attain the kind of success that he professed to have achieved, because as he was quick to say, he had become an executive director in ninety days, a rate of progress that normally takes more than a year for others to achieve.

Searcy's lack of discretion gave me the necessary forewarning about the allegation he would make at the hearing, where he intended to accuse Travis' friend and mentor, Chris Hughes, of trying to sway his testimony. This allowed me to contact Hughes, who denied the allegations and agreed to travel to Phoenix to give testimony at this hearing. After taking testimony from Searcy and Hughes out of the presence of the jury, Judge Stephens found that there was no merit to the defense's claim of prosecutorial misconduct.

With the conclusion of Monday's hearing, defense counsel informed me that Searcy would be one of two witnesses to take the stand on the following day, the first day of their case, although I had only been informed six days earlier that Searcy would be a witness at all. This was extremely late notice and left me with very little time to prepare. But at least this time they let me know he would take the stand the next day rather than refusing to identify him, as they had done for the prosecutorial misconduct hearing. I knew Searcy did not have any information that spoke to either the events leading up to or immediately following the murder, so it was hard for me to speculate what substance, if any, his testimony would contain.

Defense counsel also informed me that Darryl Brewer was the other witness they intended to call the next day.

As I sat at the prosecution table next to Detective Flores that Tuesday morning, I was on edge, hoping to hear Brewer's name called first. I was a bit disappointed when I heard that the first witness would be Searcy. The thought that ran through my mind was that something might happen between now and the afternoon when Brewer was expected to testify, because there is always the remote possibility the defense might alter their trial strategy, leading to Brewer not being called at all. But I let that thought slip by and concentrated on Searcy as the short man with thinning hair, dressed in a dark suit, yellow tie, and matching handkerchief peeking out of his jacket pocket, made his way up the aisle of the gallery to the witness box.

Nurmi rose to begin his direct examination by asking Searcy

about his affiliation with Pre-Paid Legal Services/LegalShield. "If you could, what is your position within the company? Is there a label for it?" Nurmi asked.

"I am what's called a one-hundred-thousand-dollar ring earner," Searcy replied with a smile, showing the jury the ornate gold band on his left ring finger. "I have this little ring which means I make over a hundred thousand dollars a year, whether I get out of bed or not. And I am an executive director," he proclaimed.

"Could you . . . educate us all on the hierarchy of Pre-Paid Legal or LegalShield," Nurmi followed up, "how that works in terms of where an executive director fits in . . . ?"

"LegalShield is a multilevel network marketing company that provides a legal insurance product and an identity theft product. And it has about a little over four hundred thousand associates. Out of those four hundred thousand associates, the goal is to attain a level such as myself, or some of the other people in the company, the main level that people want to get to is something called an executive director," he boasted with a bit of a grin on his face.

After talking a bit more about PPL, Searcy went on to tell jurors about Arias approaching him after a business briefing in Arizona, requesting that he provide her with some guidance on how to raise her income by increasing the number of people she could sign up as associates. He said that after their initial meeting, he saw Arias about four to six times at national and regional conferences, as well as meeting with her privately on two separate occasions. He was quick to point out that their relationship was "platonic."

His story became disjointed when he recalled one of the times that he met Arias alone, explaining she spent the night at his motor home in Las Vegas. It was during this visit, as they sat close to each other on separate couches in the motor home, that Searcy claimed to have overheard a "heated" phone call between Arias and Travis Alexander, whom he knew to be her boyfriend. Searcy recounted that when Arias answered the call, she immediately became upset, and before he could blurt out what he supposedly heard Travis say to her, I objected on the grounds of hearsay.

The court sustained my objection, restricting him from telling the jurors anything he might have heard Travis say during the call. He was left to describe how Arias took the phone outside to continue the discussion in private, which lasted about thirty minutes.

"When she came back in, she was shaking and crying," Searcy recalled.

It appeared that Nurmi had been trying to introduce aspects of that phone conversation to make it seem that Travis had said something abusive to Arias, causing her to become upset. But his effort came up short, because the judge sustained my objection that whatever Searcy claimed to have overheard could not be introduced for the jury's consideration.

With the conclusion of Searcy's direct testimony, I couldn't help but think about how strange it was that the defense had opted to call him as their first witness. As lead witnesses go, he was not impactful because he had little to talk about other than giving an overview of the PPL/LegalShield structure and talking about a phone call from Travis. Since Searcy knew nothing about the killing, I restricted myself to discussing only the areas touched on by defense counsel, as I did not want to prolong his stay on the witness stand for fear there would not be any time left for them to call Darryl Brewer that day.

My questions focused on having Searcy admit that PPL/LegalShield had many of the earmarks of a pyramid scheme, knowing that this type of affiliation would affect his credibility as a witness. I further inquired about what seemed a tawdry aspect of his relationship with Arias by asking him about the one occasion when she spent the night.

"You said that you did see her on a personal level on two occasions, right?"

"Yes."

"And one of them involved your mobile home, right?"

"Motor home," Searcy corrected me.

"Motor home, right?"

"Yup," Searcy replied in a glib fashion, as if irritated by the question.

"And she came by and she stayed two days and one night, right?"

"Correct."

"Where was this mobile home, sir?"

"Las Vegas."

Searcy was confirming that Arias spent the night in a small motor home with a man who was a relative stranger to her. By all appearances, this spoke to his bias as well as to Arias' poor judgment.

Searcy completed his testimony at around 11:30, at which time Judge Stephens called for a lunch break and indicated that proceedings would resume at 1:30 that afternoon. Even though I had time, I opted not to eat. I wasn't feeling hungry, and instead went back to my office to wait the two hours before court was set to resume. After so many months of waiting, I was finally going to have the opportunity to begin exposing Arias' self-defense claim as a sham, and I was going to use one of the defense's witnesses to do it.

Since I had already done my preparation, all I could do was count down the one-hundred and twenty minutes until I was back at the prosecution table, where I would meet Darryl Brewer for the first time.

"The defense may call its next witness," the court said.

"Thank you, Your Honor," Nurmi replied. "The defense calls Darryl Brewer."

I could feel my anticipation rising as I watched the fiftyish-looking Brewer, who was dressed in a black suit, red tie, and dark-framed glasses, raise his right hand to be sworn in. He had requested that the media not show his face, so an agree-

ment had been struck that allowed the cameras in the courtroom to record his testimony but capture his image only from
the shoulders down.

"Sir, could you introduce yourself to the jury, please?"
Nurmi began.

"My name is Darryl Brewer," he responded in a shaky voice.

"And Darryl, where do you live?"

"I live in Carmel, California."

Brewer testified that he was divorced and had one son, who
was now fourteen.

". . . And Mr. Brewer, how old are you?"

"I'm fifty-two."

"Okay, do you know this lady here in the blue shirt?"
Nurmi asked, pointing to the defense table, where Arias sat
staring blankly at Brewer.

"Yes."

"How do you know her?"

"I know Jodi because we were in love," he answered in a
somewhat rehearsed fashion.

Brewer told the court he met Arias in the fall of 2001,
when he was employed as a food and beverage director at
Ventana Inn in Big Sur and Arias came in to apply for a job
as a server. His recollection of the date he first met Arias dif-
fered from the date he previously provided to the investigator
for the defense, at which time he indicated first meeting Arias
in 2002.

"And how did she present herself during her interview with
you?"

"Outstanding. She was on time. She interviewed well. She
was dressed appropriately."

". . . Now, at that point in time you hired Ms. Arias, I would
take it to understand that you would be a supervisor to her.
Am I correct in understanding that?"

"Yes."

"Okay, and to further clarify for everyone, were you her direct supervisor? Was there a restaurant manager? How did that work?

"Jodi wasn't under my direct supervision. There were other managers involved," he said, being quick to point out that there were managerial layers between them, which would have made a romantic relationship appropriate, but he hastened to add that their dating relationship didn't start until a year later, when he was demoted to server after a change in management.

When asked about her job performance, Brewer gave a glowing report and said that "she was excelling."

"Okay. And in that time was there any disciplinary problems, any behavioral problems, anything of that nature, where she was inappropriate with customers or anything like that?"

"No," Brewer replied. His answer made me wonder whether she had acquired her bad waitressing habits, documented at Mimi's Café, P.F. Chang's and the Purple Plum, more recently.

"Okay, you mentioned there was a shift in management structure at Ventana. You were no longer Jodi's boss after that shift, is that correct?"

"That is correct."

"Okay. Did you have a new job title? Could you just kind of describe it for us?"

"Yes. I was working as a server in banquets and helping with weddings," Brewer said, affirming that once he and Arias were coworkers, they "became infatuated and fell in love."

"Tell us about who Jodi was at that point in time," Nurmi said.

"Jodi was a very responsible, caring, loving person," Brewer recounted, as if recommending her for the job of au pair. Nurmi's inquiry appeared designed to portray a softer image of Arias, and Brewer accommodated the questions, describing her relationship with his young son as "outstanding," mentioning she played a "friendly role" in the boy's life.

Brewer testified that even though the two weren't married, they bought a home together in Palm Desert in June of 2005. "The plan was somewhat uncertain, revolving around my son. We hoped to stay in the house for a minimum of at least two years. We weren't in the process of flipping houses. We wanted to establish the home and possibly resell it."

"Okay. So was this part business venture, part home, shall we say, I mean home to live in but also a business venture?" Nurmi asked.

"Not a formal business venture, a personal business venture; I mean, it was a home. But we also looked at it as an investment. Hoped to gain from it at some point."

But the venture appeared to fall apart in the fall of 2006 when "the mother of my son decided to move back to Monterey and took my son as well and he started school in Pacific Grove in fall of 2006. . . . I was going to follow [my son], and I began a strategy how to get back to Monterey. . . . I was trying to find work and as soon I found work, I was going to move back to Monterey. . . . My hope was that she [Arias] would remain in the home until we could come to a resolution so we could sell the house."

"Okay. In terms of the relationship at this point in time was it—were you breaking up? Was it going to be a long-distance relationship? What were the discussions about your relationship with Ms. Arias?"

"Let's see, the relationship was slowly deteriorating over the summer of 2006. By the fall, Jodi had—we were still together in the home, but it was becoming clear that I was moving back to Monterey and that we were not going to be together."

Brewer had decided to leave Arias behind, so that it appeared she was free to explore her options and venture into the dating market looking for another man. She also needed to make enough money to pay the mortgage and the bills associated with the ownership of the house. It looked like she was already working two jobs, and the way Brewer described it, she saw a way to get rich quickly by selling memberships to Pre-Paid Legal.

Brewer said he was unaware of Arias' relationship with Travis Alexander, and he was hoping that Arias would be back with him once they resolved the "house issue."

"Okay. After you moved to Monterey and the house went into foreclosure, what was your relationship with Jodi like during that time period . . . ?"

"I would have to say at that time the relationship was nothing more than an occasional phone call. We were not romantically involved and I had learned that she had left the house and moved to the Arizona area."

Nurmi's final question was "And so you remained friends on good terms?"

"We did," Brewer responded.

Rising from my chair, I wasted no time. I wanted to use Brewer's final answer that he and Arias had remained friends to start my questioning. Turning to Brewer, I began, "Sir, you indicated that you moved from the Palm Desert home back to [Monterey] in December of 2006, right?"

"Yes, sir."

"And when you moved back, she didn't go with you, right?"

"Correct."

"And even though time passed, you and she continued to be good friends, right?"

"We talked occasionally."

"You were friends, then, right?" I asked, continuing the questioning in a quick, staccato fashion.

"Yes."

"And she knew your phone number, and you knew hers, right?"

"Yes."

"And that continued on, for example, into 2007, right? You continued to have this relationship where you were sort of friends, where you would call occasionally, right? . . . And the same thing can be said for 2008, correct, you continued to be this sort of sporadic friend, right?"

"I had, yes, sporadic contact, yes."

"And in fact, back in 2008, she knew your number and you knew hers, right?"

"Correct."

"And if she needed something she would call you, right?" I asked, to which Nurmi objected.

"Calls for speculation," he argued, and Judge Stephens sustained his objection.

"Well, sir, isn't it true that in May of 2008, you received a telephone call from the defendant, Jodi Arias?"

"I could have, yes," Brewer replied, unaware of where my line of questioning was leading.

"Well, isn't it true that during that telephone call she was asking you for a favor? Do you remember that?" I asked, knowing what my next question would be irrespective of his answer. "Do you remember that during that favor, she was asking you for gas cans in May 2008 at the very end so that she could make a trip to Mesa? Do you remember that?"

There was a pronounced pause before his one-word answer, delivered in a quiet voice. "Yes," Brewer replied, to a palpable silence in the courtroom. It was obvious he had been unprepared for the question and was reluctant to respond because he understood the implication of an affirmative answer—Arias had planned the trip to see Travis and it had not been a spur-of-the-moment decision as she was now claiming.

Before this point, there had been times during the trial when I had observed people in the gallery checking their cell phones, looking around, or whispering to their seatmates. It seemed that now everyone's attention was on the line of questioning, as it was an untouched area, not discussed in these proceedings in either my opening statement or during my case in chief.

Moving ahead with my inquiry, I asked Brewer, "And she made more than one call asking you for these gas cans to make a trip to Arizona, didn't she?"

"Yes."

"In fact, in the first part of June of 2008, she called you again asking about these gas cans to go to Mesa, right?" I asked, feeling the deafening silence in the courtroom.

"Yes," Brewer responded, appearing tentative.

"And during the first time that she brought up this issue in the end of May of 2008, you asked her why do you need these gas cans? Do you remember asking her that?"

"I do."

"And she got really testy with you, didn't she?"

"Not necessarily testy; she said she needed them. She was taking a long trip. . . . I wouldn't say testy."

"She wouldn't answer you, though, why she wanted those gas cans, right?"

"She did answer me."

". . . And she told you she was going to Mesa, right?"

"She told me she was going on a long trip, did not say particularly Mesa, no," he said, changing his earlier answer.

"Well, sir," I said, before showing Brewer the interview summary that had been turned over to me years earlier by previous defense counsel, which contained that portion of his conversation with their investigator, "let's go ahead and mark this as an exhibit and see if this refreshes your recollection. Okay?"

Presenting Brewer with a copy of the interview summary marked Exhibit 411, I directed him to read the highlighted portion, which referred to his comment that Arias had gotten testy. "You do admit that you had a conversation with somebody representing the defendant, right?"

"I did have a conversation, yes, sir."

"And did this refresh your recollection as to the fact that she got testy with you or not?"

"No," Brewer replied.

"And with regard to going to Mesa, Arizona, does that refresh your recollection or not?" I asked.

"No," Brewer responded, appearing to dig in his heels. But it was obvious that the damage had already been done, because the jury had already heard him admit that Arias told him she was traveling to Mesa, so his backtracking was ineffectual.

"But she said she was going to go on a trip, right?"

"She did."

"And that's why she wanted to borrow the gas cans, right?"

"Yes."

"And ostensibly the reason that she wanted these gas cans is because she was going to get lost, right?" I asked the question to remind the jury of Arias' story to Detective Flores that she had gotten lost in an effort to explain the twenty-four-hour absence to him.

"I don't know that she had any plans to get lost, no."

"That's what she told you, that that was part of the reason why she needed the gas cans, right?"

"No," Brewer said emphatically.

"Sir, she did come by your house on June 3 of 2008, right, before her trip, right? . . . She came by and she had breakfast with you, right?"

"We had some food, yes," Brewer demurred in an obvious effort to avoid admitting even those facts that were undeniably true, including that food served in the morning is called breakfast.

"And your son was there, right? . . . That was around seven o'clock in the morning, right?"

"Approximately, yes."

"And while she was there you allowed her to use the e-mail

on your computer, right? . . . And she checked her e-mail, right?"

"Yes," Brewer affirmed.

". . . And before she left, though, you gave her two gas cans, didn't you?" I asked, my voice emphasizing the point.

"I did."

"They were each five-gallon gas cans, right? . . . For a total of ten gallons that would be available to put in these gas cans, right?"

"The cans would have held ten gallons, yes."

"What color were the cans?" I asked.

"They were red."

"And when you gave her these cans, at the time, did you ask her what she was going to use them for or not?"

"At the time, no," he offered, appearing to bait me into asking about the other times they may have discussed her reasons for wanting to borrow the gasoline containers.

"Okay, let me show you some exhibits," I said, referring to the ARCO receipts. Arias had made the three gas purchases beginning at 8:42 P.M. on June 3, 2008, according to the time stamp on the first receipt. ". . . It says it's pump number 2 and it does give gallons, right?"

"It does," Brewer acknowledged.

"It's 8.301 gallons, and then it gives the price and then there's a payment there, right? . . . And the time I want you to note is 8:42 P.M., right?"

"Yes," he admitted, unable to deny the obvious.

I next showed Brewer the second receipt, from the purchase that Arias made four minutes later, at 8:46 P.M. ". . . About how much gas . . . can you see, how many gallons she purchased there?"

Brewer reluctantly replied, "Looks like 9.954 gallons."

"That's approximately close to ten gallons, right?" to which Brewer responded affirmatively.

". . . Then, if we look at this other one . . . this other exhibit, we'll go with the time first. It's 8:53 P.M., right, see that in the upper left?" I asked, showing him the last ARCO receipt, driving home the point that Arias made three separate gas purchases during that stop.

"And this is for . . . ?" I asked, soliciting from Brewer the number of gallons indicated on this final receipt.

"It looks like 2.77 something," Brewer said.

"Right, and if we add, let's say, 2.7 [the amount of gas Arias bought during her last purchase] and round it [referring to the 9.954 gallons shown to have been purchased during the second transaction] up to ten . . . we're talking about 12.5 gallons, right?" This was the combined amount of gas that had been purchased with cash rather than a credit card at this ARCO station.

"Yes," Brewer replied.

". . . Let's do a little bit of basic math," I challenged. "Let's say the car she was driving had a capacity of twelve gallons"— using that number for ease of mathematical computation, although I knew the tank capacity of the Ford Focus was 13.5 gallons.

"Objection, speculative," Nurmi interrupted.

Pausing my examination, I waited for Judge Stephens, who quickly overruled his objection.

"And if you multiply that by thirty miles per gallon, let's just say that it's highway driving," I continued, "that would be 360 miles, right?"

"I imagine, if your math is correct," Brewer agreed.

After establishing the potential range of the Ford Focus, I turned to a discussion of the gas receipts from the ARCO station in Pasadena.

"On the other two exhibits [receipts for the second and third gas purchases at ARCO] we talked about, we have roughly the same amount, twelve and a half gallons, did you notice that, do you remember that?"

"Yes."

"And so, if we're talking about the same thirty miles to the gallon, twelve and a half, we're talking about roughly another 360 miles, right?"

"Makes sense."

"So, if a person fills up, for example, in Pasadena, according to the math that we're doing, and puts twelve gallons in this car and we're talking thirty miles, and I understand these are rough figures, you're talking 360, plus the other twelve and a half gallons, another 360, for a total of 720 miles, right?" I asked, knowing that the distance to Las Vegas from Pasadena through Travis' house in Mesa, Arizona, was roughly seven-hundred miles.

"Correct."

As I wound down my questions about the gas cans, I still had one more point to make. "The gas cans, sir, did she ever return them to you?" I asked.

"No," Brewer replied.

"Ever ask her about returning those gas cans to you?"

"I don't recall if I ever had a chance to ask her, no."

Moving on from the gas cans, I then turned my attention to other areas of his testimony, addressing the chronology of his relationship with Arias, with a focus on their sexual dynamic. I wanted to build off the work I'd done through Ryan Burns' testimony that showed Arias as sexually aggressive, in order to further undermine her claim that Travis was a Svengali who guilted her into submitting to his sexual whims.

I asked Brewer to confirm his earlier testimony that he and Arias had started to date in January of 2003. "And you sort of made it official . . . at the San Francisco 49ers game, right?"

"Yes."

"And . . . you spent the night together, right?"

"We did."

"And is that the first time you and she ever had sex?" I asked.

"No," Brewer replied.

"And you do remember the first time you and she had sex, though, right?"

"I do remember, yes."

"And she was very aggressive, wasn't she?"

"We were both aggressive," Brewer equivocated.

To refresh his memory about his earlier statement to the defense investigator, I showed him the portion of his interview summary in which he had described Arias as "aggressive" during their first sexual encounter.

"It says that, right?" I asked.

"That's what that says, yes," Brewer conceded.

". . . And not only was she aggressive, she was enthusiastic about it, wasn't she, the sex, I mean?"

"We were both enthusiastic, yes," he answered, in an obvious attempt to shield Arias.

"And she was comfortable with intimacy, yes?"

"Yes."

"And at some point you and she even enjoyed, I believe, on two occasions, anal sex, right?" I was forced to ask this question because Arias had maintained that the only person she have ever engaged in this type of sexual activity with had been Travis, and it was at his insistence.

"Possibly once," Brewer responded.

Ending my cross-examination of Brewer, I started back to the prosecution table, where I caught sight of Detective Flores fighting to hold back an inquisitive smile. As I sat down next to him, he broke the cardinal rule that I had established for him for the trial, which was to never speak to me while court was in session, because we ran the risk of being overheard, as the microphones at the table were very sensitive.

"What the heck was that all about?" he whispered into my ear. "You didn't tell me anything about the gas cans."

"I know," I acknowledged. "No one knew."

As I sat back in my chair, Flores and I exchanged a glance, wondering how Nurmi was going to address what was clearly a blow to Arias' self-defense claim.

Nurmi took his opportunity on redirect examination in a direction that I found perplexing. "Mr. Brewer, did your sex life with Jodi Arias involve wearing little boy's underwear? . . . Did it involve putting her in schoolgirl outfits and pigtails? . . . Did it involve bending her over a desk? . . . Did it involve ejaculating on her face? . . . Did it involve calling her a whore? . . . A slut? . . . A three-hole wonder?" to all of which Brewer replied "No."

That Nurmi chose to focus on questions about all the things that Arias had *not* done with Darryl Brewer, and in such a vulgar way, was surprising. But what I found even more strange was his failure to address the reason Arias borrowed the gas cans from Brewer and the receipts proving she had purchased gas to fill those gas cans, manifesting her intent to use them on her trip to Mesa.

"Okay, now, as related to the gas cans, and where Jodi was going on different occasions, one of the occasions you said was Mesa. One occasion you said was a long trip, so I just want to clarify that with you," Nurmi posed the question, which had the effect of discrediting his own witness.

"I believe that Jodi told me she was going on a long trip. She was going to see friends in Big Sur and Los Angeles and in Arizona and the Grand Canyon, I believe, is what she said," Brewer said, attempting to clarify his earlier testimony and cast doubt on the interview summary attributed to him by the defense investigator, claiming he hadn't approved the statement prior to it being submitted by defense counsel.

"Okay, and so when you heard Mesa or comments about Mesa when you were asked about it, that wasn't accurate to your recollection of where she was going, right?" Nurmi led Brewer to the answer, trying to deal with the fact that the witness had already admitted twice on cross-examination that Arias had told him that she needed the gas cans for her trip to Mesa.

"That's correct, she said Arizona. I didn't know of Mesa," Brewer said, looking as if he had just gotten the answer right.

And as for the gas cans themselves and what Arias wanted them for, Nurmi left that area wholly untouched.

CHAPTER 19

The assault on Travis Alexander's reputation and character, which would be the lynchpin of Jodi Arias' self-defense claim, began in earnest on the second day with testimony from the next three witnesses the defense called to the stand.

Lisa Andrews, who was now married and went by the name Lisa Diadone, had dated Travis on and off for about eight months beginning in July 2007, when she was nineteen years old. Diadone's testimony centered on an angry e-mail she sent to Travis after one of their breakups. She complained to him in that e-mail that sex was on his mind from the very beginning and they made out "too long" and "too passionately," which caused her to feel "used and dirty." The e-mail also included a concern that he had grabbed her butt in public, which upset her further when he persisted on doing it even after she asked him to stop. Throughout the direct examination by Jennifer Willmott, Diadone made it clear that she felt the intent of her e-mail was being taken "out of context," even as she was forced to admit she had authored it.

Although I had initially thought I might call Diadone as a witness, I had chosen not to, because I was concerned that she might unwittingly bring up details about her breakup with Travis, such as her belief that Arias had been the one to slash Travis' tires, or recount the night she fell asleep at Travis' house and Travis found Arias downstairs, at which time Arias admitted to having been upstairs watching the two sleep.

Any such statements touching on other misdeeds by Arias

could result in a mistrial, which would require us to start the trial all over again.

Despite the content of the letter, I didn't consider Lisa Diadone's questioning by Willmott particularly impactful, as it was based almost exclusively on a single e-mail Diadone had written to Travis early in their relationship explaining why she believed they should break up. On cross-examination, Diadone readily admitted that she and Travis had had a "high school"–type relationship, that she had expressed herself in an immature fashion in the e-mail, and that she now believed her comments were unfair. She said her complaint that he was "overly" interested in sex was in part because Travis became erect when they kissed, something she now acknowledged was a normal bodily reaction and not a result of any purposeful touching. She also mentioned that Travis only began kissing her after she made the overture by asking him to kiss her first.

During my cross-examination, Diadone expanded on her answer to Willmott that she broke up with Travis because of "strange things" that were happening by discussing two incidents that concerned her. On the first occasion, she and Travis were together at her house when someone suddenly opened the front door. She explained that the door had a security device that made a ringing noise every time it was opened, and when she and Travis heard it go off, they went to see who had come in and found that no one was there. Diadone said she became so worried that someone might have broken into the house that she asked Travis to spend the night, pointing out that during the overnight stay at her home, Travis did not make any sexual advances and they did not engage in any passionate kissing.

On a different occasion, she was at Travis' house standing in the kitchen when Arias unexpectedly walked in through the front door and, upon seeing Diadone, turned around and ran out. Diadone's testimony, far from showing that Travis was abusive in any way, instead painted a picture of an individual with values who respected his girlfriend's sexual boundaries.

After Diadone's testimony, the defense continued its attack on Travis' character by calling two of Travis' friends, Daniel Freeman and his sister, Desiree, to testify about behavior on Travis' part toward Arias that they deemed inappropriate. The Freemans were both members of the LDS church, and Daniel was also affiliated with PPL.

Desiree, the first of the two siblings to take the stand, told the jury that her brother had first introduced her to Travis, who then introduced her to Arias. In response to questions from Willmott, she recounted what she described as a disturbing exchange between Travis and Arias during a trip to Havasupai, Arizona, that she and her brother took with the couple in September 2007. Desiree recalled that at one point Arias got out of the car to take some photographs, and Travis pretended to drive away as she tried to get back into the vehicle. She said that Arias became upset and told Travis it wasn't funny, which angered Travis, whose "over-the-top" reaction shocked Desiree. While she could not recall exactly what Travis said to Arias that day, she made it clear that she found his tone inappropriate.

I initiated my cross-examination of Desiree Freeman by asking her questions about the LDS church's prohibition against sexual activities by unmarried members. This was a way to remind the jury that Arias had violated the church's doctrine by being with both Travis and Ryan Burns in a sexual way within a day of each other.

On the face of it, Desiree's testimony about Travis' accelerating the car didn't seem particularly helpful to the defense's case. His actions did not rise to being verbally abusive to Arias. Although Desiree described this incident as "over the top," she couldn't remember the words she found so offensive, and when pressed on the specifics, her memory totally failed. I didn't belabor the point, because I saw no need to get drawn into a character debate with her about what was essentially a trivial exchange between Travis and Arias.

Desiree's brother, Daniel, recounted on direct examination a fight between Travis and Arias that he said occurred
the morning the foursome was scheduled to go to Havasupai,
in the Grand Canyon, which Daniel admitted he had incited
by complaining that Arias was packing too much makeup for
the day's hike. When he voiced his concerns, he said Travis
also became upset after he realized how much she had packed,
causing Travis to raise his voice at her, and sending Arias running upstairs in tears. Daniel's testimony began to illustrate
the lengths defense counsel would go to show Travis was abusive, by blaming Travis for a situation sparked by his friend
Daniel Freeman.

The defense case took a salacious turn with the testimony
of their next two witnesses, one being a digital media expert
and the other professing an expertise in many areas, including
voice comparison and identification and photography

Lonnie Dworkin, the digital media expert, had been retained by the defense to examine Travis' Compaq Presario
laptop, seized by police during their investigation on June 10,
2008, as well as two items belonging to Jodi Arias, an external
hard drive and a Helio cell phone. The external hard drive had
been found by police during the execution of the search warrant on Arias' grandparents' house in Yreka on July 15, 2008.

The Helio cell phone had a more complicated history. Arias
had reported to the Yreka Police Department on May 18,
2008, that it had been stolen from the front seat of her car, and
police had no record of a follow-up call from Arias notifying
them that the phone had been recovered.

After confirming his educational background and experience, Willmott asked Dworkin about his examination of
Travis' laptop, specifically the Internet history and the different Web sites that Travis had visited in the early morning hours
of June 4, 2008, between 4:08 and 4:35 P.M.

"Can you tell us about the first full action," Willmott asked, referring to a listing from his report of the Web sites Travis had visited that morning. "What is it telling us?"

"Well, it's an action that documents a Web site that was visited and the date and time the Web site was visited," Dworkin replied.

"Okay. Can you tell us what Web site was visited?"

"Yes. It was YouTube.com. . . . And the date and time is June 4, 2008, at 4:08:11 P.M."

". . . Does it tell us anything else in that action?"

"Yes, it tells us the name of the file that was accessed, the YouTube file that was accessed."

"Okay, and what was that?"

"The title of the file is 'Drunk (Daft Punk—Hard Body, Faster, Stronger),' " Dworkin replied.

By providing no further details about the file, his response made it seem like Travis had accessed a YouTube Web site dedicated to pornographic materials. But I knew otherwise. These were music videos for the band Daft Punk and did not have any sexual content. Willmott's inquiry ignored that Arias had previously described this video to Detective Flores when she was questioned on July 16, 2008, and she had told him that Travis was viewing some stupid music video with people dancing with foil boxes on their heads.

". . . The next action?" Willmott continued in what seemed like a deliberate attempt to create the impression for the jury that Travis had continued to view pornography.

". . . The time is 4:11 P.M. in the morning and four seconds."

"Okay. What's the Web site? . . . What's the date?"

"The date is also June 4, 2008. . . . The Web site is YouTube. com," Dworkin said, adding, "The title of the video that was viewed is 'Daft Hands—Harder, Better, Faster, Stronger.' "

"And the next action?" Willmott elicited. "Let's start with the date."

"Okay. June 4, 2008."

"And the time?"

"It's 4:15 and thirteen seconds in the morning."

"Okay. And the Web site?"

"The Web site is again YouTube.com."

"Does it tell specifically where on YouTube?"

"The title of this file is 'Daft Hands—Double Speed (Faster, Better).'"

The purposeful way Willmott was posing the questions appeared to be a deliberate attempt to lead the jury to make assumptions, making it difficult for me to sit and wait until I could question the witness and clear up the impression being created during the direct examination.

Willmott next turned her focus to Dworkin's examination of "an external hard drive," a portable storage device that he described as "the size of a hard drive you would find on a laptop." Willmott failed to immediately identify the owner of this hard drive, leaving room for the jury to assume that it belonged to Travis, because Dworkin's testimony thus far had been related to his examination of Travis' laptop.

"Were you asked [by defense counsel] to pull photographs, everything you can off of the mirror image [of the hard drive]?" Willmott asked, to which Dworkin indicated that in addition to photos, he had also been able to access some other information from a mirror image he made of the actual hard drive.

". . . Do you recognize those as two photos taken off of this mirror image?" Willmott asked, focusing Dworkin's attention to defense exhibits 393 and 394, two 8½-by-11-inch glossy photographs, each depicting a man's penis.

The photographs were enlarged in such a fashion that the penis in one measured 8½ inches and in the other 9¾ inches, in an obvious attempt to shock whoever viewed the pictures.

". . . Defense moves—I forgot the number, defense moves to enter exhibit number—"

"Three ninety-three and three ninety-four," responded Dworkin as he held up the pictures, allowing the jury and

those in the courtroom to see that each exhibit was an enlarged photograph of a man's penis.

I stood up and objected on the grounds of relevance, pointing out that Dworkin could not identify whose penis was depicted in each of the photos. And I requested that the court
permit me to ask questions of Dworkin to show that he lacked
the foundation necessary for the pictures to be moved into
evidence.

Judge Stephens allowed me to interrupt defense counsel's
questioning so that I could challenge the foundation for his
opinion about the photographs. "Sir, with regard to the part
of the human body that's there, do you know who it belongs
to?" I asked.

"I do not."

"That's not your area of expertise, is it?"

"No, it's not," Dworkin quickly conceded.

Based on my objection, the court decided to recess for the
day, allowing Judge Stephens time to consider whether the
photos of the unidentified penises would be shown to the jury.

The defense's approach for the day was obvious; they had
planned to leave the jury with the impression that Travis Alexander could potentially have been masturbating to this
"harder, faster stronger" video and taken photos of his penis,
because the jury had yet to be told to whom the external hard
drive belonged. It was a Thursday, and court was not in session on Fridays, so the jury now had the weekend to ponder
what they had just seen when Dworkin held up the pictures.

When we returned to court the following Monday, February 4, Judge Stephens brought the jury in and instructed Willmott to continue her direct examination of Dworkin. But she
ruled that the two photographs that I had objected to that past
Thursday were not admissible in evidence. It seemed convenient to me that it was only after the judge's ruling to exclude
the photographs that Willmott asked the witness to identify
the owner of the external hard drive. "And the mirror image

that was taken of a hard drive; do you know whose hard drive that belonged to?"

"According to the document that was provided along with the hard drive . . . it appeared to belong to Jodi Arias," Dworkin responded.

"All right. Okay," Willmott continued. "I want to talk to you—want to move on a little and let's talk about a Helio phone that you looked at. . . . What is a Helio phone?"

"A Helio phone—it's actually Ocean Helio, it's an early predecessor to today's smartphones," Dworkin explained. "It has the ability to surf the Web, take photographs, record audio, things of that nature."

". . . Do you know who the phone belonged to?"

"I believe it belonged to Jodi Arias," Dworkin said.

Willmott next asked him about the audio recordings on the Helio phone.

". . . I did not just play the audio over its internal speaker and then try to pick it up with a microphone. I connected the phone directly from its audio out, or headphone jack, directly to my computer and I recorded the audio," he said.

The audio that Dworkin was referring to was a phone sex conversation between Arias and Travis that Arias recorded on May 10, 2008, without Travis' knowledge. It would not be introduced to the jury until eight days later, through the testimony of Jodi Arias herself, so it was unclear why defense counsel traveled this tortuous road to its introduction in evidence, rather than wait until Arias was on the stand for her to identify the voices and give the date it was recorded. Only then would jurors hear the soon-to-be-infamous sex tape where both Travis and Arias are heard discussing their sexual fantasies and masturbating until each climaxed, Arias twice.

Dworkin's testimony next focused on Arias' Canon camera, which police had seized during their search of Arias' grandparents' house in Yreka.

"You talked about there being a memory card that was associated with this Canon camera. . . . Were you able to pull photos off of that memory card?" Willmott asked, seeking to introduce three photographs that had been found on the memory card. The first was a close-up shot of Arias posing cheek to cheek with her sister, Angela, which was time-stamped May 15, 2008. "Okay, and in this photograph, can you tell us what color Ms. Arias' hair is?"

"I object, lack of foundation," I said. "He is not an expert on hair, and the color speaks for itself."

When the judge overruled my objection, Dworkin offered his response.

"Her hair appears to be brown," he said.

It was clear that the defense was trying to infer that Arias did not have blond hair when she rented the car at the Budget counter at the airport in Redding, California, on June 2, 2008, although the suggestion was hardly provable by viewing this photograph.

Willmott presented Dworkin with a second photograph and asked, "Can you tell what's in this photograph?"

"It appears to be a pair of women's panties, pink color, and a gray T-shirt. The gray T-shirt has 'Travis Alexander's' with a possessive—as a possessive statement, and then we have 'Travis' with a possessive statement also on the panties."

This photograph was shown on the monitors, but after all the gruesome photographs that had already been presented, there was no response, not even from the gallery.

When asked about the date and time stamp on the photograph, Dworkin replied, "We have July 12, and we have a time of 10:25:15. This is when it was taken by the camera and then saved to the memory card."

It was not lost on me that this photograph, clearly introduced to try and persuade jurors that Travis was possessive of Arias and therefore abusive, was taken more than a month after Travis' murder—just three days before Arias' arrest on July 15, 2008. Because I wasn't sure that Dworkin knew the date Travis was killed, I couldn't specifically ask him about how long after Travis's death these photos had been taken by Arias. But I could highlight the date in my cross-examination, knowing that the jury would understand the time span between the dates and realize that Travis probably had nothing to do with the imprinted words.

When the floor was turned over to me, I was anxious to dispel Willmott's illusion that she was attempting to impart on the jury that Travis had been viewing porn sites on the morning of the day he was killed.

"Sir, on Thursday, when we left off, we were talking about a number of computers," I began. "The first one that you talked about was this computer that belonged to Travis Alexander, or you gave the indication that that was Travis Alexander's, correct?"

"Yes."

". . . Somebody is going on YouTube [using that computer], correct?"

"Correct."

"Right. And what they were looking for was this 'Daft Bodies—Harder, Better, Faster, Stronger,' right?"

"Correct, that was the title."

"And Daft Bodies is a rock group, right?"

"That, I don't know," Dworkin replied sheepishly.

"Well, don't you think that you should have gone on, because this sort of seemed a little bit salacious, doesn't it? It looks like it may be porn, doesn't it?"

"It potentially may or may not be."

"Right. But if I told you that Daft Bodies was nothing more than a rock group, would you disagree with me?"

Willmott interjected with an objection, trying to preserve the impression she had attempted to create for the jury over the last two days, saying that my question called for speculation. But Judge Stephens overruled her objection.

"I have no way of agreeing or disagreeing because I have

no knowledge of it," Dworkin replied, beginning to show that perhaps his testimony had been less than complete.

"And 'Harder, Better, Faster, Stronger,' do you know that that's the name of a song that this group has?"

"Again, I have no knowledge of this particular video or group."

Because I knew that these videos had no sexual content, I made the point through my questions, spelling out for the jury that introducing the titles of the videos was an attempt to mischaracterize what Travis had been watching.

From there, I turned my attention to whether he had made the decision to print the penis photographs from the hard drive.

"Well, you picked certain photographs from the other hard drive . . . didn't you?"

"No," Dworkin replied, explaining that he had provided the reports of his analysis, which contained all photographs, to defense counsel, but had played no part in choosing which ones would be shown in court.

"With regard to the photographs that we were talking about Thursday," I asked, referring to the two pictures of a man's penis, "did you print those photographs, yes or no?"

"No. I did not print those photographs," he said.

"With regard to the Canon camera, there were some photographs that were taken and this is one of them, right?" I said, showing Dworkin the photograph of Arias in the monogrammed T-shirt and pink underwear.

"Yes."

"And this one says, 'Travis Alexander's,' the possessive, on the shirt, correct? And then it says 'Travis' on the shorts? . . . It looks a little bit posed, don't they?"

"Yes," Dworkin agreed, voicing what probably everyone in the courtroom was thinking.

Addressing the photograph of Arias posing with her sister, Angela, in which Dworkin testified that Arias had brown hair, I asked, "Sir, you're really not an expert on hair, are you?"

"I have been asked for my opinion in the past on body features including hair, but as an advertised expert on hair, specifically, no," Dworkin replied in what sounded like a worried
tone. Perhaps he was concerned that my next question would
be whether he was an expert on penises.

"So . . . when you were asked about hair color . . . were you
just giving us the opinion that—the same opinion that anybody in this courtroom would have given us?"

"Yes."

"So, it's not that you're any better or any worse than people
here, right?"

"Probably not," Dworkin conceded.

"In terms of the hair, do you know when this hair color was
applied to the defendant?"

"No, I don't," Dworkin replied.

When I indicated that I had no more questions for this witness, the judge asked Willmott, "Do you have an extensive
redirect, or is it brief?"

"Judge, it may take longer than five minutes . . ." Willmott
replied, turning to look at the clock.

"All right," the judge said. "We'll take the noon recess at
this time."

When we returned from lunch, Willmott completed her redirect examination of Dworkin.

Defense counsel's second witness this day was Bryan Neumeister, a self-professed expert in voice identification and photography analysis. Neumeister, dressed in a black dress shirt,
black sports coat and a reddish tie, started his testimony by
reading from his CV as if he were unfamiliar with his own
qualifications. Neumeister then talked about his role in en-
hancing the audio on the May 10, 2008, conversation between
Travis and Arias that Arias had recorded on her Helio cell
phone.

Neumeister was able to say that he had compared the male
voice on the recording and identified it as Travis', and he iden-

tified the other voice, a female voice, as belonging to Arias, even though he had not done a voice comparison with her voice and was basing it on the other person in the conversation calling the female speaker "Jodi." To explain the process he followed in his analysis, he went through a number of graphs that were more boring than informative, and as he was quick to point out, basking in self-aggrandizement, "And, again this is just for the record. You may not understand or you could ask questions . . ."

Defense counsel ended Neumeister's testimony without moving to enter the audio recording into evidence, which would have to wait until Arias herself was on the stand, which as I was about to learn, would be immediately, as she was the next witness they would call.

Defense counsel had not indicated that they would have any other witnesses for that day. But, I was not surprised that Arias was called to the stand without providing me prior notice, because it has become accepted practice for defense counsel to wait until the last minute to inform the prosecution when or if they will call a defendant to testify.

Okay, I thought. Let's see what she says now about how she killed Travis.

CHAPTER 20

The defense calls Jodi Arias."

Nurmi's announcement resulted in a perceptible stillness settling over the courtroom that Monday afternoon. This was the moment everyone had been anticipating, and it came earlier than I had expected. Typically, the defendant is the last witness to take the stand. Being the last to testify carries with it the advantage of knowing what every other witness has already said, affording a defendant the opportunity to address any troublesome issues that require further explanation, so for Arias to testify before the defense had presented the rest of its case was a bit of a surprise.

While I had not been given notice that Arias would be taking the stand until minutes before she was called that afternoon, I had time to voice an objection to her walking from the defense table to the witness stand in view of the jury. As a security measure designed to prevent an escape, all inmates attending trial are fitted with a leg brace that locks at the knee should the person try to run away. The brace is worn underneath the pant leg and is not visible but causes a noticeable limp when the person is walking.

To avoid the jury seeing Arias walking in this fashion and possibly feeling sympathy for her, Judge Stephens granted my request that Arias should already be in the witness box when the jury was brought back into the courtroom.

As she waited in the witness chair for the proceedings to

begin, Arias took a deep breath, pulled the microphone closer, and gazed at the dozens of faces staring back at her.

I thought back to the status conference five years earlier, when I had seen her in the courtroom for the first time, sitting in the jury box looking somewhat out of place dressed in horizontally striped black-and-white jail garb apparently not having any need for glasses back then. Today she would play a different part, the lead role as an abused woman. Her short-sleeve black sweater was appropriately conservative and paired with baggy light-colored slacks several sizes too big for her slight frame; it was an ensemble that had surely been chosen to make her appear smaller and somewhat fragile, with the wispy bangs and thick-framed glasses completing the librarian look.

"Ms. Arias, please stand to be sworn," Judge Stephens directed when the jury returned to the courtroom just after 2 P.M.

As we were all about to see, swearing to tell the truth, "so help me God," meant nothing to Jodi Ann Arias.

I imagined her testimony would immediately focus on the crime itself, because before this point all we had heard from the defense's witnesses was what a cad Travis had been. But it quickly became clear from Nurmi's initial questions that his direct examination would take an indirect route.

"Hi, Jodi," he began in a friendly tone.

Arias managed to eke out a "hi" in a voice so faint she was barely audible.

"How are you feeling right now?" Nurmi asked.

Before Arias could answer the very first question posed, I objected, and the judge sustained my objection, because Arias' feelings were irrelevant to the truthfulness of her answers.

Nurmi rephrased the question. "I want to ask you—let me ask you this, is this a position you ever thought you would find yourself in?"

"Objection, relevance," I said again, because the question was along the same vein as the previous one.

And with that, Judge Stephens switched on the white noise, a computer generated sound specifically designed to prevent others in the courtroom from hearing bench conferences between court and counsel. The white noise had already begun to dominate the proceedings as there were countless bench conferences called throughout the trial.

While the judge considered my objection, Arias became the focus of the TV cameras and of everyone in the courtroom. Even under such intense scrutiny, she remained unflappable, looking relaxed and at ease as she sat facing the gallery with her hands folded in her lap.

After a quick discussion, during which the judge sustained my objection, Nurmi returned to the floor to resume his direct examination. "Let me ask you a couple of important questions before we get back and start talking about who you are and why you're here, okay?"

"Okay."

"Did you kill Travis Alexander on June 4, 2008?"

"Yes, I did," she replied in a matter-of-fact tone and without a trace of emotion.

"Why?"

There was a pregnant pause before Arias delivered what smacked of a rehearsed response. "The simple answer is he attacked me, and I was defending myself."

"Okay, it was brought up during these proceedings that you gave an interview to *Inside Edition*. Do you remember seeing that tape?"

"Yes, I do."

"And in that tape, you said that no jury would convict you, something to that effect, do you remember saying that?"

"Yeah, I did say that," Arias admitted, looking down at her lap.

"Why?" Nurmi posed.

"I made that statement in September 2008, I believe it was, and at that time I had plans to commit suicide. So I was extremely confident that no jury would convict me because I didn't expect any of you to be here. I didn't expect to be here, so I could have easily said no jury would acquit me, either," she said, taking a statement that showed her in a negative light and attempting to turn it into a sympathetic moment.

"I couldn't say that, though, because there was an officer sitting five feet behind me. Had I told them the reason no jury would convict me at that time, I would have been thrown in a padded cell and stripped down and that would have been my life for a while until I stabilized.

"So I was very confident that no jury would convict me because I planned to be dead. Probably the most bitter words I'll ever eat," Arias added in a subdued voice, as if to show regret—not for killing Travis, but for making the seemingly pompous statement on national television.

"I'm sorry, what was that?" Nurmi asked, appearing eager to have Arias repeat the statement to emphasize her regret.

"I said, those are probably the most bitter words I'll ever eat."

Nurmi's inquiry moved to questions about Arias' life, beginning with her immediate family, followed by questions about her childhood in Salinas, California.

"I lived there until I was twelve," Arias said. I found it ironic that this was the city where she had chosen to buy the third gas can.

"Okay, what was life like in Salinas?"

"The first years of my life, it was really good."

"When you say that—before you continue, let's clarify. What do you mean by first years?"

"I would say until about age seven it was a fairly ideal childhood," she explained, without elaborating.

"Okay, different people have different meanings when they say ideal, so why don't you describe for us what you mean by ideal childhood?"

"I have predominantly positive memories of my childhood

at that time. My brother and I lived in—when I was about four years old, we moved to a house in a cul-de-sac. We had the center lot, so it was a huge backyard. We had a lot of places to play there. There were trees to climb and there were other kids in the neighborhood . . . that we played with. . . ."

Arias explained that while she and her brother Carl were two years apart in age, they were just a grade apart in school because Arias had been left back in kindergarten.

"And tell us about your parents at that time, to your recollection. Were they both working? Was your mom at home? Tell us about that."

"Yeah, when I was younger, I remember my mom used to work. I guess she was working as a server with my dad. He owned restaurants my whole life. Then, when I was around eleven or twelve, she became a dental assistant."

". . . Jodi, one of the things that you said a couple of questions ago when we were speaking is that your life was pretty ideal up until about age seven. Is something different after age seven, or . . . ?" Nurmi asked, signaling Arias to change topics and begin discussing the alleged physical abuse by her parents.

"It seemed like, well you know, my parents would just, you know, spank us or hit us, discipline. So it seemed like at age seven it started getting a little bit more intense . . ." Arias responded.

"Okay, you said they started spanking you?"

"Well, I was spanked before on occasion. It seemed like the frequency and the intensity of it increased around that age."

"What do you mean by that, frequency and intensity?" Nurmi pressed. It was becoming clear that defense counsel was working to depict Jodi Arias as a victim of childhood abuse.

"Well, just—there were—I think that's the first year my dad started using a belt," Arias said, starting to tear up. "My mom began to carry a wooden spoon in her purse."

"Objection," I said. "Relevance."

"Sustained," Judge Stephens ruled.

"May we approach?" Nurmi asked the judge.

"You may," Judge Stephens said, flipping on the white noise once again.

After a brief discussion at the bench, the judge ruled that Nurmi could continue with his line of inquiry.

"You were just now telling us that your mother carried a wooden spoon with her. What did she do with that spoon?" he asked.

"It was a wooden kitchen spoon that she would keep in her purse, and if we were misbehaving, my brother and I, this was before Angela and Joseph were born, although it continued through that point, if we were misbehaving, she would use it on us. Sometimes, she would pull the car over and, you know, like if we were being brats or something . . ."

"What do you mean by use it on you?"

"She would hit us with it."

"She hit you hard?"

"It felt pretty hard, yes. It left welts."

Arias' mother, Sandy, was in the front row of the gallery next to her twin sister, Heather, and appeared to be fighting back tears as she listened to her daughter's account. Across the aisle were Travis' sisters Samantha and Tanisha. Samantha, in particular, glared at Jodi Arias, in apparent disgust at what appeared to be an attempt by Arias to blame Travis' murder on her parents' discipline.

"It left welts on your body?" Nurmi repeated.

"Yes."

"When your dad hit you with the belt, did that leave welts on your body?"

"Objection. Lack of foundation. Time. Date," I said.

"Rephrase," Judge Stephens advised Nurmi.

"You told us your dad hit you with a belt? . . . After age seven? . . . Did he leave welts?"

"He didn't leave welts as often as my mom," Arias replied.

"She also used a belt," Arias continued. "My dad was very

intimidating, so I don't think he needed to hit us quite as hard to get the point across. My mom didn't carry that fear factor with her, so I think she used more force. Her blows felt a lot worse, actually."

"Physically or emotionally?"

"Both."

". . . Can you discern for us how many times a week your mother would beat you with the spoon?" Nurmi asked, substituting Arias' word "hit" with the word "beat" to describe the punishment.

"I don't recall how many times, particularly, but it seemed like it could go anywhere from four times a week to once every two weeks. It just depended."

Arias claimed the "beatings" from her mother and father "increased" in frequency and severity, "I'd say all the way through my teenage years."

Focusing on the discipline meted out by her parents was an unexpected approach to her self-defense claim. The issue to be resolved by the jury was whether she had premeditated Travis' murder, not whether she had been mistreated by her parents. Arias ran the risk of alienating the jury by appearing to complain about every single alleged act of abuse, which could make her come across to the jury as less a victim and more a spoiled child.

"Okay . . . you've talked about frequency and severity; did the level of the brutality increase?" Nurmi inquired, incorporating an even more severe term in his question.

"Yes. My brother and I would—we didn't like being hit. . . . I know I didn't, so we would squirm around a little. The more we squirmed, the harder they would try to whack us.

"So, just, that progressed. Things would increase. You know, at one point, I don't think she meant to, but my mother broke my brother's vein in his wrist as he was putting his hand behind his back to block one of her blows. And, you know, as

I became a teenager, my dad would get rougher and rougher," Arias answered.

"Okay, before we go on to rougher and rougher, let me ask you this, and I'm not simply talking physically: How did you feel? How did you feel when your own mother was beating you?"

"When I was younger, I remember feeling—I didn't have a word for it then, but I can describe it as betrayed and confused. And as I got a little bit older, it would just really make me mad because I just—I didn't get why. I don't know, I understood I was being punished, but I would just be mad at her a lot because it hurt."

"Because you still loved her?" said Nurmi, apparently providing Arias with the reason for the anger directed at her mother.

"Yeah. I loved my mom."

"Even though she was still beating you, and you still loved her?"

"Yes. It put a strain on our relationship, but I still loved her, of course."

". . . Going back to what you said about your dad and the beatings getting rougher and rougher, could you describe for us what you mean by that?"

"Yeah. He never beat me with his fists or anything, he would just shove me into furniture, sometimes the piano, or things like that, into tables, chairs, desks, whatever was around. He would just push me really hard, and I would go flying into that.

"One time I hit a door post on the side of my head, hit the post, and it knocked me out momentarily. I just remember waking up on the ground. My mom was there. We were all arguing. I was arguing with my mom and he got involved. So I remember waking up, and she was telling him to be careful."

". . . Do you remember how old you were when this happened?"

"By then, I was age seventeen, maybe sixteen, but I think I was seventeen."

As I sat listening, I noticed that Nurmi had avoided asking about visits to the doctor or hospital, times when police or school officials might have initiated an investigation, or discussions among family and friends about any injuries or possible bruising they might have seen. Arias' testimony on the alleged beatings would remain unconfirmed for the rest of the trial, with no corroborating witnesses or documents to support these allegations.

Nurmi proceeded to introduce a second line of inquiry that centered on the many moves Arias' family made after they left Salinas when she was twelve.

Arias testified that after living in Santa Maria for a couple of years, the family moved to Yreka, where she attended high school, beginning in the ninth grade.

". . . Okay. And just to give us a sense of things, how far was Yreka from Santa Maria, where you moved from?" Nurmi asked. "So you were several hours away?"

"Yeah, ten hours," Arias replied in a voice barely above a whisper, adding that she didn't know anybody when she moved there.

". . . Now, you mentioned that when you moved to—based on what you told us before, are we correct in understanding that the beatings, the pushing of the furniture, that sort of thing with your dad, continued throughout your high school years?" Nurmi asked.

"Yes," Arias confirmed.

"Okay. Were those the incidents that you were talking about before about being pushed into the post and the furniture, or were there other incidents?"

"That happened when I was in high school. There were a few things that happened right before we moved," Arias recounted. "A bunch of my friends and I one night decided—like the last night we were there we decided to sneak out of the house and hang out and my parents woke up and found out.

"So, when I came back, my dad asked where I had been. And I had fallen asleep. He woke me up around 6:00. So, when I sat up I was disoriented because I had been sleeping. I didn't give him a satisfactory answer, so he hit me across the face, and I fell back down.

"Then he sat me back up and asked me again, and I didn't give him a satisfactory answer, so he hit me across the face again, and I fell back down."

"When you say he hit you across the face, did he punch you?" Nurmi asked.

"No. It was an openhanded, hard slap."

"Do you recall, did you bleed?"

"No, I didn't. Not that I recall."

"Did you bruise?"

"Not that I recall."

"Did it hurt?"

"Yes."

". . . Your dad is a pretty big guy, right?" Nurmi said, presenting a menacing impression of Arias' father.

"He was pretty big at that time," Arias affirmed. "His health is—he's frail now, but he was very big at that time. . . . I don't know his weight, but he's about five eleven. He used to bench-press 520 pounds. . . ."

". . . To your knowledge, was your mom aware—I know you mentioned the one incident where your mom was present; was your mom aware of your dad beating you?"

"Well, she was present, yes, of course. Sometimes we were on road trips together, and they would take turns if they, you know, had to pull the car over, or something. . . ."

". . . Did your mom's beatings with the wooden spoon, did they continue in high school as well?"

"They continued for a short time, but I think as I turned sixteen, seventeen, she—I don't recall her carrying the wooden spoon around, but she just started grabbing whatever was available, like a hairbrush.

"She had acrylic nails, so sometimes she would grab me and dig her nails into my skin, and things like that."

After determining that Arias did not graduate high school, Nurmi asked, "Why didn't you graduate high school?"

"Well, it's kind of complicated," Arias replied, initially hesitating to acknowledge her failure before discussing her excuses for not having earned her diploma.

She explained that she was no longer living at home when she dropped out of high school, and had moved in with her then boyfriend in a town about six miles from Yreka.

"Okay, why did you leave your parents' home to go live with your boyfriend?"

"I was kind of tired of the discipline, and it was three months until I was eighteen. And one day, they decided to ground me until I was eighteen. I was—I skipped one period in high school because there was a final for my—I was taking a college history class, U.S. history, and I wasn't—I didn't feel like I had adequately studied, so I skipped that period to study for the exam and decided I would make it up the next day.

"So, I parked my car in the parking lot at Rite Aid and just cracked open the window and I was studying it for that hour, and my dad—somehow found me. It's a small town.

"So, I guess the school notified him I wasn't present for that class, so he found me. And at that point, they didn't use physical discipline that day, but I was grounded until I was eighteen. I couldn't fathom being grounded for three months.

"When you were grounded in my house, it meant no phone, no TV, no friends, no social functions of any kind, and you're in your room, period.

". . . And I thought, I wasn't going to wait until I was eighteen to move in with him. It was three months away, and it just made sense to me at that time, as I was seventeen years old, so I just moved out."

Arias sounded like a rebellious teenager who would do things her way irrespective of the consequences and then complain that it really wasn't her fault because, as in this case, she needed to cut class to study for a test.

The trial had now become the Jodi Ann Arias life story. As she and Nurmi told it, her mother had been quick to beat her, usually with a spoon, while her father would push her down and slap her in the face. She portrayed her parents harsh in grounding her for cutting class.

The success of the approach being employed by the defense hinged on the jury believing Arias' words and developing sympathy and positive feelings for her—and forgetting that she had problems telling the truth.

CHAPTER 21

Once the defense finished discussing in detail how Jodi Arias was allegedly mistreated by her parents when growing up, they turned their attention to Arias' relationships with men, starting with her high school boyfriend, Bobby Juarez. It appeared their goal was to expose for the jury what they believed to be a pattern in her relationships, which would begin with a honeymoon period during which Arias supposedly committed herself fully only to be hurt after she discovered that the other person was either unfaithful or did not want to commit to her.

Rather than be grounded for missing school, Arias moved out of her parents' house and in with Bobby, whom she had met at a carnival when she was fifteen and he was eighteen. She testified that the relationship started off as a friendship, with the two dating on and off over the next three years. Arias said she and Bobby had been back together for about seven months when she moved in with him. At the time, Bobby was living in Montague with an elderly couple he addressed as "Mom" and "Dad," but Arias believed they were his grandparents.

"I got a job at another restaurant and began working full-time," she recounted. ". . . To me it made more sense to work so I could support myself and my boyfriend. He didn't have a job." This response typified Arias' style of emphasizing a point by being critical of others.

Arias testified that she believed things were going well in their relationship until she discovered that Bobby was supposedly cheating. She described his frequent telephone conversations with a woman he claimed was just a friend. "They had been interested in each other in the past," she said. "He would talk to her a lot, actually, in my presence. So I figured if he's doing it right in front of me, there's nothing going on there.

"So then, one day, he went to the library. That's where we went for Internet access, and he would e-mail her a lot. And I took—I had to go to work at the Purple Plum. And I dropped him off at his friend's house. . . . And before going to the Purple Plum, I went back to the library. And I clicked—this is—he had a Hotmail account. This is in 1998. So I clicked the—I don't know if they had different security things for Hotmail at that point. But I clicked the 'back' button to see what was really going on with her, because I had suspicions. And I found a whole bunch of love letters that he was writing her that were all contemporaneous with the time that we were together.

"So I printed them out and I called in sick for work, because I was not well emotionally. And I drove back out to his friend's house, and I didn't want to create a scene or drama. So I said, 'Can I talk to you?' So we went into the bathroom, and I pulled them out of my pocket and handed them to him, and he opened them up and read them and—he felt kind of shocked."

This story showed what appeared to be the jealous side of Arias, who would go to any lengths in an effort to confirm her suspicions, including snooping into a library computer to access her boyfriend's e-mail account.

Arias said she broke up with Bobby after that, but then agreed to get back with him after he promised to break off contact with the other woman, someone we would later learn he had never met in person.

In response to Nurmi's question as to whether Bobby ever physically abused her, Arias recounted an argument the two had in the fall of 1999, when Bobby came to see her at the home of a friend where she was staying.

"Our argument escalated and he approached me and spun

me around, and he was very much into martial arts. So he had some kind of hold. I guess it's called a stranglehold. So he started strangling me just for a few seconds and then he let go. I almost passed out. I fell on my knees."

". . . I was trying to get to the phone to call 911 and he got my arm in some kind of lock and was putting pressure on my forearm and I thought he might break it because that seemed to be what the goal was. So I managed to grab the phone and I called 911, and he grabbed it out of my hand and hung up.

"And I was crying. He kept telling me to shut up because they were going to call back. So he was right. The phone rang and he answered and he gave the operator an excuse like, he said, 'My girlfriend was trying to program 911 into the speed dial and accidentally called it.'" Any vestige of truthfulness in Arias' answer was now shrouded in doubt because 911 operators are trained to ask to speak with the person who called, and not simply accept the word of the boyfriend offering an excuse as to why the emergency number was dialed.

"But did you stay together after that?" Nurmi asked.

"This was really toward the end of our relationship. . . . We didn't stay together much longer after that."

Arias' answer was apparently not the response that Nurmi was hoping to elicit, because he followed up with similar questions.

"Why did you stay together with him after this incident?"

"Well, I don't know if we were still together," Arias replied. "But he would still come over to the house where I lived. . . ."

"Why would you hang out with him in that regard?"

". . . During all the years I've known him, that had never happened before. So I just didn't think it was something that was a pattern of his or that would continue."

"Did you ever engage in sexual behavior with him after this incident?" Nurmi asked.

"I don't remember, maybe," she said tentatively, ". . . maybe once or twice. I don't remember, honestly."

"And why was that okay with you after this incident?"

"I still loved him," Arias answered.

Perhaps this was the answer that Nurmi wanted, because he now left this topic and turned to asking questions about her next boyfriend, Bobby Juarez's roommate, Matthew McCartney. Bobby and Matt were sharing a studio apartment in Medford, Oregon, about fifty miles north of Yreka, where Arias was a frequent visitor. She said she was still trying to make things work with Bobby when she discovered something about Matt during a visit to Medford that made her take notice. That weekend, Matt had a female visitor.

"And it was a real eye-opener because I saw how Matt was treating her, and he was very chivalrous and very polite, and he was a gentleman, and he just treated her with a lot of respect," Arias recounted. "And that's not something I had received, but I had seen it on TV and that kind of thing. So, it was just jarring to see that and then consider my relationship."

". . . But you lived with your parents for the first seventeen years or your life, right? Did you not see your father treat your mother in this way?" Nurmi asked, creating an opening for Arias to once again disparage her father, this time claiming that he treated her mother in a degrading manner.

"One I recall specifically is my mother used to be very thin, and I think she is a size 10 now. . . . He used to put up photos of her on the refrigerator when she was thinner. And he would make comments about her weight . . . he would put things like that around the house to remind her that he would prefer her with less weight. . . ."

Although Arias believed that her relationship with Bobby Juarez was no longer going as she hoped and he was indicating a desire to break up, Arias testified she decided to move to Medford, where he was living, ostensibly because there were more job opportunities. Further complicating her move, Bobby would no longer speak to her after an incident where he "came around the corner and saw us [Arias and Matt] all, like, just hanging out and having fun."

Jumping from one lover to the next, especially when Matt was Bobby's roommate, made her seem an opportunist, rather than the victim she was attempting to portray.

When court resumed on Tuesday morning, Arias continued her testimony by describing the initial period of her relationship with Matt McCartney in glowing terms. About five weeks after the two started dating, the couple moved into a small apartment together, with Arias finding a job at Applebee's and Matt working as a manager at Subway.

"I see that period of my life as probably one of the best times in my life," Arias recalled. "He treated me very well. He was very kind. He was very respectful. He was very spiritual," she recalled.

". . . At the time you met Matt, where were you spiritually?" Nurmi asked. "Was there a particular religion you were a member of? . . ."

"I was not a member of any denomination. I considered myself Christian. I didn't attend church. And I didn't obey all the commandments that Christianity espouses."

"Okay, so when you talk about Matt and the spirituality, did you become more affiliated with his beliefs . . . ?"

"We sort of explored together and opened up to other beliefs. We began taking meditation seminars, kind of New Age–type seminars, but they had their roots in Hinduism and Buddhism, maybe some kind of, like, a more modern version of transcendentalism, things like that. We took these little courses and classes and we would drive to Portland or the Bay Area."

"Okay. Was that a big part of your relationship?" Nurmi inquired.

"Yes, it was," she answered, perhaps not realizing that she was describing the identical path she would later take with

Travis, where she fully immersed herself in Mormonism to align herself with him.

"This may go without saying because you had lived together: Was this also a sexual relationship?"

"Yes."

"Did you love Matt?"

"Very much. Yeah, I was in love with him."

Arias explained that she and Matt lived together for about five months in Medford before moving to Crater Lake, Oregon, where they found seasonal work and dorm accommodations at the Crater Lake Resort.

"How long in total in terms of relationship were you together with Matt?"

"I think approximately a year and eight months."

"And in that year and eight months, did he ever hit you?"

"No."

"Did he ever call you a whore?"

"No."

"Slut?"

"No."

"Three-hole wonder?"

"No."

By this point, Nurmi had asked this same set of questions so often that the words had begun to lose their intrinsic power to shock the listener.

"What brought the end of your relationship with Matt McCartney?" Nurmi continued.

Arias recounted that after their summer at Crater Lake, they rented the same small apartment in Medford, but after a couple of months, they began to argue over little things.

"It wasn't anything serious, but it wore on our relationship because it made things not enjoyable," she said, explaining that at one point, the two decided to take a break, with Matt returning to Crater Lake for one season and Arias moving to

Ashland, Oregon, about fifteen miles south of Medford. "We saw each other on weekends. He would come into town in Ashland and stay with me.

"And I remember I was with his dad's girlfriend . . . and we were trying to download pictures onto his dad's hard drive, and on the desktop there were some other pictures of this girl. And I didn't recognize her. But I recognized the setting. And it was inside the lodge at Crater Lake.

"And the date was also current with the season, which would have been 2001 . . . and a few weeks later, I was working at Applebee's. . . . I was walking past this table and two people said, 'Hi, Jodi,' and I stopped, and I didn't recognize them. And they explained that they worked with Matt at Crater Lake, and they were just in town for their days off. . . . And they said, 'We took a vote. We think you should know something.' And they told me he was seeing another girl named Bianca at Crater Lake. . . ." The chance meeting with two of Matt's Crater Lake coworkers, who were so in tune with democratic principles that they even took a vote before telling her of his relationship with another woman, strained credibility. Arias' story was especially troublesome because she failed to explain how these strangers would even have recognized her.

"What did you do when you had this information?"

"I was reeling, because, I mean, of all the boyfriends I had, I would have expected him to not be the one that cheated on me. He was very loyal. I trusted him completely, like implicitly. He could have said the sky was falling and I would have believed him. I think I would have just looked out the window to see what it looks like."

Arias testified that she asked her boss to leave early that night, went home, changed her clothes, and set off for Crater Lake. "I decided I wanted to find out if it was true. So . . . I drove up to Crater Lake to see if I could find out. . . . I didn't want to continue the relationship if that was the case."

Arias described her quest to find Bianca's room, and what she did when Bianca answered the knock at her door. "I said, 'Hi, are you Bianca?' and she said, 'Yeah.' So she invited me in because she knew who I was. And so we sat down."

Arias claimed that they had a ninety-minute conversation, during which she confirmed that Bianca and Matt were together.

"Now, in this hour-and-a-half conversation, were you yelling at her?" Nurmi asked.

"No. It was just chitchat, actually. I mean, I was not trying to freak out or get upset, you know, because she had no idea. She was under the impression that he and I were no longer together. I didn't look at this as her fault."

"How did it feel when you had this information confirmed?"

"I didn't really allow myself to have much emotion until I left her presence. And at that point, I allowed myself to cry."

Arias explained that a confrontation with Matt came soon after, in September 2001. "I went over to his dad's house. I knew the day he was getting back. And he was on the phone with Bianca when I came over. And he hung up, and he said, 'I know what you want to talk about.'

". . . And basically our relationship was over and it was kind of sad," she said, describing the outcome of their conversation.

Arias testified that she left the Medford area soon after, because there were "too many memories," but said that she and McCartney remained friends.

Her next stop was the Big Sur–Carmel area to seek employment at the Ventana Inn & Spa, where she met the man who would become her next love interest, Darryl Brewer.

In response to Nurmi's questions, Arias described her growing feelings for Brewer, whom she said she began dating about a year into her employment at the Ventana Inn.

"Now, at that point in time, how old are you . . . and how old was Mr. Brewer?"

"I was twenty-two . . . he was forty-two."

"How did you feel about dating someone that much your senior?"

"I wasn't so much concerned about dating him as I was concerned about how other people might view it," Arias replied. "I found Darryl very attractive. He was tall. He was, you know, handsome, beautiful eyes, that kind of thing. We were very compatible, our personalities. I don't know, I saw him as, like, a George Clooney type, like, he's older but attractive. And we had lots of similar interests."

Arias also testified in detail about their four-and-a-half-year relationship, which included their decision to buy a house together, and the events that led up to their breakup.

"Right off the bat, he told you that he didn't want to get married?" Nurmi suggested.

"He made his intentions very clear that he liked me and he was attracted to me and he was okay with being with me, but he said, 'I don't see myself getting married again.' "

"And how did that sit with you?"

"I was young at that time. So it didn't bother me. I figure I'll have many years left. And I enjoyed being with him so that's what I did. I just enjoyed the time we had together."

After discussing the house Arias and Brewer bought together in Palm Desert, Nurmi moved on to the status of their relationship. "Okay . . . the fall of 2006 . . . what was going on with your relationship with Mr. Brewer?" Nurmi inquired. "Were you still happy, or describe that for us?"

"I still loved him. We weren't really progressing in our relationship. I was no longer twenty-two. I was twenty-six now, so I began to question where I was going with my life. Was I going to have a family with this person? And so it really didn't seem that way. And at the time my goal was marriage and children, at least someday. . . . And so at age twenty-six, I was more than halfway through my twenties, and I wanted to begin focusing more on that. . . ."

Things got worse when Brewer informed her that he wanted

to move to the Monterey area to be closer to his son from his first marriage, who would now be attending school in Pacific Grove, meaning she would soon be without a boyfriend as well as a financial partner.

Arias said she began actively looking for ways to get on her feet monetarily. She thought she had found the answer in March 2006, when she was cleaning out her closet and came upon a DVD about Pre-Paid Legal Services, which had been given to her months earlier by her manager at the California Pizza Kitchen, where she had worked for a time.

"He asked me where I saw myself in five years," she recalled of their exchange. "He said he was going to be retired. I thought it was a bold statement because he was about my age."

Arias said she had planned on throwing the video away, but after watching it, she liked what she saw. "It seemed like something that . . . I might have success with," she said, recalling that she promptly went online to sign up and purchase a membership.

Her online membership resulted in a call from a woman named Michelle, an associate of PPL who gave her "tons of supplies, DVDs to pass out to other people, magazines, marketing materials." Arias admitted she didn't do anything with the materials. And when Michelle called a few months later to invite her to a PPL event in Daniels Summit, Utah, she couldn't go because she was attending her cousin's wedding. But when Michelle phoned again in late summer to invite her to the PPL convention taking place in Las Vegas that September, she agreed to attend. Arrangements were made for Arias to carpool from Southern California with Michelle and another woman, Lenore, and the three would share a room at the MGM Grand, where the event was being held.

"I had never attended a convention, so I didn't really know what to expect," Arias said, explaining that she hadn't packed items such as a fancy dress for the more elaborate events or a bikini to enjoy the outdoor swimming facilities.

"While you were at this convention, did you ever meet an individual by the name of Travis Alexander?" Nurmi inquired, mentioning the subject of this criminal prosecution for the first time in nearly two days, signaling an end to the extended tour of Arias' life.

The narrative she would spin about her relationship with Travis, via Nurmi's questions, was akin to Cinderella's story, with Arias playing the lead role. In her telling, when she first encountered her Prince Charming, she was standing at the Rainforest Café, in the lobby of the MGM Grand, watching the crowd of people part.

"I saw somebody walking toward me, kind of fast paced, and I noticed it was a guy," Arias began. "And I thought he was going somewhere, because he had a purpose. So I stepped out of the way. I thought he needed to walk past me. But he stopped right in front of me and stuck his hand out and introduced himself."

Arias seemed to be reliving the magic of the moment from the witness box as she recounted how Travis invited her to be his guest at the prestigious executive director banquet, a function similar to a formal ball, scheduled for that evening. Arias remembered that she at first turned him down, because she didn't have a dress appropriate for the occasion and there was no time to shop for one. Her rendition even included a fairy godmother in Travis' friend Sky Hughes, who just happened to have a dress that Arias could wear that night.

"Okay. Tell us what the banquet was like for you?" Nurmi inquired.

"It was nice," Arias related. "I was somewhat accustomed to that level of dining because of my serving experience, but I was always the server, never the guest. . . ."

"It sounds to me like, then, that you were to some degree getting intoxicated by the success you were seeing. Is that fair to say?"

"I don't know if intoxicated would quite be right, but it definitely made a big impression on me."

Arias said that at the PPL event the following day, Travis invited her to sit by his side on the floor with the executive directors, which was "special pass" seating, where she would sit with him over the next two days of the convention.

At the end of the weekend, Travis indicated he would call her, and Arias admitted, "I didn't really expect him to call, but that's kind of where we left it."

"And you talked about breaking up with Mr. Brewer. When did you do that?" Nurmi asked.

"I got back from the convention on Sunday and I broke up with Darryl on Thursday that week."

As she had done when she started dating Matt, Arias was leaving her current boyfriend as soon as she had another man in waiting, someone she saw as a prince. But there would be no glass slipper waiting for Arias when she returned to Palm Desert, as Travis was unwilling to play the role of Prince Charming, a part she wanted him to play. So, Arias made sure that Travis would never have any happily ever afters.

CHAPTER 22

The prosecution of Jodi Ann Arias had been a hot topic of nightly cable news shows since the trial started on January 2, 2013, and people traveled across the state each day hoping to secure a seat in the gallery. Demand was such that those wanting to get seats, which were available on a first-come, first-served basis, started to line up hours before court started. But interest from both the media and court watchers heightened when Arias' testimony turned to graphic details of her sexual relationship with Travis Alexander, culminating in the introduction of the sexually explicit phone call Arias recorded on May 10, 2008, where the two are heard moaning and squealing in the throes of a masturbatory climax.

I was surprised at defense counsel's decision to question Arias in such painstaking detail about her sexual behavior with Travis, turning the trial into a Masters and Johnson sex clinic while avoiding the issue of her premeditation of the murder. It seemed Nurmi was attempting to emphasize Travis' involvement in the sexual activity, while at the same time, minimizing Arias' participation by saying it was not her choice to have sex, but rather a result of her inability to say no.

But although he wanted the jury to see Travis in a negative light, Nurmi failed to acknowledge that Arias was enjoying these encounters and, as she would be heard lamenting in their sex tape, she was concerned that the sexual growth that she had enjoyed so much with Travis would be stunted by being with a less adventuresome partner.

"I worry that I might feel like a wilting flower is all, who never really blossomed to her full potential, at least in the sexual world. . . . I still have plenty of blossom time left. . . ."

The jurors endured what seemed like endless testimony about each and every sexual episode Arias and Travis had, no matter how embarrassing the details. Her recollection of their first time together centered on the weekend they spent at the Murrieta, California, home of Travis' friends Chris and Sky Hughes, approximately a week after Arias met him at the convention in Las Vegas.

"Did you feel uncomfortable going to Murrieta to spend . . . a couple of days in this home with people you barely knew?" Nurmi began.

". . . It had been discussed ahead of time . . . that I could stay the night," she replied dispassionately. "They had an extra bedroom and they wanted me to attend church with them in the morning. So I agreed to that."

"When did you first kiss Mr. Alexander?" Nurmi asked.

"We all went to bed," Arias recalled. "And he came into the bedroom I was staying in. I assumed there was probably going to be some kissing or some kind of talking or hanging out. We talked every night that entire week. So, that's when we kissed."

". . . Was there conversation first? Did he just come in and start kissing you?"

"There was no conversation. I thought there was going to be, but there was no conversation," Arias said.

". . . Okay. Was he touching you?"

". . . We were getting intimate. We were making out, basically. . . . At that point, we were laying on the bed. We were side by side, facing each other, kissing. . . . It began to lead to more."

"What do you mean by 'more'?"

"Well, I don't really recall how it happened, but he began to remove my clothes."

". . . When he began to remove your clothing, was that surprising to you?"

"It was really surprising, but it was more—I felt apprehensive, but I was going with it. . . . I wasn't expecting that. So I didn't want to tell him no. So I was just going with it," she answered.

"Why didn't you want to tell him no?" Nurmi asked.

"I didn't want to do anything that would displease him, not because I feared, like, he would get angry or anything. But I didn't want to—I didn't want him to feel rejected. And I didn't want him to get his feelings hurt. I didn't want to spoil the mood. . . ."

"Why would rejecting him at this point in time be such a big deal to you?"

"At this point in time, I wasn't really accustomed to saying no. . . . It was hard for me to tell somebody no. . . ." she answered, obviously forgetting that she had already testified that she was the one who refused to have sexual relations with Darryl although they were living under the same roof.

This response was apparently designed to illustrate Arias' vulnerability in her relationships with men, which ignored how assertive she had been in relationships with her previous boyfriends. She broke up with Bobby after snooping and finding letters he had sent to another woman using the library computer; drove hours to chat with Bianca, who she believed was involved with Matt, before confronting him and breaking off the relationship, and ending it with Darryl to be with Travis.

Arias testified that at some point during their evening escapade in Murrieta, Travis removed his clothing, which included his temple garments, undergarments worn by Mormons beneath their clothing.

"This is embarrassing," Arias said coyly, before matter-of-factly regaling the court with minute and intimate details of her sexual encounter with Travis.

"I understand how it might be, but it's important to share this with us. So, if you could please tell us what happened next?" Nurmi asked in a reassuring tone.

"He began to perform oral sex on me," she replied in a low whisper.

"And was this comfortable?" Nurmi prodded. ". . . Were you comfortable when this oral sex was going on?"

"I was comfortable. It was dark. I mean, the lights were off, so that made it a little bit more tolerable . . . I mean, I knew what he was doing, for sure. But it was just—it felt like it was much too soon. And I mean, I couldn't exactly rewind at that point."

". . . Why didn't you voice your discomfort?"

"I didn't want him to have that impression. I wanted to at least appear like I was enjoying it as much as he seemed to be. . . ."

"So you were attempting to give him the impression that you were enjoying things?"

"Yes."

". . . Okay. What happened after he performed oral sex upon you?"

"He asked for reciprocation."

"And how did that request make you feel?"

"At that point, I had taken it that far. I was kind of glad he was done. And I was just willing to reciprocate at that point," she answered, describing her sexual response as if it were an act of charity.

Without pausing, Nurmi asked Arias to outline the details of her next meeting with Travis, which occurred several days later. Travis phoned to say that he would be passing through the Palm Desert area and wanted to give her a copy of the Book of Mormon. Uncomfortable with Travis coming to the house she shared with Darryl Brewer, Arias said she arranged for the two to meet at a nearby Starbucks, where they ordered drinks and Travis told her about the Word of Wisdom, an LDS doctrine that prohibits the consumption of coffee, tea, alcohol, tobacco, and illegal drugs, after which the two agreed to find a place because, according to her, "he was horny."

Arias claimed that they drove to a park near the Starbucks and Travis told her he wanted to "receive oral sex," so she complied. "I felt an attraction to him and the feeling was mutual. . . . I don't know, I wanted to do what he wanted to do," she said, ignoring that she didn't have to drive to the park to be with him.

Arias admitted to feeling disappointed in herself, especially because Travis left within minutes of ejaculating, but she felt better after he called her later in the day apologizing for the way he had treated her.

Arias said that after her encounter with Travis at Starbucks, she began receiving visits from Mormon missionaries, hoping to introduce her to the church and relate their beliefs. She said she spoke to Travis on the phone almost daily, but the two didn't see each other again until a month later, when they met at a hotel in Ehrenberg, Arizona, a small town just across the Colorado River from California. Arias said they chose that location because it was a halfway point between Mesa and Palm Desert and admitted that sexual intimacy "was kind of the purpose of the trip."

Her stated disappointment with his having left right after he climaxed during the previous encounter did not deter her from agreeing to meet him at a hotel to spend time together, which seemed hypocritical if, as she claimed, she really didn't want to just have sex, but also wanted some romance.

She described the weekend as being more about sex than romance. "There was oral sex that weekend. . . . We did what I guess he called—at the time he called it grinding . . . just being together but not actually having intercourse. It's something that I guess a lot of Mormons do. But they're not supposed to. . . . There are different terms for it, [such as] the Provo Push. . . ."

"When you weren't engaged in sexual activity, how was he treating you?" Nurmi asked.

"He wasn't treating me bad. He just seemed checked out, you know, the whole time we were checked in, he was just kind of distant. I thought we connected a lot over the phone. And it was different when we were together . . . there wasn't much of a mental or emotional connection like there was on the phone.

"It was just primarily physical," Arias added in a voice so low that Nurmi implored her to speak up so the jury could hear her response.

When he asked if she considered herself to be in a relationship with Travis at this point, she said, "No," adding, "It was definitely not anything defined. We were sort of seeing each other, but we were definitely not boyfriend and girlfriend."

Not ready to leave the hotel encounter behind, Nurmi pressed her to list the number of times she and Travis engaged in sexual activity that weekend. When Arias said three, he asked her to again describe them.

"The first night it was the grinding, and the next night it was the oral sex," she recounted.

"Okay. And what was the third night?"

"It was oral sex also, before we left."

"Okay. Did he ever express a desire during this weekend to engage in anal sex with you?" Nurmi asked, to which Arias said, "Yes."

She further asserted that after the weekend in Ehrenberg, she felt "a little bit used."

"What do you mean, though, that you felt used?" Nurmi pressed.

"Well, you know. He gets a hotel room. I show up. We hang out. We have sex. He's not really there, present, he's not really mentally present. I'm getting a lot of attention, but only while we're engaging in sexual activity. And then we check out. And he takes off. And I kind of feel like a prostitute."

Arias testified that she called Travis several times after the weekend, but didn't hear back from him until Tuesday, when he left a "very nice message" on her phone, and the two resumed their frequent phone calls, which she said were both "spiritual" and "sexual" in nature.

The trial became even more lurid when Nurmi showed Arias the first of two photographs that Dworkin had found on her hard drive, and asked her to identify what the picture contained. "It's an erect penis," she said, which she claimed Travis sent to her cell phone on November 11, 2006.

"Is this something that you solicited?" Nurmi asked, as he displayed the first photograph on the monitor so that it flashed up on all the courtroom screens.

"Not directly," she replied, looking down. "I didn't expect a photograph, but we were flirting."

". . . This was a picture of his erection that he sent you, is that right?"

"Yes," Arias said, explaining that she was at a PPL event listening to speakers when she and Travis began texting. "It turned flirty and then it turned sexual. And it went on for hours, actually, back and forth, just trying to be witty and top each other's last comments."

". . . So he sent you two photos that day?" Nurmi solicited, showing Arias the second photograph, also featuring a man's erect penis.

"Yes, consecutively," Arias said matter-of-factly, telling jurors she had left the meeting and was in a restaurant with others when she opened the photo files and then quickly closed her phone so no one could see them.

Because these photos were sent during Travis and Arias' courtship, more than a year and a half before Arias killed him, there didn't appear to be a reason to introduce the pictures and make them part of the case other than to denigrate Travis in front of the jurors.

Arias testified that fifteen days later, on November 26,

2006, Travis baptized her into the Mormon Church during a small service in Palm Desert. After the ceremony, she said, Travis followed her back to her house in his car and the two were again intimate, this time engaging in anal sex for the first time. But the two didn't start dating exclusively until February 2007, although even then, Arias claimed that Travis hid their relationship from most of his friends.

Arias testified that they broke up four months later, on June 29, after Arias went though his phone while he was napping and found numerous text exchanges with other women, leading her to believe he was being unfaithful. Still, she claimed that Travis called her the day after their breakup, telling her that he was horny and promising to change. Less than a month later, Arias moved to Mesa, and according to her, the two continued their sexual relationship.

"Were you acting as a couple in public?" Nurmi asked.

"No, we were even more clandestine," Arias said, claiming the two had late-night rendezvous about three or four times a week.

She also alleged that Travis started being physically abusive to her, beginning with an incident in October 2007, when he pushed her down on the ground as she tried to leave the bedroom during an argument. "We were arguing, and I got up to leave, and he wasn't done making his point, and he wanted me to stay, so I guess he could finish yelling at me."

"What did Mr. Alexander say when he pushed you down?" asked Nurmi.

"He said—he said 'no,' like, five times fast, 'no, no, no, no, no, you're not going anywhere.'"

According to Arias, the two made up and their sexual relationship continued, during which time she alleged to have witnessed something so disturbing on January 21, 2008, that it changed the course of their relationship.

"I walked in and Travis was on the bed masturbating. And

I got really embarrassed, even though we have been intimate more times than I could count, it was just kind of awkward walking in on him like that.

"And I was headed toward the dresser, but then I stopped and I was trying to think of something funny or witty to say, like, do you still need my help or something. And he started grabbing at something on the bed. And I realized they were papers and as he was grabbing the papers, one kind of went sailing off the bed and it fell in that chaotic pattern that paper falls and it landed faceup near my feet. And it was a photograph."

"What was in the photograph? What was the photograph of?" asked Nurmi.

"It was a picture of a little boy."

"Could you guess how old the little boy was?"

"Five-ish—five, six," Arias alleged. "I'm not a good judge of age."

Arias' testimony about this incident actually occuring was contradicted by what she had previously written in her journal, seized by police from her grandparents' Yreka home on the day she was arrested.

In the entry for January 20, 2008, Arias acknowledges her failure to attend a friend's baptism because she and Travis were exploring their "naughty fantasies" that day. She does not write again in her journal until January 24, 2008: "I haven't written because there has been nothing noteworthy to report (for January 21, 22, 23)." The three-day gap where she found "nothing noteworthy to report" happens to include the day she claims to have seen Travis masturbating to the picture of the little boy.

"Was the little boy dressed?" Nurmi inquired without addressing the journal entries during the direct examination.

"He was dressed in underwear, like briefs," Arias said.

She recalled being frozen for a moment, not sure how to react. "It kind of seemed like one of those dreams where something is really off, but you just can't figure it out. . . . And I turned to go and he called my name, and I just ran. . . ."

Instead of calling the police or speaking with a Mormon bishop after leaving the house, she decided to return that same day, whereupon she said the two engaged in anal sex.

Nurmi asked, "Why, Jodi, were you willing to submit yourself to sexual interaction with Mr. Alexander having seen and having heard everything you saw and heard that day?"

"It's hard to describe because it's very embarrassing. But he seemed very ashamed with himself. And he, like—he didn't want to be that way. It was something he struggled with. And that's not who he wanted to be. It's not who he wanted to be in the future. And he was trying to deal with it.

"And when he had sex with women, he felt like a normal heterosexual man. And that's what he wanted to be. And that's what he said he was. And that's what I believed him to be. And so when he had sex with women, he felt more normal and it was preferable to his other deviant urges."

"So were you doing this, having sex, to help him?"

"Yes, you could say that," Arias answered. According to her testimony, she also helped by giving him some pamphlets that she found at the mall that she believed could be useful.

Arias claimed that the following day, January 22, Travis was physically abusive toward her, although according to her journal "nothing noteworthy" occurred that day. She testified that on that day she was preparing to leave on a trip to California to see friends. "We were talking in his bedroom and he told me he needed to borrow, I think it was two hundred dollars. But I didn't have it. I'd just lent him six hundred and ninety-nine dollars and—like a few days prior. And I had just enough money to get—to pay for the gas on my trip, maybe some food, and get back.

". . . I didn't really snap at him because he had reacted very badly in the past when I snapped at him. But I did say—I said, I lent you seven hundred dollars . . . and when I said that, he got angry and he crossed the room and he started shaking me. He said, 'I'm fucking sick of you.' And he's screaming real loud and some spit got in my face . . . and he body-slammed me on the floor at the foot of the bed.

". . . It didn't hurt, but it startled me . . . and I kind of let out an unexpected sound, I guess it could be best described as a yelp . . . and I think he misinterpreted because he said, 'Don't act like it hurts.' He called me a bitch. He kicked me in the ribs. And that hurt for real. But he kicked me and I put my hand out to block his foot and it clipped my hand and hit my finger." Arias described the ring finger on her left hand as being swollen and likely broken, as she held it up for the jury to see that it was bent at an angle. However, she admitted that she didn't seek medical attention or call the police in response to this supposed injury.

Arias also claimed later in her testimony that in April, just days before she was set to move to Yreka, Travis "just flipped his lid and blew up. And he threw me on the ground and got on top of me and started choking me."

Arias went on, "He squeezed my neck and I couldn't breathe— everything turned gray really fast and then went black. . . . I didn't have time to think, oh, my God, he's going to kill me. I just—the only thought I could think is, I can't breathe, I can't breathe, like I didn't have any air."

When court resumed on February 12, Arias' fifth day of testimony, Nurmi introduced into evidence the sexually explicit conversation Arias had recorded on May 10, 2008. Arias explained that she made the recording while she was at her grandparents' house in Yreka, where she was living at the time. She also claimed that she made the recording at Travis' request, although this request is not on the recording.

To properly prepare those in the gallery, Judge Stephens asked that they have "no reaction whatsoever to anything that is played for this jury," and if they believed they could not do so, they were asked to leave the courtroom. I had already played the audio recording for Travis Alexander's family and they had determined that they wanted to be in court while it was played.

Arias was on the witness stand when Nurmi began to play the approximately forty-five-minute recording over the courtroom loudspeakers, and an awkward placidity fell over the courtroom. The first voice we heard was Arias', sounding a lot more animated and playful than she had throughout her testimony.

"Okay, what did you say, I'm sorry," Arias says, opening the conversation, to which Travis responds in a groggy voice, indicative of just being awakened from sleep, "I said, why don't we just talk for a little bit about happy things and get normalized for a moment and then we'll see where that takes us."

Arias breaks into a giggle. "We'll see where it takes us. I like that . . ."

The conversation started off slowly, with the two discussing their individual travel plans for the coming month, postings on the Internet made by mutual acquaintances that they believe were inappropriate, and Travis' intention of coming to see her before he takes his trip to Cancún with Mimi.

Arias steers the conversation to the sexual adventures they've enjoyed in the past: "There have been a few times where I've been bold enough to just pull you onto the bed and start . . . and . . . oh my gosh, remember that time when I came to visit you when I was still living in California and I fell asleep on your chair next to your bed and you woke me up by pulling my pants off and totally licking my pussy."

". . . Yeah, ah, you've got to admit, though, there's not many guys like that would do that just for fun . . . wake you up with a . . ." Travis replies, now clearly more engaged. ". . . I'm going to tie you to a tree and put it in your ass all the way."

Arias responds with a beguiling laugh and says, "Oh my gosh. That is so debasing. I like it."

Spectators in the gallery exchanged awkward glances, and

it seemed like some were biting back laughter as the recording progressed, with the conversation becoming more graphic and the two growing even more uninhibited.

". . . Before I met you, I never jacked off. Once I started . . . once, ah . . . once we started meeting, I don't know, it was once a month, once every two weeks, like since you've left I jack off every day, sometimes two, three times a day," we hear Travis tell Arias, who responds with an invitation.

". . . I wish you were here. If you were here, my grandparents are asleep. I'd let you right in my bedroom. We would shut and lock the door and we'd just have a big fuck fest. We'd go at it all night." Arias continued in a whisper, "You make me feel horny. I seriously think about having sex with you every day, several times a day. I think of how it feels to have your cock deep inside me. I remember it . . . and I want it again."

"Is it wrong that I am glad we started fucking?" Travis asked.

"Well, if it's wrong, then I don't want to be right," Arias replies.

At this point it is clear that Arias is masturbating and approaching an orgasm, becoming breathless as she instructs Travis, "Don't come yet, okay, cause then I'll come two times and you can come the second time."

As the impending orgasm approaches, her whispering rises into what seems like an interminable shriek as Travis quietly listens. Once she is done, he compliments her. "Now that was hot. Naturally the way you . . . the way you moaned there, it sounds like . . . you're a twelve-year-old girl having her first orgasm. It is so hot."

". . . Sounds like what?"

"A twelve-year-old girl having her first orgasm," Travis repeats, at which Arias laughs gleefully. Even she sounds as if she understands that this is a comment made in the heat of the moment, not to be taken seriously.

Clearly unaffected by the comment, Arias continues the

sexual tenor of the conversation, coaxing him on by saying, "Yeah, I want you. I like the way your dick feels against me. It's one thing that you're smooth everywhere, and of course your dick is way smooth. When I have your dick in my mouth, I like putting my lips all over it. I really, really, really want to suck your dick right now, so bad," she says in a sultry voice, and the two gradually reach their orgasm at the same time, with Arias screeching so loudly that she drowns out Travis' moans.

As much as it seems like the recording should end, the sexual dialogue continues. Travis discloses that Arias is the one who introduced him to using K-Y personal lubricant. "Oh . . . you introduced me to K-Y, you know that?"

". . . Yeah," Arias responds. "And K-Y is made for that, so it's good for you."

Even though in her earlier testimony Arias had painted their time in Ehrenberg as less romantic than she had hoped, on the recording, she romanticizes the moments they had shared there.

"Remember the first time you and I grinded, ah, um, at Ehrenberg and we both . . . like I ended up just coming and you're like 'wow.' . . . I came, you came at the same time, I looked around, there's jizz all over. It was so hot," she said with a giggle. "We came together. That was so cool."

At the end of the recording, Judge Stephens called a recess, instructing all parties to be back in the courtroom by 2:50 P.M. When proceedings resumed, Nurmi questioned Arias in detail about what jurors had just heard in the recording. His examination paid particular attention to Travis' comment that Arias' orgasm sounded like that of a twelve-year-old girl reaching climax for the first time.

"Let me ask you this," Nurmi posed. "When you recorded this tape and you're living in Yreka in May of 2008, were you twelve?"

"No," Arias replied.

"Was this your first orgasm?"

"No," she again answered, in what seemed an admission that she had indeed climaxed during their phone conversation.

But later in the redirect examination, when Nurmi asked her if the orgasms heard on the tape were real, she said no, claiming she was only pretending to climax. "I was faking it because I can't—well, when I'm on the phone—when I do something like that, like, masturbating requires both hands."

Arias continued her attack on Travis' character from the witness stand by alleging that he had once told her he wanted her to dress up in a schoolgirl's outfit and wear her hair in braids to act out one of his fantasies, reminiscent of how she willingly posed during their last sexual encounter memorialized in the photographs taken on June 4, 2008.

━━━━━━━━━

CHAPTER 23

The lurid details of Arias' and Travis' sex life had all but dominated Arias' testimony during her six days on the witness stand, with Travis' murder feeling more like an afterthought than the reason we were here in the courtroom. Questions about her trip to Mesa finally surfaced on February 19, toward the end of her direct examination, when Nurmi began asking about Arias' movements in the days leading up to the murder.

Arias denied staging the burglary at her grandparents' home to obtain the .25-caliber semiautomatic handgun she had used to shoot Travis. She also claimed that her decision to rent a car in Redding, instead of Yreka, was based on a good deal she found on the Web.

She recounted her drive south to Santa Cruz, where she met her ex-boyfriend Matt McCartney for an evening of karaoke. After spending the night at Matt's apartment in Monterey, she made an early-morning visit to Darryl Brewer in Pacific Grove.

"And did you borrow anything from Mr. Brewer while you were there?" Nurmi asked.

"Yes, I borrowed his gas cans."

"And how many did you borrow from him?"

"Two."

"Why did you borrow two gas cans from Darryl Brewer?"

"So that I could—well, gas in Yreka at that time was $4.78 a gallon for regular unleaded. This was 2008. It was very expensive. All gas in California is a little more expensive because they have stricter regulations. So going to Nevada and Utah would have been cheaper, so I wanted to fill up."

With one question and a single answer, the issue of the gas cans had seemingly been laid to rest. Arias' explanation for borrowing the gas containers appeared plausible, especially since she even knew the price per gallon being charged in California for unleaded gas back in 2008. Her carefully crafted response failed to mention the third gas can she had purchased in Salinas, which cost $12.96, plus tax, negating any possible savings from the purchase of gasoline at the cheaper price in Nevada and Utah.

"You didn't tell him 'keep this a secret'?" Nurmi asked of Arias' conversation with Brewer that day.

"No."

"Okay. And when you were having breakfast with Darryl and his son, do you remember telling Darryl that you were going to Mesa?"

Nurmi's question failed to address that the conversation Arias had with Brewer about going to Mesa had not occurred that morning at breakfast, but during a telephone conversation the two had in late May, when she first asked about borrowing the gas cans.

"I had no plans to go to Mesa at that point, so, no I wouldn't have told him that," she responded.

Arias claimed she next went to Salinas to get a manicure, so that her nails "looked good" for Ryan Burns. In Pasadena, she stopped at Starbucks, and then at ARCO, "because they had cheaper gas," where Arias claimed she "filled up the tank and I filled up the gas cans, too."

Apparently Arias was not mindful of her previous answer about needing to fill the gas cans in Utah and Nevada, as she was now admitting that she filled them in California, where the gas was more expensive.

"Okay. So at this point in time, you have your car full of

gas, you have your gas cans full of gas, right? . . . And the plan is to go to Utah, right?"

"Yes," Arias said, recounting that she then called Ryan Burns to tell him she was on her way.

". . . Did you go to Utah directly after you spoke to Ryan Burns?" Nurmi asked.

"No . . . I had been talking to Travis intermittently throughout that time, and the weeks prior when he discovered that I was going to Utah, he started saying, 'Why are you going to Utah?' . . .

"On the very last time I called Travis, it was kind of like—I don't know how to describe it. He had been—he had been very sweet. He had been guilting me, kind of making me feel that I was taking this big trip and that I wasn't going to see him. . . . And since I was driving south, he wanted me to come to Mesa.

"I told him no the first few times. During one conversation, he became angry. During the others, [he] stayed calm; he has this way of, like, talking in this really sweet voice . . . and making me feel guilty, and he sounded so very sweet, and so it was like, when I called him one more time, it was just like, All right, I'm going, so I went."

". . . Okay. When you arrived at Mr. Alexander's house, did you have a gun with you?" Nurmi asked.

"No," she answered, although she had told Detective Flores on June 10, 2008, that Travis did not have a gun at his house and had only his two fists for protection.

"Did you have a knife with you?"

"No."

Arias claimed she entered the house through a side gate, because she knew that Travis locked the front door at night.

"Why wouldn't you just knock on the front door?" Nurmi inquired.

"I had always just come and gone without knocking. . . . It was just easier to walk in."

Arias said once inside the house, she found Travis in his office on the first floor, with his dog Napoleon sitting on the floor next to him. "He had his back to me and he was on his laptop, watching music videos or something on YouTube." He didn't see her initially, she said, so she stood in the doorway looking at him until Napoleon's bark alerted him to her presence. "That's when Travis turned around and got up out of his chair and came over and greeted me. . . . He had a big smile on his face and he kissed me on the lips."

Arias said the two continued watching the videos for a bit before going into the kitchen, where he implied he wanted to have sex, but she was too tired from the drive, so they went up to his bedroom where they slept, with Arias waking at noon and Travis sleeping until 1:00 P.M.

Nurmi next asked Arias to describe their sexual interactions that afternoon, which Arias claimed involved Travis binding her wrists as part of their foreplay, indicating that Travis then used a knife to cut the ropes in order to free her hands. This was an obvious attempt to account for the knife she would later use to stab him.

Her recollection also included their picture-taking session and "regular vanilla" sex. Jurors again viewed the photographs of Arias posing naked on Travis' bed, her hair in braids, with Nurmi directing their attention to Arias' shaved pubic region in the photograph.

"Travis didn't like hair," she said. She also talked about a sex video that she claimed the two recorded on his Sanyo camera that they deleted after viewing it together.

Arias claimed that after the sex, she took a shower and got ready to "hit the road," adding that she put the sheets from Travis' bed in the washing machine, as they typically did each time the two had sex.

Even though her car was packed and she was ready to depart Mesa at 2:00 P.M., Arias said she stayed around for a bit to view the CDs containing photographs taken during their trips that she made for Travis that had been "hanging around" in her briefcase "for months."

She described Travis growing angry when the CDs wouldn't play on his computer, saying that when they finally did, he noticed that they were scratched and blamed her for holding on to them for too long. To blow off steam, she said Travis threw one of the CDs at the wall, causing it to ricochet and land on the desk, and then roll off onto her head before ending up on the carpet.

According to Arias, she was now worried, "because I feel like the trip had gone pretty well at that point, now he's going to get angry or I've done something stupid again, and . . . the trip is going to get ruined. . . ."

Arias alleged that in his anger, Travis grabbed her by the arm, spun her around, bent her over the desk, pulled down her pants, and pressed his groin against her buttock.

"Based on that movement, did you believe that he wanted to have sex with you again?"

"Yes, I could feel that he had an erection."

"Okay. And at that point in time, did you want to have sex with Mr. Alexander?"

"Well, yeah, actually I did because it was better than him getting mad. . . . I didn't want his anger to escalate to the levels that it had in the past. . . ."

Nurmi inquired, "So, your mind-set on June 4, 2008, was 'anything to avoid a fight,' is that what you are telling us?"

"Yes, in that moment, yes," Arias said, claiming Travis was now a lot calmer.

"Did you leave then?" Nurmi asked.

"No . . . We decided to go upstairs and take pictures, more pictures."

According to Arias, this impromptu picture-taking session was at her insistence after she convinced Travis that the photographs would show off his recent weight loss. ". . . The Cancún trip was announced in 2007, I think right before I broke up with him. And so he assumed he was going to win the trip and so he was getting into shape. . . . The prior summer he was almost 240, and so he had lost a lot of weight and he was down to, like, a little over two hundred. . . . His goal was to have a six-pack. . . . He wasn't quite there yet, but he was close . . . and when he got to that point, he wanted photos taken of what he had accomplished."

Court ended that afternoon with Arias testifying that she had wanted their visit to end on a positive note, and since the pictures on the CDs were ruined, she wanted to do something else to make him happy.

Arias' testimony was in its eighth day when she returned to court on February 20, to finally testify to Travis' killing.

Nurmi opened his examination by asking Arias about the photo shoot she and Travis had decided to conduct in the late afternoon of June 4.

"And this was to take place in the bathroom?"

"Yes."

"And why was the shower area selected?"

"It was selected for the water. We were going to go for a certain effect with the pictures and the water," Arias said.

". . . Tell us what happens once he gets in the shower."

"I was taking pictures of him. We were trying out different poses . . . and at one point he was sitting and I was taking pictures. I was probably a few feet from the shower so that the water didn't get on the camera. And . . . I was showing him the photos, and we were deleting some. And at one point, when I went to delete the photo, as I moved the camera it slipped out of my hand . . . like, it bounced, and I almost caught it. But I didn't catch it, and it landed on the mat and then it rolled onto the tile."

"Where were you when this took place, relative to the shower?"

"I was crouched by the shower. I might have been on the mat, or the edge of the mat. . . . At that point, Travis flipped out again. And he stood up and he stepped out of the shower and he picked me up. I was crouching, but he lifted me up. As he was screaming that I was a stupid idiot. And he body-slammed me again on the tile.

"He told me that a five-year-old can hold a camera better than I can—and when I hit the tile, he was—I rolled over on the side and started running down the hallway. And I don't know why I didn't run out of the room. I ran to the closet be-cause the door was open, was my thought.

". . . I could hear his footsteps chasing me . . . so I ran into the closet and I slammed the door. And I intended to run through the opposite end of the door because it had an exit. And as soon as I got in there and began to run, I remembered where he kept the gun. So I grabbed it.

"I jumped up on the shelf. He kept it on the very top. I grabbed it and I ran out the other door as he was opening the door. And he ran chasing me and I turned around and pointed it at him so that he would stop chasing me.

". . . We were in the middle of the bathroom. I pointed it at him with both of my hands. I thought that would stop him. . . . He got like a linebacker. He got kind of low and grabbed my waist. But, before he did that, as he was lunging at me, the gun went off."

Arias claimed she didn't mean to shoot Travis. "I didn't even think I was holding the trigger. I just was pointing it at him and I didn't even know that I shot him. It just went off. And he was—he lunged at me and we fell really hard against the tile toward the other wall . . . so at this point, I didn't even know if he had been shot. . . . We were struggling and wrestling . . . and he was getting on top of me . . . he's grabbing at my clothes and I got up. And he's just screaming angry. And after I broke away from him, he said, 'Fucking kill you, bitch.' "

Although to this point, she had been able to recall even the minutest details of her relationship with Travis, her memory of the events in the bathroom as she fought for her life became fuzzy. "There's a lot of that day that I don't remember," she said. "There are a lot of gaps."

"Okay," Nurmi said, seemingly working to jar her memory. ". . . Once you broke away from him, what do you remember?"

"Almost nothing for a long time. . . . There's like a huge gap. . . . And the most clear memory I have at that point is driving in the desert. . . ."

"Let me ask you this, do you remember stabbing Mr. Alexander?"

"I have no memory of stabbing him."

"Do you remember . . . dragging him across the floor?"

"No, I just remember trying to get away from him."

"Do you remember placing him in the shower?"

"I'm sorry. That's no. . . . I have a vague memory of putting the knife in the dishwasher. . . ."

"What else do you remember?" Nurmi asked.

"Not much," Arias stated flatly, claiming that the next thing she remembered was driving west. "Because I remember the sun was in my eyes for a while. I didn't know where I was going. I didn't have GPS anymore. . . . I hit a lot of stoplights. And then eventually, I was in the desert."

Arias testified that she did recall taking the gun with her when she left Travis' house that day. "I remember throwing it . . . in the desert."

". . . Explain to us if you believed that Mr. Alexander was alive or dead? . . ." Nurmi asked.

"I didn't know. . . . But I didn't think he was . . . I thought he was not alive at that point."

As part of her direct examination, Arias detailed her movements in the hours, days, weeks, and months after the killing, including the many lies she'd told along the way, something Nurmi sought to address in his final questions to her on the stand.

". . . Since Mr. Alexander's death was discovered, you told

one version of events in which you weren't there and another version of events where intruders came into the home, killed Mr. Alexander, and you escaped. Why did you then now decide to tell us what really happened?

"Why did you decide to come forward with all these things that you've been hiding? Mr. Alexander's sexual interests, the sexual relationship, the violence: Why did you feel comfortable coming forth with that information?"

Arias paused, readjusted herself in the chair, and looked at the jurors. "It wasn't an overnight decision by any means," she began. "From day one, there's a part of me that always wanted to but didn't dare do that. I would rather have gone to my grave without confirming that I could have done something like that.

"I was extremely ashamed of it. It wasn't in line with who I am or how I had been living my life all the way up to that point. So as the years went by, however, I began to—it feels very fraudulent from day one, especially when there are so many nice people reaching out to you and they believe you or they believe in you. . . . It feels wrong.

". . . It was a process that happened over a long period of time. But by the spring of 2010. . . . I confessed."

"When you say you confessed, what do you mean by 'confessed'?"

"I basically told everyone what I could remember of the day and that the intruder story was all BS, pretty much."

"That's all the questions I have, Judge," Nurmi said, paving the way for me to begin my cross-examination.

—————————

CHAPTER 24

Cross-examination is a bit of an art. The evidentiary rules allow questioning beyond matters raised in the direct examination as long as the inquiry touches on facts in dispute. So, my approach is to always ask questions that are germane to the case, but I like to start by inquiring about matters that are not expected by the defendant, avoiding rehearsed answers.

In the case of Jodi Ann Arias, I don't think she anticipated that I would begin her cross-examination, on the morning of February 21, by talking about unflattering names she had called family members in conversations with Travis that had not been discussed in her direct examination. I wanted to begin by showing jurors she had a double standard, which she believed allowed her to make demeaning comments about others while expecting those around her to refrain from engaging in the same type of name calling. I also planned to weave into the first part of my questioning that the injury to her left ring finger she claimed to have sustained during an assault by Travis on January 22, 2008, the day after she alleged to have found him masturbating to pictures of young boys, had actually happened during *her* attack on Travis on June 4, 2008. I knew these two topics were unrelated, which is why I chose them, because it would make it difficult for Arias to predict the questions I would pose.

I had learned from her interviews with Detective Flores that conducting my cross-examination in a linear fashion would be ineffective. That was the approach he had employed during his interrogation, which allowed Arias to became comfortable and weave the story about intruders killing Travis. Preparing scripted questions in advance, even as to minor points, would have been counterproductive, because Arias ad-libbed even as to undisputed facts, rendering useless the next question on the scripted page.

"Ma'am," I began, showing Arias Exhibit 413, a close-up photograph of her and her sister, Angela, with a date stamp of May 10, 2008, that defense witness Lonnie Dworkin had recovered from the memory card of Arias' Canon camera. "Do you recognize this exhibit?" I asked, knowing that she was familiar with the photograph because her witness had introduced it into evidence on her behalf. "That's a picture of you, correct?"

When Arias agreed, I asked her about the teen with the dyed red hair in the photo with her. "And the other one is a picture of your dumb sister, correct?"

"That's my sister," she affirmed, her clipped response indicating her displeasure with my characterization of Angela. "She's not dumb."

"Well, do you remember having a conversation with Travis Alexander back on May 10, 2008?" I asked.

"Yes."

"And during that conversation isn't it true you said, 'but I honestly think,' talking about Angela, 'she's a little dumb.' You said that, right?" I asked, referring to comments she made about her sister during the May 10, 2008, sexually explicit phone call with Travis.

"Yes, I called her dumb and stupid."

"Did I ask you whether or not you called her stupid?" I countered, in an effort to prevent her from controlling the questioning.

"No."

"I asked you whether or not you called her dumb, right?"

"Yes."

"Now take a look at Exhibit 452," I instructed, showing Arias another photograph of her and Angela, taken from a different angle that showed more than just their faces. "Do you recognize the two people?"

"Yes," Arias replied, enabling me to move it into evidence.

". . . And what date was the photograph taken?" I asked, directing Arias to look at the date on the back of the exhibit, which read May 2, 2008. "And with regard to this photograph, it also features you and your sister, the one that you said was stupid, correct?"

"Yes," she said, admitting to engaging in name calling, which allowed me to point out that she was upset with Travis for engaging in this very same behavior.

"Now, with regard to this name calling . . . your text message was that you were upset at some point because Mr. Alexander said that you were going to turn out just like your mother, or you were acting like your mother. Do you remember that text?"

"Yes."

I followed up by referring to a portion of her direct examination where she had detailed the bad words Travis supposedly said about her mother.

"I don't remember."

"Do you have a problem with your memory, ma'am?"

"Sometimes," she responded.

Citing memory issues would become one of the ways Arias would attempt to avoid answering my questions when it appeared that her responses might reveal an inconvenient truth.

". . . And you can tell us, for example, what type of sex you had with Mr. Alexander many years ago, but you're having trouble telling us what you said a couple of days ago?" I asked.

"When I'm under stress, yeah, it affects my memory," Arias retorted, refusing to back down from the excuse.

"I thought you said the relationship with Mr. Alexander was very stressful?"

"Some of the sex wasn't."

"Pardon?" I asked, not sure if I had heard her answer correctly.

"Some of the sex wasn't," she repeated.

Before this point in the trial, Arias had attempted to present herself as someone who was meek and compliant in her sexual dealings with Travis, someone with religious values.

She had spent an inordinate amount of time on direct examination describing the sordid details of her many sexual moments with Travis, replaying them for the jury as if they were musical pieces with different beats and tempo, but all with the same bad note—she just could not say no.

She had spoken of their first encounter in Murrieta, California, where she claimed he foisted himself on her, performing oral sex until thankfully he moved his mouth away. She even lamented their time in Ehrenberg, where she expected a weekend of romance only to have the time spent "grinding" or having oral sex, but all the while Travis seemed distant, making her feel like a prostitute. She avowed that her willingness to engage in anal sex after she allegedly discovered Travis masturbating to images of young boys was nothing more than a self-sacrificing act on her part, done only to calm Travis' pedophilic urges. So, it was quite revelatory that she was now saying that she had liked some of the sex in direct contradiction of her answers when she was questioned by defense counsel.

"So, you did enjoy the sex then, is that what you're telling me?"

"At times I did," she admitted blandly.

"But you did indicate as part of your examination that Mr. Alexander at some point said something about your grandfather also . . . That he made some pejorative comments, some bad comments about him, right?" I solicited, switching back to a specific comment Arias made during her direct testimony in an attempt to attack Travis' character and paint him in a bad light.

"My grandfather," Arias answered. "Yes, his name," she said, making sure the jury knew that Travis allegedly belittled her grandfather's good name.

". . . One of the things that seems to be coming out here is that you seem to have a double standard here with regard to making comments about people, don't you?" I asked.

Judge Stephens overruled Nurmi's objection that my question was argumentative, allowing Arias to respond.

"I do," she said, but then immediately backtracked, offering justifications for her responses.

When she became upset over Travis' comment about her grandfather, it was because she was already upset about something else that day. As for calling Angela "dumb" and "stupid," she made those statements at a time when she was feeling "sentimental."

". . . You have a different standard for Mr. Alexander, correct? Yes or no?"

When Arias responded "No," I continued this line of questioning by referring to another, more illustrative, example of her double standard when it came to Travis, recalling an incident that happened less than two months after she broke up with him.

". . . Back in August of 2007, you went over to Mr. Alexander's house . . . and at that time you were broken up with Mr. Alexander, right?"

"I had broken up with him," Arias replied.

". . . And you broke up with him on June 29, 2007, right? . . . But you felt that it was okay for you to go over to his house in August 2007, didn't you?"

"After he told me," she said, in an attempt to justify her action.

"Yes or no," I asked, my voice rising. "Did you feel it was okay to go over to his house?"

"I said yes," Arias challenged, even though she had not previously provided me with an affirmative answer.

Arias' answers were being delivered with a perceptible edge, and on numerous occasions, she appeared to scold me, "I said yes" or "I said no." The tone in her responses ordained my continuing use of a stern approach to overcome her obvious unwillingness to give straightforward answers.

"And . . . you started to peep into the house, didn't you?" I continued, my voice still raised.

"Yes."

"So you went around the back to look, right?"

"I went around the back to get in," she admonished me.

". . . But when you got to the back to get in, you started to look at what was going on, right? . . . You saw something inside that upset you, right? You saw Mr. Alexander, right?"

"I did not know it was him at first," she replied, appearing reluctant to provide a more definitive answer.

When I pressed, she admitted that she saw Travis and he was with a woman she "did not recognize."

". . . And you were able to see that they were making out, right?"

"Oh yeah, they were."

". . . So what happened then is you were actually watching what they were doing then, right?"

"Briefly, yes."

". . . And after you saw this, one of the things you did was that you took off, right?"

"Yes."

"And you felt strongly enough about this that the next day you called your father, right?"

"I called my parents' house and my dad answered."

"Yes or no. You spoke to your father?"

"I did speak to him."

"And you were crying, right? . . . And you were upset about this, right? . . . And you told him why you were upset, right?"

"Yes."

"I thought you said before that you didn't discuss these issues involving you and Mr. Alexander?"

"Not typically."

". . . You said you didn't yesterday and all the days before. Remember telling us that?" I asked, referring to her previous testimony in response to Nurmi's questions.

"The violence, yes," she replied, her way of clarifying that she had simply been referring to the alleged domestic violence in her relationship with Travis, not Travis' behavior with other women.

"Oh, I see," I said. "But you did discuss the fact that you saw him kissing somebody else to your father, right?"

"Yes."

"And as a result of that, you decided to go talk to Mr. Alexander about it, right?"

"Yes."

"What in the world gave you the right to go talk to an ex-boyfriend?" I probed. "According to you, you had broken up with him. What right do you have?"

Nurmi objected that my question was argumentative, and his objection was sustained by the judge. I rephrased the question, forcing Arias into acknowledging her double standard. "Weren't you broken up?"

"Yes."

"You were being territorial with him, weren't you?"

"No."

"Then why in the world would you even care what he was doing?" I asked.

"Because he was trying to court me back," she snapped, justifying her unannounced appearance at his house that evening.

"... And so you could have left that situation alone, but you decided to confront him anyway, right?"

"Of course."

In keeping with my nonlinear approach, I asked Arias about her sexual encounter with Ryan Burns immediately following the sexual interlude in the afternoon of June 4, 2008, with Travis Alexander. "At the end, right when you killed him, you indicated that you were monogamous with him, right?"

"Yes."

"And at that time you then left the killing scene, if you will, and you went right to Utah, right? . . . And you went up to Utah, ma'am, you ended up with somebody named Ryan Burns? And you ended up in his bed, right?"

Arias admitted laying down with Burns, clearly unfazed at the audacity of rendezvousing with him after just having slept with and killed another man.

Arias contended that she wasn't sure if Travis was actually dead when she arrived in Utah on June 5, 2008, to meet with Burns, claiming that she didn't know Travis was dead until she received confirmation on June 10.

"So if you didn't think he was dead . . . then it's okay for you at that point . . . to sort of roll around with Mr. Burns . . . ?"

"I'm single," Arias answered in a snit, ignoring that Travis was also single at the time when she confronted him about kissing another woman.

I believed she had been taken sufficiently off course that I could now circle back to the reason I had begun my cross-examination with the photographs of her and her sister, Angela—the injury to the left finger.

"With regard to Exhibit 452, it does show you, right, correct?" I asked, showing her a photograph that had been taken on May 15, 2008.

"Yes."

"Shows something else on there, though, doesn't it? Doesn't it show your hand?"

"Yes," Arias replied, unaware of where I was going with my inquiry.

"And in fact, let me show you another close-up of your hand," I said, presenting her with Exhibit 453, which was an enlargement of her hand pictured in the previous photograph.

Directing Arias' attention to the ring finger on her left hand, I asked, "Do you remember that you testified that on January 22, 2008, you and Mr. Alexander were involved in some sort of violent encounter? . . . And you told us that during that encounter, he threw you down. . . . And while you were down, he kicked you. . . . And when he kicked you, ma'am, one of the things that happened was that you put up your left hand. Do you remember telling us that?"

"Yes, both hands," Arias replied, now embellishing her story to include both hands.

"Well, you told us specifically about your left hand. . . . And when you put up your left hand, according to you, he kicked you and he damaged your ring finger on the left hand. . . . And in fact, you even held it up for us, didn't you?"

"Yes."

"And it was crooked when you showed it to us, wasn't it?"

"It's bent, yes."

Instructing her to hold her finger up for the jury once again, I asked her why, if Travis had injured her finger on January 22, 2008, it did not appear bent in the photo of her and her sister taken almost four months later, on May 15, 2008, less than one month before the murder.

"My finger *is* bent there," Arias insisted, even though the photograph showed otherwise.

". . . Hold up your finger again," I directed, "sideways so we can all see it."

"When my fingers are straightened, this one stays bent," she said, raising her left hand and showing her ring finger bent at a ninety-degree angle.

". . . Well, you talked to Ryan Burns about it, didn't you?" I asked. "And you told him that that finger, the left ring finger, had been damaged, right, injured, didn't you?"

"I don't know if it was the left," Arias submitted.

"You don't remember telling him it was the left ring finger, ma'am? . . . Again, do you have a memory problem?"

"Occasionally," she replied, latching on to the parachute I was apparently providing.

"And so some of the things you told us, for example, then, about things in the past, you may have also had memory problems, right? . . . And so whatever you told us in the past is somewhat suspect, then, because your memory is lacking?"

"I only told things that I remember clearly that are crystallized in my mind."

I reminded Arias of the bandage she was wearing on her finger when she arrived in Utah on June 5 and she and Ryan Burns joined friends at a restaurant. "And it was your left finger, wasn't it?"

"No."

"It was your right finger then . . . is that what you are saying?"

"It was two fingers," Arias maintained. ". . . Two right fingers."

"Do you remember your conversation with Detective Flores about this issue involving the finger? . . . And that you told him that on June 4, 2008, you had been over at Mr. Alexander's home . . . and that some girl had come in. . . . And during whatever happened on June 4, you told Detective Flores that it was your left finger that had been damaged, do you remember that?" I asked, requesting to move into evidence the portion of the video containing Arias' conversation with Flores on July 16, 2008, so that the jurors could view her contradictory statements for themselves.

After playing the video, I directed Arias' attention to the comments she made to the detective that day, indicating that the supposed female intruder had cut her "right there," as she pointed to a specific location on her left ring finger.

"Look at it there," I said, directing her attention to the monitor. "The finger had the same aspect or the same angle to it that your finger does now, doesn't it?"

"Yes," Arias conceded.

"Ma'am, the injury to your finger happened on June 4, 2008, not January 22, 2008, didn't it?"

"That's not correct," she pronounced in a dictatorial fashion even after having viewed herself admitting to Detective Flores that the finger had been injured on June 4, 2008.

To further discount her claim and show she was being untruthful, I pointed to two entries in Arias' journal, dated January 20 and January 24, 2008, which I asked her to review. "And nowhere do you mention either in this January 24 of '08 or January 20 of '08 document, you don't mention anything about this physical encounter with Mr. Alexander that you told us happened on January 22 of 2008, do you?"

"No, I would never."

"I'm not asking if you would ever. Do you mention it there?"

"I said no," Arias sniped.

". . . You do say in Exhibit 456 [the entry dated January 24, 2008], 'I haven't written because there is nothing noteworthy to report,' right? . . . So to you, getting this injury to the left ring finger, that's no big deal, right?"

"That's not what I'm saying."

". . . Well, you didn't call the police? . . . You didn't get medical care for it, right?"

"Not professional medical care."

"Ma'am, did you go to the doctor to get it looked at? . . . Did you go to the hospital to get it looked at?"

"No."

". . . And with regard to your conversation that you had with Detective Flores on July 16, 2008, you didn't tell him

anything about that, did you? . . . In fact, you told him a different story, didn't you? . . . You told him something about these
two people and how you got that injury to your finger, right?"

"Yes."

"So, you're saying that what you told the detective was a
lie?"

"Yes," she conceded, knowing that she had nothing to lose
because she had already admitted that she had been untruthful
with Flores about who killed Travis.

"So, in your view, when do you decide to tell the truth,
when you're in this court and no place else? . . ."

"No."

Touching on Arias' claim that she walked in on Travis masturbating on January 21, 2008, I reminded her of the testimony she gave on direct examination claiming to have been
"concerned" about Travis spending the night at a friend's
home, knowing that the friend had a child. "You made it
sound like there was such a big problem . . . and yet you didn't
go to that person and tell them, 'Hey, he's got this issue,'
did you?"

"No."

"You didn't go to the police and tell them anything?" I
posed, pointing out that she also did not report Travis to Child
Protective Services, instead choosing to keep this allegation to
herself for two years after his death.

"I think it's almost three years ago at this point," Arias said,
changing the reference point, seemingly oblivious to how her
response might be construed by jurors.

As the first day of my cross-examination wore on, I continued to chip away at the credibility of her claim that Travis
was a pedophile. To further discount her allegation, I wanted
to pin her down by soliciting more precise details of her movements on January 21, 2008, the day she claimed to have caught
Travis masturbating to the photo of the little boy, something

that she would make excruciatingly difficult with her vague responses.

"What time do you claim that you saw this masturbatory activity?" I asked.

"I don't know the exact time, but it was afternoon, well before it was dark. It was still light out."

"Okay, can you be more specific?"

"It was afternoon."

"All right. Was it two o'clock? If it was so noteworthy, why can't you remember the time?"

"It's kind of traumatic."

". . . Weren't your senses heightened at that time that you saw this? . . . Were you angry?"

"I was sick to my stomach. . . . I mean, it's something I'm never going to forget, but I wish I could."

"You are never going to forget it . . . but you have forgotten the time?"

"I know it was afternoon."

". . . You worked at Mimi's Café. . . . You had been working that day. . . . Your shift was over. . . . What time did your shift start?"

"It varied."

"That day, what time did your shift start?"

"In the morning."

"What time?"

"Some time in the morning. I don't know the exact time."

"You don't know the exact time, yet you knew you had to be there that day at a certain time. . . . What time does Mimi's open?"

"I've never opened Mimi's, so I'm not sure, but they open early."

". . . Was it an eight-hour shift, then?"

"No, they aren't eight-hour shifts."

". . . How many hours was your shift?"

"It depends on the flow of business."

"I understand that it may depend on that. How many hours did you work on January 21, 2008, on this day that this horrible thing you claim happened?"

"I would only be able to tell you a range. . . . I know the range, but not the exact hours."

"Ma'am . . . you had a lot of memory for a lot of events involving sexual instances with Mr. Alexander, yet you seem to be having problems with your memory here today. . . . And you also alluded to a little bit that you have problems with your memory. . . . Your problems with the memory, is this of recent vintage?"

"Define recent," Arias countered sharply.

". . . Since you started testifying?"

"No, it goes back further than that. . . . I don't even know if I'd call it a problem. . . . I just . . . I don't remember every single thing that's ever happened to me in my whole life."

"Ma'am, your memory issues—"

"I wouldn't call them issues," Arias corrected me again.

"Well, you don't want to call them problems. . . . You don't want to call them issues, right?"

"I didn't say I didn't want to . . ."

"All right, we'll call them issues, then. . . . With regard to these memory issues that you claim to have, when did you start having them?"

"It depends on the type of memory issues."

"If it benefits you, you have a memory issue," I asked, to which Nurmi objected. "Or by virtue . . ." to which Nurmi also objected.

"Well," I began, about to formulate my next question when Arias blurted out a response.

"When it hurts, sometimes," she admitted over Nurmi's objection.

". . . You say that you have memory problems but it depends on the circumstances, right?"

"That's right."

"And give me the factors, I don't want to know about the specific circumstances, what factors influence you having a memory problem?"

"Usually when men like you are screaming at me or grilling me, or someone like Travis is doing the same," she retorted, her body tensing angrily.

And with that flash of anger, everyone in the courtroom, including the jury, could now imagine Jodi Ann Arias wearing the pants with a vertical stripe running down the leg standing just outside the shower moments before she took out her knife and stabbed Travis Alexander in the chest.

——————

CHAPTER 25

Jodi Arias' responses to questions posed by the media had been beautifully worded and elegantly delivered, falling from her lips like water flowing down a clear stream. She had been just as persuasive in her presentation to family, friends, and police, even if her tale had changed several times. Although she had been just as impressive in her performance on direct examination, she was now missing her cues as she tripped over her lines during the first day of cross-examination. There would be no critical acclaim as she defended her most recent story, because reality had started to set in with almost every answer that she gave—Arias had a problem with the truth.

In formulating my cross-examination, I had been careful to emphasize only major areas rather than quibble with her about trivial matters, which would have been a waste of time. The sexual relationship with Travis had been a mutual experience, so I necessarily had to question her assertion that Travis always forced her into having sex because she could not say no. She had been implicit in her testimony that she was no longer being untruthful, because she had sworn to tell the truth, causing me to expose how she manipulated her words.

"Ma'am, you have a problem with the truth, telling the truth, don't you?" I began.

"Not typically," Arias replied.

"Well, when it's to your benefit you will lie, right?" I asked, drawing an objection from Nurmi, which was sustained by

Judge Stephens, forcing me to take a different approach to illustrate the point.

"Ma'am, do you remember having a conversation with Detective Flores of the Mesa Police Department back on July 15, 2008?" I continued, drawing the courtroom's attention to the video monitors. I played an excerpt from the videotaped interview in which Arias tells Flores that she would "help" police with their investigation in any way she can.

Turning to Arias, I asked, "That's not true, is it?"

"I don't know," she responded. "I guess it depends on what 'help' means," she answered.

"Yes or no?" I pressed. "Were you there to help him?"

"I don't know," she resisted.

"Were you there to tell the truth?"

"No," she said, finally admitting what she could not deny.

"And in fact you were there for a different purpose. You were there so that he wouldn't get the truth, right?"

"No, I was there against my will," Arias argued, insinuating that being arrested for Travis' murder had been an unlawful violation of her personal freedom.

". . . So, if being arrested had already occurred, why not tell the truth?" I persisted.

"I was ashamed," Arias uttered, looking down at her lap in a move obviously intended to garner sympathy.

"And the reason you were ashamed of killing Mr. Alexander was because that was going to have some repercussions for you?"

"Part of the reason, yes," she answered.

". . . And the other reason was that you were feeling scared, right?"

"That's part of the reason, too."

"So, if you feel scared, you believe then it's okay to lie?"

"No, that's not true," she said, suggesting there was an altruistic motive to her deception.

"Well, that's what you did, though, right?"

"Yes," Arias replied, adding that her concern for her family was part of the reason she had lied to Flores that day.

"And so you were thinking more of yourself when you made this statement to this detective, right?" I asked, unwilling to accept her answer.

"I'm not sure about that."

"Well, other than you, who would be sure about your statement?" I inquired, not expecting the response she offered.

"God," she said.

"Well, God's not here. We can't subpoena him, right?" I answered her back, signaling her suggestion was outrageous and not the end of the inquiry.

"I don't think so," she replied, refusing to admit the obvious.

"Do you remember that you lied about the murder of Travis Alexander?" I asked. ". . . Because the detective had already told you about the fingerprints, hadn't he? . . . And he also told you about the hair that was there. . . . You guys talked about DNA analysis, didn't you? And he showed you the photograph with the foot in it. Do you remember that?"

I asked this series of questions to demonstrate how adept she was at creating innocuous explanations for the evidence linking her to the crime scene.

"Yes," she replied to all of my questions.

". . . And you don't deny that that is your foot in the photograph, do you?"

"I don't deny it."

"And that's when you changed your story . . . to conform with the forensic evidence that he was telling you about, right?"

"That's right."

"And that was because you wanted to make up a story to conform with what he was telling you, right?"

"Yeah, as much as possible."

". . . Well, ma'am, your goal was not to go to prison, then? And in fact it was something you were trying to avoid, right?"

"I don't know. I was trying to kill myself, I think," she answered, attempting to portray herself in a fragile state.

"One of the things you told us about was that when you were in the Maricopa County Jail that you tried to kill yourself, right?" I followed up.

"No, Siskiyou Jail," she corrected me.

"Siskiyou Jail," I amended. "You do remember that when you tried to do that, you took Advil . . . and that . . . you took some razors . . . and you cut yourself, right?"

"It was a nick," she corrected me again.

". . . And you nicked yourself and it hurt . . . and I think that the word you used was stung, right?"

"Yes."

"To use your standard, ma'am, of how you stopped because it stung, can you imagine how much it must have hurt Mr. Alexander when you stuck that knife right into his chest, that really must have hurt?" I asked as a way to remind the jury that this was a murder prosecution, not a cathartic exercise for Arias.

Nurmi interjected with an objection—"Relevance, argumentative"—which the judge sustained.

Moving the inquiry back to the subject of Arias' continuing lack of truthfulness, I asked, "The detective isn't the only person you lied to, right?"

"That's right."

". . . You lied to a lot of people, right?"

"Everyone," she replied coolly, appearing to have finally found a comfort zone.

". . . And in fact one of the people you lied to was Ryan Burns . . . this individual that you had a romantic interest in? . . . In fact, in order to see if the spark was there, you went all the way to Utah, right?"

"That was my goal . . . but not for the reason that you stated."

". . . So you're saying that he was an afterthought?"

"Yeah, he was."

"So he was just an alibi, then?"

"Well, no, not an alibi . . ."

"Mr. Burns was an afterthought, though, right?"

". . . He was an afterthought after June 4."

"Okay. So before that he was a priority, though?"

"He was the reason for the trip."

". . . And the reason for the trip to go and see him was to see whether or not there was a romantic interest, right?"

"That's why I planned the trip," she replied, something she was eager to point out, knowing that her answer countered the allegation that she took the trip as part of her plan to kill Travis.

". . . And when you got there, one of the things that you said was that, 'Well, I needed to keep up a façade.' . . . So you lied about getting lost, right?"

"Yes," Arias affirmed, although she was quick to add that she had actually gotten lost during the trip.

". . . Oh, so it's true, then, that this trip that you went to see Mr. Alexander, it was because you got lost?" I asked, trying to clarify that it was no accident that she had detoured to Arizona to visit Travis.

"That's not why," Arias said, beginning to appear rattled.

". . . Ma'am, when was the first time you realized you were lost?"

"When I couldn't power on my phone, it was dark," she recounted, claiming that she pulled off the road somewhere in Arizona and made a series of phone calls, the first being to her ex-boyfriend Matt McCartney to tell him that she was lost.

". . . So, you're out there and you try to call Mr. McCartney. And so you say that you are lost. But one of the things that you say you do is that you get out of the car . . . and you clean up . . . because you knew what you had done, right?"

"I don't remember thinking that."

"Well, you knew you had killed Mr. Alexander at that point, right?"

"It's hard to describe," she answered, refusing to admit what was a fait accompli.

"So in your mind back then when you're on the side of the road, you don't know if you killed him, right? That's what you're saying?"

"I don't really know if it was in my mind like—it was kind of not there . . . in my head."

". . . You were there enough to pick up the phone and call Matthew McCartney. . . . You were there enough to call Ryan Burns, right?" I asked, casting doubt on her story that she was disoriented.

"Yes."

"And you were there enough to make a call to Travis Alexander, weren't you?" I asked, referring to the voice message she left on Travis' phone in an attempt to cover up that she had killed him.

"Yes."

"How about the time when you got out and you started to wash your hands?" I asked, mentioning the blood that she claimed to have washed off with some bottled water she had in the car when she stopped somewhere in the desert.

". . . I just knew something awful had happened because I had blood on my hands and feet."

Arias claimed that when she arrived in Utah on the morning of June 5, she was in a "strong state of denial" at having killed Travis. But when pressed, she conceded that she "believed [she] knew he was dead."

". . . And when you went to see Mr. Burns, you were the same person that you had been before, you were happy, smiling, right?" I asked, knowing that her friends in Utah had described her demeanor as being normal, with her smiling.

"I was not," she claimed. "But I was trying to portray that."

". . . And during the afternoon when you are with Mr. Burns, you begin to kiss him, right?"

"Yes," she replied.

". . . Knowing that Mr. Alexander was dead, right?"

"I guess so. . . . It's hard to explain," Arias said, appearing to want to parse out the killing.

"Ma'am, what is hard to explain about a person breathing or not breathing? . . . Why is that a difficult concept for you?"

"Because I never killed anyone before," she sniped, suggesting that perhaps she should be shown latitude because it was her first time.

Returning to the topic of the sexual encounter she had with Ryan Burns, I asked Arias to tell the jurors when the intimate kissing had taken place.

"I think it started first in the afternoon and then in the evening, or I guess it would be early morning, on the fifth or the sixth . . ."

"He also placed his hands between your legs, right, at some point?"

"Not that I recall," Arias said with an air of indignation.

". . . You were here when he testified . . . so it could be that he did place his hands between your legs, right?"

"No," she snapped edgily. "Could be that he was full of crap," she answered in a flash of anger.

"So you're saying that Mr. Burns is full of crap?"

"When he said he got near my vaginal area, absolutely."

Arias' testimony on direct examination had portrayed her sexual relationship with Travis as more obligatory than pleasurable, implying that he had been the sexual aggressor and she the passive partner, a victim of sorts who had only gone along to avoid displeasing or offending him. I wanted to show the jury that she had been a willing participant, who had enjoyed their sexual interludes and had even encouraged and initiated some of them.

"One of the things that you kept saying on direct examination was that he [Travis], you know, 'I felt that I liked him

[Travis] and I didn't want to hurt his feelings.' . . . Do you remember saying that you didn't want to hurt his feelings?"

"I felt that way, like it would have been a blow to his ego," Arias said, referencing her and Travis' first sexual encounter at the Hugheses' house in Murietta.

". . . You cared about his ego even though you had only known him for approximately two weeks?"

"Yes."

"So does that mean you were more invested in him than you are telling us? In other words, you really had strong feelings for him?"

"They weren't strong, but there was an attraction there."

"So, you were attracted to him then, and you wanted this sort of activity to continue?"

". . . Well, I didn't stop it," she said, in keeping with her earlier script.

"Well, when you say you didn't stop it, it just sounds again like you're saying it was all him, not you, right?"

"It takes two to tango," Arias admitted.

"That's right. And it was a mutual activity. . . . So that means, for example, that when you and he were involved the very first time that it was mutual, right?"

"Yes, it was."

"And when you were involved any time after that, it was also mutual, right?"

"I believe it was . . . when I told him to stop, he did," she answered, removing the insinuation that the sexual activity was forced upon her by Travis.

As my queries grew more pointed, so did Arias' responses. This reached an apex with questions about text messages she had found in Travis' cell phone when she sneaked a peek while he was napping, conduct similar to her returning to the Yreka library and snooping into Bobby Juarez's e-mail account.

"The messages, what did they say? . . . What was the subject matter?" I asked, not knowing what Arias had in store for me.

"Things referencing specific sexual body parts interacting with other sexual body parts . . . and plans in the making of meeting up at hotel rooms or his house . . ."

"And you were very offended by that, right?"

"Yeah. Offended would be accurate," she offered, conceding for the first time that I had chosen the right word.

"Right. And you were so offended that you still decided to go on vacation with him, right?"

"That wasn't why."

"Well, no, you were very offended. You just told us that, right?" I followed up, using the same verbiage from the inquiry initiating this line of questioning.

"I didn't say 'very,' but yes, I was offended . . . I was hurt," she said, now taking issue with the modifier to the word "offended." It appeared she was turning her focus to the words in order to avoid answering a question that might portray her in an unflattering light.

"Ma'am, didn't you just say 'offended'?" I asked in a raised voice. "And did you just say it was a good word?"

"Yeah, there are many descriptors to use."

"But you just said it was a good word, right?"

"Yes, I think," she replied.

"You 'think' means you don't remember what you just said."

"I don't know."

"What do you mean you don't know? You just said 'offended' is a good word. And when I used it, then you took issue with it. Is it a good word or is it not a good word?"

"It depends on how you use it."

"I asked you the question, you were offended, and you said 'offended' is a good word, right? . . ." I continued, knowing I had to expose what appeared to be a word game to her.

"I think so, yes."

"Well, you 'think so' means you don't know, right?"

"I don't know," she confirmed.

"This just happened. How is it that you are not remembering what you said?" I asked, implying that it was not a memory problem.

"Because you're making my brain scramble," Arias said.

"I'm again making your brain scramble," I said, referring to earlier questioning when she had used the same excuse. "So in this case in particular, the problem is not you, it's the question being posed by the prosecutor, right?"

"No."

"Yes or no," I continued, talking over Arias.

"I was saying 'no' when you interrupted me," Arias sniped, in what seemed an attempt to wrest control of the questioning.

"So, in this case, you're looking to point the finger at somebody else again?"

"No, it's my fault," she said in what appeared to be a change of attitude, if only for the purposes of this question.

"Well, you're saying it's the prosecutor that's asking you the questions and creating a problem for you, right? . . . You said, 'it's the way you're posing the questions,' right?"

Knowing she had painted herself into a corner, Arias again said she didn't know.

"So, how is it, if it just happened, you can't even remember what you just said?"

"I think I'm more focused on your posture and your tone and your anger. So it's hard to process the question," she said, trying to deflect the attention away from her answers and onto my conduct.

". . . You're saying you are having trouble telling us the truth on the witness stand, right?"

"Absolutely," she remarked without pausing, finally admitting what had been obvious from the beginning of her testimony.

"You're telling us you're having trouble telling us the truth because of the way the questions are being posed, right?"

"I have no problem telling the truth," Arias shot back, returning to earlier form.

". . . And you indicated that the prosecutor's posture is aggressive, right?"

"I didn't say aggressive. . . . It's not the problem with your posture, it's that it creates a problem with me processing what you're saying, because I'm focused more on your posture than the content of the questions," she answered.

". . . Ma'am, with this issue of posturing, do you remember back on July 15, 2008, when Detective Flores interviewed you? . . . And he was sitting down, right?" I asked, knowing that I could prove that she had a problem answering questions truthfully irrespective of the posture and demeanor of the person making the inquiries.

"Yes."

"And his voice was very quiet, right?"

"Yes."

"And when he was asking you these questions and his voice was very quiet, you still lied to him, didn't you?"

"Yes."

"So, it doesn't have anything to do with the volume of the questions then, does it, as to whether or not you'll tell the truth?"

"I will always tell the truth," Arias replied, without realizing she had just been untruthful.

". . . So you told the truth to Detective Flores back then, right?"

"I mean here under oath," she clarified.

Much has been made of the assertive attitude I adopted during my cross-examination of Arias, as this exchange illustrates. But any other approach would have been ineffective, as she would have controlled the questioning by picking and choosing the questions she would answer.

Recalling Arias' direct testimony about the photographs of

a man's erect penis that Travis had allegedly sent to her cell phone, I asked if she had found the photos "offensive."

"Not at all, actually," she said.

". . . And so when you were telling us about how it was that you received this, you didn't mean to tell us that you were offended by it, right?"

"No, I was not offended."

"In fact, it was something that you liked, right?"

"I did like it, yeah," she admitted, which served to cast doubt on the validity of including the photographs as part of her case.

". . . And you also sent him pictures of yourself?" I said, referring to several photos of Arias topless that she sent to Travis.

"Yes, I did," she admitted, agreeing that she didn't find anything wrong with exchanging pictures of this nature.

Arias also acknowledged that she had been the one to introduce K-Y personal lubricant into their relationship. "And it was used as part of these sexual encounters that the two of you had?"

"Yes . . . It made our activities more enjoyable," she explained, which called into question the defense's claim that sex was something Arias engaged in because she couldn't say no.

". . . When you say that you felt like a prostitute, that's at odds with what you're telling us or what we're hearing here about the K-Y?"

"Well, you're talking about two different incidents, so, yes, it would be at odds," she clarified.

"So your participation, if you will, in these activities was equal to his, right, wasn't it? . . . So, any derogatory statement such as 'I felt like a prostitute' isn't really representative of what was going on, right?"

"It was. But it was my fault for feeling that way, because I allowed it," Arias answered.

"Well, I know that you allowed it, and you felt that way . . .

and you say that you felt like a prostitute, but when we hear, for example, these partial clips of this sexual conversation," I said, referring to the graphic sex tape that Arias recorded on May 10, 2008, "it looks like you're the one that's moving it along, not him?"

"Is that a question?" she challenged.

"It is a question," I replied.

"What's the question?" she posed, seemingly eager to chastise me in front of the jurors.

"The question is, isn't it true that you were the one to move it along?"

"I'd say it was mutual," Arias said, clarifying that she didn't feel like a prostitute during the sex, just afterward.

"Well, this is suggestive of you being as much of a participant in these activities as he was, right?"

"Yes. And I was."

To drive home the point that Arias had not only been a willing participant, but that she had enjoyed her sexual relationship with Travis, I pointed to another event that she had described on direct examination as making her feel like a prostitute. According to Arias, the two engaged in oral sex on the porch of her house in Mesa, fulfilling one of their fantasies, during which Travis supposedly ejaculated on her face, threw some chocolates at her, and left.

"Well, when he jizzes on my face and throws candy my way and walks away without a word, it kind of feels like I was a prostitute," Arias remarked, at which time I moved to introduce several text messages the two had exchanged about carrying out this same scenario for a second time, with the only difference being now Arias was the one soliciting it.

"And this is what the text message reads . . . 'the reason I was asking about later tonight is because I want to give you a nice BJ.' BJ stands for what?" I asked.

"Blow job," Arias said matter-of-factly.

". . . Right, and in addition to it, you say, 'and I'd like a generous facial in return' . . . that means you want him to ejaculate on your face, right?"

"That is correct," she admitted.

Directing Arias' attention back to the May 10, 2008 phone call that she recorded, I suggested that it also provided a glimpse into what her views were about the sexual relationship between her and Travis. "And in fact in it you indicate that you want to blossom sexually, right?"

"Yes."

I was able to have Arias admit that she had been the one to propose dressing up like a "horny little school girl" in a text message she sent to Travis in February 2008. "Okay, let's read it: 'I want to fuck you like a dirty, horny little school girl.' So that implies that you're dressed up in a certain fashion, right?"

"Yes."

"And it also implies or indicates that it's you who likes this sort of activity and looking like a horny little schoolgirl, right?"

"Yes," Arias replied, casting doubt on the legitimacy of her earlier claim that it was Travis who preferred this activity.

Arias also conceded that part of what the two discussed during their phone conversations was just fantasy and had not actually occurred. "And so that if he says he wants to tie you to a tree and stick it up your ass, that could also be seen as fantasy, right?" I said, referring to a comment made by Travis that Arias took issue with on direct examination.

"Yes."

"That never happened, did it?"

"No."

She had now admitted that she was not victimized by Travis and was a willing participant in their sexual games, using her words and actions to fan their heated flame. In her haste to prove that she was always right, Arias had also exposed herself as someone who was unduly combative, unlike the victim she was trying to portray. The pillars of sand supporting her self-defense claim had started to crumble under the weight of her assertiveness. Her need to always be right had blinded her, and she could not stop herself from turning her back on the role of victim, a critical part of her defense.

CHAPTER 26

On Wednesday, February 26, Jodi Ann Arias described her trip to Arizona to kill Travis Alexander as a "road trip" that was "partially vacation, partially a business trip," unaware that her portrayal would provide the entry point for my inquiry about the gas cans. I had purposely waited until I was near the end of my cross-examination to introduce the existence of the third gas can, in order to maximize the impact. This irrefutable evidence would prove that Arias had premeditated Travis' murder, so I wanted it to be the last testimony the jury heard from Arias.

Arias' admission that her trip had been partially for business allowed me to ask questions about the receipts police had found in the Airwalk shoebox seized during the search of her grandparents' house on July 15, 2008. And while I made it appear that my interest in the receipts had to do with Arias' plan to use them as deductions on her income tax, I was actually paving a path to the topic of the gas cans.

"When you say partially a business trip, what you're saying is, for example, that if you went to buy gas, that's something that could be deductible, correct?" I solicited. ". . . In fact, since you were going to go to Utah, going to a gas station, it would make sense to save the receipts so that you could deduct them from your income taxes, right?"

"That's right," Arias replied, clueless as to what my inquiry was about to reveal.

"And in this particular case, it wouldn't matter whether you paid with cash or a credit card, right?"

"Yes."

". . . So you did at least pay attention to the receipts you got, for example, from the gas station, right?"

"What do you mean, pay attention?" Arias asked warily.

"Kept them."

"Yeah, I threw everything in a shoebox," she confirmed.

She discussed renting the car at the Redding airport, saying that either her brother's neighbor or sister-in-law dropped her off on the morning of June 2, 2008, although she could not recall for sure whom it had been. Arias agreed that she rejected the red car first offered to her by Ralphael Colombo because she had heard that drivers of red cars "get more tickets."

After establishing that the white Ford Focus she ended up renting that day had a gas capacity of just over twelve gallons, I reminded her of her calls to Darryl Brewer in late May, when she had asked to borrow the two gas cans. "So you did have these discussions with Mr. Brewer and you decided to get the gas cans. Why didn't you just go and buy some gas cans?"

"Because they were expensive," Arias replied.

"When you say they were expensive, how much is a gas can today?"

"I don't remember. But it wasn't in my budget for my travels."

"And you wanted two of them, right?"

"I don't know. I guess whatever he had."

"So if he would have had six, you would have taken six?"

"No, they wouldn't have fit."

"And these gas cans, when you picked them up, where did you put them?"

"In the trunk."

". . . And what color were the gas cans?"

"They were red."

Arias testified that after leaving Brewer's house, she drove to Salinas, where she had a manicure.

"And then you left Salinas and continued on your trip, right? . . ."

"That's correct."

"About what time was it?"

"Afternoon. But I don't know what time," she answered, believing she had anticipated my next question.

"You told us about the gas cans from Mr. Brewer, right?"

"That's right."

"But you forgot to tell us something else, didn't you?"

"You haven't asked me yet," she stated smugly.

"Well, isn't it true that there were more than two gas cans involved here, right?" I asked. I had waited almost the entire trial to ask this question.

Arias' face had a noticeable reaction. I could see her eyes widening behind the lenses of her glasses. "Yes," she answered.

"You never testified about a third gas can, did you?" I said.

"No," she answered, some of the smugness leaving her face, at least for the moment.

"This third gas can, you actually bought it in Salinas, didn't you?"

"Yes," Arias answered. And for that one instance, I saw a cornered look in her eyes.

"And you bought it from Walmart, didn't you?"

"Yes, I did," Arias said with a hint of trepidation in her voice.

"And not only do you have two five-gallon gas cans, you have another gas can. What's the capacity of this one?" I asked.

"It was the same—no, I think it was—I don't know. It was the same size, I think," Arias said appearing as though she was trying to regain her composure.

"You think—so now you have a capacity of fifteen gallons, right?"

Arias remained impassive. "At that moment I did," she said.

"Well, you're saying at that point you had that capacity. Was there something involving these gas cans that would not allow you to fill them up to their capacity later on?"

"Yes, there was."

"And what is that?" I asked, curious to see what she would come up with in her attempt to discount this evidence.

"I returned the gas can," she said flatly, staring back at me, unwilling to back down. I took a second to stare back, knowing that nothing could be further from the truth.

Amanda Webb, a loss-prevention supervisor at Walmart, where Arias admitted she bought the third gas can, had already checked their records and determined that Arias had not returned to the store for a refund that day, as she was now claiming.

Chelsey Young, a manager with Tesoro Companies Inc., had examined the gasoline transaction records at my request and found that Arias had made three separate purchases of gasoline during the same visit at their Salt Lake City, Utah, gas station in the early morning hours of June 6, 2008, starting at 3:54 P.M. The first purchase was a pay-at-the-pump transaction where Arias paid $41.18 for 10.672 gallons of gasoline. The second transaction, which was initiated seven minutes later at 4:01 P.M., was also conducted at the pump, where she purchased an additional 5.091 gallons at a cost of $19.65. The third and last transaction, which took place at 4:05 P.M., was performed inside the station's minimart, where Arias bought an additional 9.583 gallons, which cost her $36.98.

In all, Arias stocked up on 25.346 gallons of gasoline, paying a total of $97.81, during that single visit. This large amount of gas could only have been pumped if she had three five-gallon gas cans, because the maximum amount she would have been able to carry with two gasoline cans and a full tank of gas in her car was approximately twenty-two gallons. It seemed that the cost of killing Travis Alexander had been relatively cheap, because it only cost Arias around $100.

"You returned it back, right?" I continued, giving her a last chance to back away from her previous answer.

"Yes," she replied, refusing to grab the olive branch I offered.

"So that now you have a capacity of still ten gallons, right?"

"Yes."

"Maximum, right?"

"Yes."

". . . Ma'am . . . one of the things you were telling us is that you were very financially strapped, for lack of a better phrase, right?"

"That's right."

". . . So if you want to save on gas, why is it then that you are willing to pay thirteen dollars for a gas can, which would increase, if you will, the price of travel . . . by thirteen dollars?"

"That wasn't a calculation I made when I bought it. That's why I returned it."

"Do you have a receipt that you took it back?"

"I didn't get a receipt," she answered, expecting the jury to believe that Walmart had suspended its practice of issuing receipts for refunds, at least for that one transaction.

"So Walmart didn't give you any documentation whatsoever that you took that gas can back?"

"I don't think so," she said, reverting to her fallback response.

". . . I just want to be clear about this. You believe when you took that gas can back, Walmart did not give you any written documents evidencing that or showing that?"

"I don't recall," she said, resorting to the other tried and true response she employed to avoid giving an answer.

Wanting her to believe that she was in the clear, I moved the cross-examination to other parts of her trip, knowing that I was going to come back and address the gas cans one more time.

Arias admitted that she stopped at Starbucks, where she bought a strawberry Frappuccino.

"And while you were there, you called Mr. Burns, right?"

"I don't know if I called him from Starbucks. I know we talked a few times that night."

"And the plan was for you to still go up to Utah, right?"

"Yes."

"And if you were to leave Pasadena at about that time you said you were going to leave, you would have arrived up in the West Jordan area about maybe ten, eleven o'clock the next morning, right?"

"If I drove straight through, I think that's right," Arias said, agreeing that the drive would take about twelve hours.

"But in talking to Mr. Burns, you never told him that you were not going to go straight to Utah, did you?"

". . . No, I didn't tell him that," Arias conceded.

Returning the inquiry to questions about Arias' stop at the Starbucks in Pasadena, I asked her to describe what happened after she purchased her drink and used the restroom, and after she came out to her car and found some skaters hanging around in the parking lot. "When you come out, you see there were these skaters laughing near your car, correct?"

"Not like laughing loud, just kind of snickering," Arias maintained, appearing unwilling to agree with anything I said.

". . . How many were there?" I asked.

"There were three," Arias said.

"And as you get ready to leave, you turn your lights on . . . and as you turn your lights on something catches your eye, right?"

"Not till I begin to back out," Arias corrected me.

"Why do you care that something's out in front of you if you don't know anything about your license plate?"

"Because it was a reflector. It was reflective. I just kind of put two and two together like maybe I should check what that is real quick before I hit the road."

Arias claimed that she pulled back into the parking space, turned off her lights and got out of the car to investigate, finding a license plate that was covered in bugs lying on the ground. When she looked at the front of her car, she noticed her license plate was missing and a ton of bugs similar to those on the license plate were on the front bumper area, prompting her to throw the license onto the floorboard of the car before getting on the road that night.

"Did it ever occur to you to investigate the license plate in the back to see whether or not it matched?"

"Not right there," Arias answered. "I was more concerned with getting in my car and locking the doors."

Arias admitted that after her stop at Starbucks, she called Travis to let him know that she was coming to Mesa. She blamed him for her last-minute decision, claiming he guilted her into coming to Arizona.

"One of the things that you told us was that the reason that you came out here was that he had an ability, according to you, to just basically guilt you into doing things, right?"

"Yeah. But in a sweet way," she responded, romanticizing Travis, whereas before she spent the majority of her time on the stand vilifying him.

"Well, guilt is guilt, whether it's sweet or bittersweet, wouldn't you agree?"

"Yes."

"And so it's not a very positive thing to be guilted into something, right?"

"I don't know. . . . It kind of felt good when he was doing it," she replied.

I wasn't sure why she was now taking this position. Perhaps she wanted to make herself more sympathetic to the jury, or perhaps she just wanted to be contrary with me.

"Why call him after you already gassed up and everything and you're on your way to Utah? . . ." I asked.

"Why? Because I was calling him prior to the trip; he kept guilting me, would be the term. And to be honest, it was flattering and I enjoyed hearing it."

Arias claimed that Travis had begun guilting her into coming to Mesa since learning about her trip to Utah about one week before she was scheduled to depart.

"And it's something that you keep saying that he keeps guilting you, that's the phrase you're using, right?"

"Yes," Arias replied with an inappropriate grin.

"And you know, you smiled there like it was something pleasant."

"Yeah. He was very sweet about it."

". . . If he's guilting you and you already have another beau or another person out there, why do you keep exposing yourself?"

"Well, Travis had that effect on me, I guess you could say," she told me, blaming it all on his charm.

"Well, it was because you liked it, isn't it?"

"I did like it."

". . . And so you decided that instead of going to see Mr. Burns, you were going to instead come to see Mr. Alexander, correct?"

"Yes."

"And it was your decision, solely, right?"

"Yes," Arias admitted, contradicting her claim on direct examination that Travis' hold over her was so great that he had somehow convinced her to abandon her trip to Utah and come to Mesa for him.

———

February 28 marked the fifth and final day of my cross-examination of Jodi Ann Arias. This would be her thirteenth day on the stand, during eight of which she had been under direct examination by defense counsel Laurence Nurmi. She was beginning to appear weary, likely as a result of our heated exchanges as I pressed her on topics she wanted to avoid, prompting her to engage in verbal fisticuffs, exposing the woman behind the librarian look.

Historically, jurors do not like when defendants are oppositional with the prosecutor, because it appears they have something to hide. Yet Arias continued to evade the specifics of the killing claiming she didn't remember as I began to wind down my cross-examination with questions about Travis' murder.

On the courtroom monitors I displayed a police photograph of Travis' body on the floor of the shower and asked, "Where were you taking the photographs when this happened?"

"Outside the shower," she replied, her voice laden with apparent emotion.

"Pardon?" I asked.

"Outside the shower," she repeated, this time breaking into sobs.

I didn't want jurors to be left with this sympathetic image of Arias on the witness stand crying, so I continued with a string of questions to focus on what she had done to Travis. "Ma'am, were you crying when you were shooting him?" I asked.

"I don't remember," Arias responded, keeping the story straight through her tears.

"Were you crying when you were stabbing him?" I continued, unswayed by her display of emotion.

"I don't remember."

"How about when you cut his throat, were you crying then?"

"I don't know."

"So take a look, then," I said, again directing Arias' attention to the photograph on the monitor. "And you're the one that did this, right?"

"Yes."

"And you're the same individual that lied about all this, right?"

"Yes," she admitted, tears falling onto her cheeks.

At this point Judge Stephens called for a lunch break, instructing all parties to be back in the courtroom by 1:25 P.M. By then, Arias would have had time to prepare responses to my questions about where she was standing in the bathroom just before the killing, so I abandoned this line of inquiry.

That afternoon, I questioned Arias about her version of what happened while she and Travis were alone that resulted in her killing him. She recited the same lines she had delivered on direct examination, saying that she was in a fog and could not remember anything except that he said, "Fucking kill you, bitch!" and that she had to defend herself.

I had not expected that she would deviate from the script, she had followed on direct examination where she admitted that she had taken with her the rope they used in their supposed sexual playing, the gun she had used to shoot him in the face, and the knife that she used to slash his throat, and that she had deleted the photographs from the camera, all things she could not deny.

My last line of questioning involved the three messages Arias left for Travis after she killed him. She called while on the road to Utah around midnight of June 4, 2008, leaving him a voice message which I played for the jury. "And that's you lying on the message, right?"

"Yes," Arias admitted.

The next day, June 6, she sent him a text message inquiring about when he was going to deposit the $200 check she had given him as a partial payment for his BMW. "And you did that, again, so that you could cover up what you had done, right?"

"Yes."

On June 7, she sent him an e-mail discussing her imminent travel to Arizona and asking to stay at his house while he is away in Cancún. One of the reasons she claimed she wanted to stay at his house is because of the "cozy" bed. ". . . You're sending it to him even though you know he's dead, right? It's a way to stage the scene, right?"

"I think so, yeah. That was my goal, I think," Arias answered, her response emblematic of the way she had answered most questions on cross-examination, where she failed to fully take responsibility for her actions.

And with that, I ended my cross-examination.

When court resumed on March 4, Nurmi conducted his redirect examination of Arias, which went on for almost two full days, taking us to March 6, the day Judge Stephens began to read the more than one hundred questions jurors had for Jodi Arias.

Among the jurors questions were several insightful queries about Arias' claim that she had returned the third gas can in Salinas.

"What happened to the gas cans after the road trip in June of 2008?" was a question from one of the jurors.

"They went back to my grandmother's house where I went back to eventually. And I was taking a road trip to Monterey and had intended to bring them to Darryl. But I never made it to that road trip," Arias contended.

"When you purchased the gas at the ARCO in Pasadena, why didn't you just fill everything up at the pump so that it was all under one transaction? Why do three separate transactions?" another juror posed.

"What, what I do recall is when I filled the gas cans, rather

than have just a loose gas hose somewhere, I didn't have anywhere to put it. So I hung it up. And when I hung it up, that
ended the transaction. So, that's probably why," Arias said.
"If I could have, you know, put them back in the trunk or
whatever and then started the car or vice versa, I didn't want
to just set it on the ground, so I hung it up. I know that ended
the transaction. So that's probably why there was more than
one and maybe I was topping off the gas tank for another."

"In testimony on March 5, 2013, you mentioned filling a
third gas can," another juror began. "When and where did
you get this can?"

"Can you repeat that?" Arias asked apologetically.

When the question was reread by Judge Stephens, Arias
hesitated, as if trying to conjure up a plausible explanation.
"March 5?" she repeated slowly. "I believe that was—that was
a hypothetical. I didn't get—I had a third can when I originally
purchased one in Salinas. I returned it before leaving Salinas.

"So what we were doing is throwing out a hypothetical as
to why would I only put two gallons in a third tank or third
can. So that was a hypothetical. I only had two gas cans with
me," Arias asserted.

On March 7, Nurmi conducted a follow-up direct examination of Arias, seeking to clarify answers she had provided to
the jury questions. When he was done, I began my follow-up
cross-examination. I had waited until the last possible moment
to expose that Arias had actually taken the third gas can on
the trip, which helped prove that she had premeditated Travis'
murder.

"One of the things that we know, ma'am, is that you told
us that, well, when you decided to take this trip, that you
contacted Mr. Brewer because you wanted to take some—get
some gas cans from him, right?" I began.

"Yes."

"It's been established that there were two gas cans, each
with the capacity of five gallons or a little bit over, right?"

"That's my understanding."

"Well, you were there, right?"

"Yes."

Over repeated objections from Nurmi, I pressed Arias about her gas purchases and her claim that she had returned the third gas can to Walmart the same day she purchased it.

"And, ma'am, one of the things that you said was that the reason that you did this was because you—it was expensive, and it didn't seem to make sense to you to get that gas can, right?"

"In hindsight, I realized it didn't make sense," Arias answered.

"All right," I said. "So why is it—why is it, then, ma'am, that you showed up with three gas cans in Salt Lake City?" I asked the question because the amount of gas Arias bought at the Tesoro gas station was more than the capacity of the car's fuel tank and the two gas cans and required an additional five-gallon can.

"Objection," Nurmi snapped. "Beyond the scope of the question . . ."

Judge Stephens called a sidebar to explore Nurmi's position, ruling that I could proceed.

"So why is it you had the three gas cans in Salt Lake City, ma'am?" I asked one more time, eager to hear how Arias would respond.

"I don't even recall going to Salt Lake City," she claimed, her answer compounding the egregious harm she had already done to her credibility. "I went to West Jordan. And I went—"

"Hold on," I said, stopping her midsentence. "First, let's break that down. You're saying you don't remember ever even going to Salt Lake City ever on June 6, 2008?"

"I don't even know where the city limits end and begin. To answer the gas can question. I went to Mesa with two gas cans."

I first took Arias through the receipts from the Tesoro gas

station in Salt Lake City, forcing her to admit that she had indeed stopped there before confronting her with the bank statements from Washington Mutual detailing her transactions. "And when we are talking about this exhibit, do you see three transactions to the Tesoro in Salt Lake City?"

"Yes, I do," Arias conceded.

"You were in Salt Lake City, Utah on June 6 of 2008, weren't you?"

"Yes."

". . . And you did indicate to us that you did buy a third gas can in Salinas, didn't you?"

"Yes, I did," Arias reluctantly confirmed.

". . . Ma'am, would it surprise you that Walmart in Salinas does not have any record of any refund—"

"Objection," Nurmi spoke over me. "Argumentative. Beyond the scope." Judge Stephens called the parties to the bench for another sidebar, then ruled that I could continue with my inquiry.

". . . You said you got a refund in cash, didn't you?"

"Yes, I did."

"Would it surprise you that Walmart doesn't have any record for [the return of] a gas can on that date of June 3, 2008?"

Even faced with this undeniable evidence, Arias stuck to her script. "Considering that I returned it, that would surprise me."

"Pardon?" I said, after she equivocated on an answer that should have been indisputable. ". . . It would surprise you? Because you claim you returned it on that date, right?"

"Yes, I did, and I received cash for it," Arias continued to argue to the bitter end.

And she refused to admit that she had used the third gas can in Salt Lake City even though Tesoro representative Chelsey Young would testify in rebuttal as to the three transactions and the amount of gasoline she purchased, and Amanda Webb would tell the jury that Arias had not returned the gas can for a refund.

After Jodi Arias had finished her eighteenth day of testimony, which included answering questions for the jury, the defense opted to call two additional witnesses, Richard M. Samuels, a psychologist, and Alyce LaViolette, a social worker, in what appeared to be an effort to bolster Arias' testimony that she couldn't remember the specifics of the killing and had been physically and verbally abused by Travis.

Samuels was a clinical and forensic psychologist, who had been in practice for thirty-three years and had conducted over one thousand psychological assessments. He administered a number of tests to Arias, including the MCMI-III (Millon Clinical Multiaxial Inventory–3) and Post-Traumatic Stress Diagnostic Scale (PDS), which is a forty-nine-item self-reporting instrument designed to aid in the diagnosis of post-traumatic stress disorder (PTSD). As Samuels explained it, PTSD can result from a person's experiencing, witnessing, or being confronted by a traumatic event that involves death or serious injury, and responding with intense fear, helplessness, or horror.

After speaking with Arias in a clinical interview in which she discussed negative aspects of her relationship with Travis, reviewing documents such as Arias' diary and the police report, and hand-scoring the PDS, Samuels had arrived at the opinion that she met the diagnostic criteria for PTSD, identifying the major traumatic event in her life to be the death of Travis Alexander.

Samuels' opinion was not well founded and was easily discounted because Arias reported in the PDS that the traumatic event that triggered her PTSD was the killing of Travis by two strangers, one of the other stories she told before she admitted the "truth." Arias' lack of candor during the testing voided any results on the PDS and called into question Samuels' opinion based on its results.

Alyce LaViolette was a psychotherapist with a master of science degree who billed herself as an expert in marriage and family therapy. LaViolette was not licensed as a doctor, which prohibited her from administering any personality tests. Her opinion was based solely on a review of documents such as the witness interview summaries conducted by the defense investigator and LaViolette's own interviews with Arias.

Her approach in deciding whether Arias was a victim of domestic violence required that she forget Arias' past trespasses against the truth. She applied something called the Law of Attraction to decode Arias' writings, determining that Arias' failure to mention any physical and verbal abuse meant that it *did* exist. Not having interviewed Travis was not a problem for her because, as she testified, "ninety percent of all communication is nonverbal." She based her conclusions on what Arias told her about Travis' actions.

In support of her opinion, LaViolette relied on a self-created Continuum of Aggression and Abuse, which she argued showed that Travis had abused Arias. Her lengthy list of speaking engagements spoke to her bias, which included offering keynote addresses with titles such as "Was Snow White a Battered Woman?" and "Snow White, Gender and Domestic Violence."

And when I cross-examined her about secondary gain, the concept that an individual may be deceitful if it is to their benefit to not tell the truth, she answered, "If you were in my group, I would ask you to take a time-out, Mr. Martinez."

Both of these experts appeared to have done more harm than good to the defense case, because Samuels was duped by Arias into giving an opinion based on a story that she had already admitted wasn't true, and LaViolette was further undermined, as she seemed to believe that even Snow White was a battered woman. Both of them had relied on the word of Jodi Ann Arias, someone who had been proven a liar.

Besides Chelsey Young and Amanda Webb, one of the other witnesses I called to testify in rebuttal was Janeen DeMarte,

Ph.D. I had retained Dr. DeMarte, a licensed clinical psychologist, to assist in determining the accuracy of Samuels'
PTSD diagnosis and LaViolette's Battered Woman Syndrome
finding.

Dr. DeMarte interviewed Arias on three separate occasions,
reviewed a tome of documents and viewed Arias' interviews
with *48 Hours*. She also administered a battery of psychological tests.

Based on her examination, Dr. DeMarte concluded that
Arias' presentation did not meet the diagnostic criteria
for PTSD as indicated by Samuels, and instead determined
that Arias' symptom presentation was best characterized
by Borderline Personality Disorder. People with Borderline
Personality Disorder are often adolescent-like, engaging in
childish behavior with simplistic problem solving strategies.
Dr. DeMarte also opined that Arias did not fit the profile of a
woman suffering from Battered Woman Syndrome, as LaViolette had found.

After the rebuttal witnesses completed their testimony, the
presentation of evidence for both sides came to an end.

Closing arguments began on May 2, 2013, and ended the
next day at 3:35 P.M., at which time the jury retired to consider its verdict. The jury deliberated for two days, May 6 and
May 7, before informing the court on May 8, at 11:23 P.M.,
that they had reached a verdict.

The court announced that the jury's verdict would be read
after the lunch hour at 1:30 P.M.

But there would be no lunch for me. I just didn't have an
appetite. There had been so many other times during the trial
that I had gone back to court after the recess without having
eaten so it almost felt normal to miss the noontime meal one
more time.

I don't ever speculate on a verdict—it seems to serve no
purpose. But there is always apprehension associated with the
return of a verdict, so it was a relief to finally be back at coun-

sel table as the jury filed into the courtroom having reached its decision.

At 1:48 P.M. the clerk of the court stood up with the verdict in hand. And, as the electric tension in the courtroom climbed to an even higher pitch, the clerk announced that the jury had found Jodi Ann Arias guilty of premeditated first-degree murder.

———————————

It was around 8:15 on the morning of April 13, 2015, and I was already in the victim room next to courtroom 5C, waiting for the sentencing hearing of Jodi Ann Arias to begin. This room had been hallowed ground during trial, where uninhibited discussions between Travis' family and me had been the norm. Today no one else was around, and I sat at the round table in the company of approximately ten empty chairs crowded into the room. Over the course of the trial, these chairs seemed to routinely find their way into the gallery just on the other side of the inner door to the courtroom.

As I sat waiting for the proceeding to get under way, my attention was drawn to the framed "Victim Notification" poster hanging on the wall, defining the rights of victims in criminal prosecutions. It had always been there, but today I actually took note of it, concluding that it was probably the reason this room had gotten its name. With fifteen minutes to waste, my thoughts wandered back to the proceedings that had taken place over the past twenty-six months in the courtroom on the other side of the door. I wondered if Arias had already been brought up to the holding cells so that the sentencing proceeding would start on time.

Arizona law provides for the possibility of three phases in cases where the death penalty is a sentencing option. In the first phase, known as the guilt phase, the jury is asked to decide whether the prosecution has proven the crime of first-degree murder beyond a reasonable doubt. If the jury finds a defendant guilty, then the trial proceeds to the aggravation phase, where the state must prove the existence of at least one aggravating circumstance before a defendant is eligible for the death penalty. Only if the jury finds an aggravating circumstance will the trial proceed to the last and final phase, the penalty phase, when the jury is asked to decide unanimously whether the penalty will be death or life in prison.

Arias had been found guilty of first-degree murder on May 8, 2013. One week later, on May 15, the jury returned its verdict finding one aggravating circumstance, that the murder was especially cruel, meaning that they agreed that Travis had suffered extreme physical pain or mental distress or anguish before he lapsed into unconsciousness and died. Although a majority of the jurors decided that death would be the appropriate sentence, they could not reach a unanimous verdict as required by law, and the court declared a mistrial on May 23, 2013.

A second jury was empaneled approximately one and a half years later to decide the sentence. The court allowed the delay to give the defense more time to conduct further investigation into Arias' claims. The retrial of the penalty phase started with opening statements on October 21, 2014, and lasted thirty-eight trial days over the course of approximately four months. The defense had a lengthy presentation in support of their belief that Arias should be sentenced to life in prison as opposed to receiving the death penalty. Although a majority of those jurors, this time eleven out of twelve, voted to impose the death penalty, they were not unanimous, and the judge declared a second mistrial on March 5, 2015. The law does not permit any further retrials under these circumstances, meaning that the judge would now determine Arias' sentence, either life in prison with the possibility of release after twenty-five years or natural life in prison with no possibility of release.

As I rose to enter the courtroom to hear the sentence, it occurred to me once again that had I chosen to pass off the

8:30 A.M. call to the prosecutor whose shift had just begun that June morning, these last years would have been different. Like so much about this case, that one small decision had profound ramifications.

Looking back, I've come to see that the attitude I brought to this prosecution had nothing to do with Jodi Ann Arias and the bestial way she ended Travis' life. To the contrary, my approach was a product of a time passed and the values and teachings of the small town where I grew up, a place that I still remember leaving.

It was September 1974 when I traveled south on Interstate 15 away from my home in Victorville, California, a small town in San Bernardino County about eighty-five miles northeast of Los Angeles. I was driving a 1964 Chevrolet Impala, a car that I'd bought for $250. It didn't matter that it was ten years old and not in the best mechanical shape. I wasn't going very far, only about ninety miles. I was on my way to begin college at the University of California, Irvine.

As I glanced in the rearview mirror, I was treated to the verdant landscape characteristic of my hometown. Trees lined the streets, including Seventh Street, the main road that ran from one end to the other. It was a very small town back then, with a population of only around twelve thousand; at least, that's what the sign said. My rearview mirror also showed off the green fields alongside the Mojave River, which flowed through the outskirts of town. That's how I remember seeing Victorville through nineteen-year-old eyes as I drove away that afternoon. I say that I remember seeing it that way because that's how it seemed to me as I left it behind. But nothing could be further from the truth.

Victorville sits in the high desert in Southern California. There are few trees and no green fields, and the river mostly runs underground away from the sea. The climate is arid, and the wind blows almost every day, rolling tumbleweeds into yards in bunches. It is hot during the summer, with high temperatures above the hundred-degree mark, but cold in the winter, when the temperature drops into the teens. There are very few days that may be deemed pleasant. But it was my hometown and a place where I made memories, some good and some bad.

I attended the only high school in town, Victor Valley High. The student enrollment was low, so I knew almost everybody. It made belonging easy. We formed friendships, some stronger than others. Although time eroded those friendships, the same cannot be said of the values I learned. There were lessons taught in the home as I was growing up. In my family, my father's edict was the last and only word. As I've gotten older, I have grown to understand the logic of his reasoning and have come to respect his decisions.

Perhaps Victorville was not as bucolic as I remember it, but it was the place where I learned right from wrong. And what Jodi Ann Arias did to Travis Alexander on June 4, 2008, was wrong.

For that, Judge Sherry Stephens of the Maricopa County Superior Court sentenced her to prison for the rest of her natural life.

It didn't surprise me that Jodi Arias remained stone-faced during the reading of her sentence, wearing the same blank expression she had worn throughout much of the trial. Nor did it surprise me that she used her allocution prior to being sentenced, not to ask for forgiveness or to show remorse, but as a platform to point the finger at me, Detective Flores, and everybody else she deemed guilty of causing the injustice that she felt was now being foisted upon her.

To the end, Arias maintained her posture as a victim. It was her parents' fault because her mother hit her with a spoon and her dad slapped her, and Bobby and Matt's fault for cheating on her. It was Travis' fault that she detoured to Mesa that day, and my fault for scrambling her brain with my questions. According to her, Detective Flores and I had even tampered with the evidence.

Trials are life-changing experiences, not only for a defendant who is convicted and must pay for his or her crime, but also for people like me who see the underside of life on a daily basis and are always in the maelstrom. This includes those who have assisted in bringing these cases to their completion—people like Detective Esteban Flores, who saw his duties through even though he suffered the loss of his fifteen-year-old son, Tony, during the course of the second penalty phase of the trial.

With a crime as highly-publicized as this one it is challenging to avoid the media coverage and it is sometimes important to turn your back on it all. This is especially true for me after having been scrutinized publicly in a way I've never been before and often in a negative fashion. In spite of the notoriety and criticism, nothing much has changed in my day-to-day work as a prosecutor with the Maricopa County Attorney's Office. I am very much the same person I was when I answered that 8:30 P.M. phone call, and I remain committed to my role as a prosecutor in the criminal justice system.